THE VIOLENCE OF GOD
AND THE WAR ON TERROR

THE VIOLENCE OF GOD AND THE WAR ON TERROR

Jeremy Young

SEABURY BOOKS
an imprint of
Church Publishing Incorporated, New York

© 2008 by Jeremy Young

Published in 2007 by Darton, Longman and Todd Ltd
1 Spencer Court
140–142 Wandsworth High Street
London sw18 4jj

First published in the United States in 2008 by
Church Publishing, Incorporated
445 Fifth Avenue
New York, New York 10016

www.churchpublishing.com

A catalog record for this book is available from the Library of Congress

ISBN: 978-1-59627-085-5

5   4   3   2   1

For my parents,
who have always supported me,
even when they disagreed.

Contents

Foreword

This is a stunning book that many readers like yourself will resist at the start. If you persevere, you will find a whole new way of looking at what may be the leading issue of our era: the so-called "war on terrorism." But the topic of terror is only the endpoint of a quest for the roots of the notion of "redemptive violence," by which individuals and nations seek to set matters right in the world by physically destroying evil.

We Westerners will have little trouble seeing that Islamic jihadists resort to violence to exterminate evil as they see it. Young will bring us to our senses as he shows how that myth of redemption through violence is just as forcefully expressed in Jewish and Christian traditions as it is in Islam. As a family therapist, Anglican priest, and pastoral theologian, the author demonstrates how a cycle of abuse, familiar in domestic violence, infuses biblical tradition, theological speculation, ethical practice and political behavior down to the present day.

Along the way he incorporates the views of biblical scholars such as Walter Brueggemann and Walter Wink, as well as the work of the analysts Heinz Kohut and Erich Neumann in a compelling work that, in its aspiring reach, approaches the level of "a grand theory."

Young begins with a careful delineation of the cycle of abuse with which he is familiar as a therapist. He then shows how this endless cycle of repetitive aggression is duplicated in the biblical accounts of God as the abuser of his people, shown in quixotic shifts between blessing and punishing Israel, in a totally controlling manner. How are we to account for the extreme, often arbitrary, violence of God as narrated in the Hebrew Bible and the New Testament as well?

Young contends that God the Warrior is a byproduct of the violence that ancient Israelites endured both at the hands of foreign nations and their own native elites. Calling on the extensive literature on the cycle of one-on-one abuse among individuals, he reminds us that, once abused, social and political groups are unfortunately prone either to blame themselves for the abuse or to become abusers in turn. The central symbols of Exodus-Conquest and of the crucifixion of Jesus contain large dimensions of divine violence that are often uncritically celebrated as exemplary acts of God.

At the same time, there is in the Bible counter-testimony that takes exception to the violent behavior of God, even boldly challenges it, particularly in Genesis, Psalms, Job, Ecclesiastes, Ruth, and Jonah, as well as in the teaching and ministry of Jesus.

This brings Young, as a Christian believer, to an agonizing assessment of the relationship between the alarmingly abusive and truly liberating aspects of the Bible. He finds that many features of the Bible are double-edged, containing elements of God as abuser side by side with elements of God as nurturer and respecter of human autonomy. Young is keenly aware that the problem is not simply what the Bible says, but the often abusive and violent conclusions that people draw from the Bible. He struggles seriously with the extent to which we can take the Bible as actual divine revelation rather than a human projection.

Young goes on to trace the legacy of this biblical violence into Christian history and theology and on to the conflicts in today's world entangled with Jewish, Christian, and Islamic beliefs and behaviors that share in this myth of redemptive violence. He notes the baleful results of church-state alliances that give religious validation to destructive acts of states. He observes the contributions of the theological notions of "original sin" and "predestination" to the cycle of violence among groups and nations. He tangles with the myth of American innocence as a dangerous premise for the use of our military power, for it is typical of the abuser to claim innocence. He takes the Israeli government to task for abusing Palestinians, in a clear reversal of victimhood after the Holocaust. And of course there are Islamic jihadists, equally caught up in the cycle of violence.

Books of this type are sometimes a mere lament or a stormy rant. Not so this one. Every step of the way, Young presents carefully reasoned arguments and exhibits humility in the face of so much that we do not really know about God or ourselves. It seems to me he has given us much to think and do something about.

Norman K. Gottwald
Emeritus Professor of Biblical Studies
New York Theological Seminary
and Adjunct Professor of Old Testament
Pacific School of Religion

Acknowledgements

This book is a much extended version of a paper which I originally gave to the Annual Conference of the British and Irish Association for Practical Theology at Dublin in 2004, entitled Battered Believers. That paper drew attention to the comparison between the behaviour of violent and abusive men and the biblical depiction of God. My awareness of their similarity first developed during the training that I received in the dynamics of violent relationships while I was working as a family therapy trainee and, later, as a qualified therapist at Hesed House, Inchicore, Dublin. It was there that I first worked therapeutically with both victims and perpetrators of violence. I am extremely grateful to the staff and clients there and, especially, to Sister Jo Kennedy and Rebecca Gibson for their insight and sensitive encouragement.

Amongst individuals who have either encouraged me in this book or read and commented on the manuscript, I would particularly like to thank Deborah Wilde, Hana Kende, John Mills, Judith Chavasse, Anthony Battersby, Rachel Fielden, Therese Hicks, my editor Virginia Hearn, and, above all, my wife Anne, whose resilience, encouragement and love towards a book-writing husband, struggling with a project which proved much more demanding and time-consuming than anticipated, have been extraordinary.

Author's Note

Please note that there is a problem in knowing what term to use to refer to the Scriptures which are accepted as canonical by the Jewish religion. On the one hand, they are a self-sufficient collection of documents. On the other hand, they are the first volume of the Christian canon, of which the New Testament is the second. In order to deal with this ambiguity, I shall refer to these documents as the Hebrew Bible or Scriptures when considering them in their own right as Jewish documents, and as the Old Testament when viewing them as Christian documents through the interpretative lens of the New Testament and Christian doctrine.

Another dilemma is what name to give to the ancestors of the Jewish people. According to archaeological and historical research, the origins of the tribes who settled the land of Canaan and eventually formed the people of Israel are obscure. For this reason, it is not accurate to refer to them as Jews. Instead, I shall describe them as Hebrews or Israelites or the people of Israel or by some other appropriate term depending on context, and shall reserve the terms, Jews or Jewish people, for the historical period after the conquest of the kingdom of Judah in 587 BCE, when the temple at Jerusalem was destroyed and the leaders of the people of Judah were sent into exile in Babylon. The religion which we now call Judaism only developed into a recognisably modern form in the centuries following that disaster. One reason for this usage is that I will be saying some critical things about the Hebrew Scriptures which I am anxious should not be taken as criticisms of contemporary Jews. It is, therefore, helpful to distinguish between Jewish people alive now and their very distant ancestors in order to avoid any impression of blaming them for what their ancestors wrote or did. For too long Christians have blamed their contemporary Jews for 'murdering Christ' and I do not want to be guilty of a modern equivalent.

In this regard, it is important to distinguish between anti-Semitism, anti-Judaism, anti-Zionism and opposition to the policies of the State of Israel. Anti-Semitism is an irrational prejudice against Jewish people, whether or not they are religious. It is expressed in antagonistic attitudes to Jews as such and, at its worst, gives rise to persecution, the worst example of which was the Holocaust in which six million Jews perished. Anti-Judaism is opposition to the Jewish religion rather than the Jewish people. Anti-Zionism is opposition to the political ideology known as Zionism, which is based on the belief that the Jews will never be safe from persecution until they are established in an independent Jewish state in which they can defend themselves. The place chosen for this state is the ancient biblical kingdom of Israel, otherwise known as Palestine. Zionism has been successful to the extent that the State of Israel was founded in 1948 and was recognised under international law by the United Nations. However, many Palestinians and other Arabs have never accepted the right of Israel to exist and, since the conquest of the Occupied Territories in 1967 and their illegal administration by Israel, the behaviour of successive Israeli governments, especially towards Palestinians, has become increasingly controversial and subject to criticism from many sources, both outside and within the Arab world.

Thus, it is possible to be opposed to Israeli policies towards the Palestinians whilst still being in favour of the existence of Israel, or to reject the right of Israel to exist whilst still respecting the Jewish religion and the Jewish people, or to disagree with the beliefs and practices of Judaism without being anti-Semitic – that is, prejudiced against the Jewish people as such. Of course, those who are anti-Semitic are likely to hold negative views of Judaism, Israel and the policies of the Israeli government. There are, therefore, multiple possibilities of confusion between these different categories, which is why discussion of Israel is so difficult. These complex debates are made much more fraught by the deliberate use of accusations of anti-Semitism against those who dare to criticise Israel's policies by its supporters in order to silence them. In my opinion, both anti-Semitism and the use of accusations of anti-Semitism to foreclose debate of these matters are totally unacceptable.

A further difficulty is knowing what gender to use when referring to God. Although Christian theology states that God is without gender, the terminology used about the deity in the Christian tradition is almost exclusively masculine, including the masculine pronoun. There are, it is true, some instances of female imagery being used, but these are very definitely exceptions that prove the rule. The 'maleness' of the Jewish and Christian God has become hugely problematic in recent years as a result of the challenge to the patriarchal organisation of society origi-nating in the women's movement, which has been incorporated into the-ological debate by feminist theology. In this study the gender of God is of critical importance. Because God is represented as male and behaves like an abusive male assuming all the privileges of a male in a tradition-ally patriarchal society, it would be misleading to attempt to use any other terms than masculine ones to refer to 'him', especially since it is precisely this depiction of the deity which is the conundrum that I am examining. Hence, I will refer to God by the masculine pronoun when investigating the image of God as an abuser, but will use other pronouns at other times. In doing so, I do not intend to suggest that there is any essential link between abusive behaviour and men. Women are just as capable of behaving abusively as men. Whether any particular man or woman becomes abusive depends on many different factors which will be described in detail in this book.

Chapter 1

IS GOD AN ABUSER?

We live in a world in which political conflict and violence linked to religious beliefs and religiously identified communities are becoming more and more prominent. Most visibly this applies to the so-called 'war on terror', the invasions of Afghanistan and Iraq, and the growing tensions between the Western world, especially the United States of America, and Islamic societies. Mistrust, suspicion and hatred are also frequently encountered in other conflicts associated with religious divisions, many of which involve Jews, Christians or Muslims – for example, the Balkans, Northern Ireland and Israel–Palestine. If we are to end or mitigate the violence associated with these divisions and move towards reconciliation, we need to understand the religious roots of this violence and how they feed the continuing bloodshed. The biblical witness to a God who is violent has encouraged and been used to justify innumerable human acts of violence, including much of the violence perpetrated in the so-called 'war on terror'. This is the problem for both belief and politics which this book will examine.

In my previous book, *The Cost of Certainty* (Young, 2004), I argued that the theological structure of Christian belief promotes the appalling record of violence, persecution, hatred, intolerance, bigotry, abuse and hypocrisy associated with the Christian churches over the past two millennia. This is because it encourages believers to deny or repress their doubts, sins and failures in order to be acceptable to the God who, Christian doctrine declares, will condemn those whom he finds unacceptable to eternal punishment. Consequently, the faithful are liable to project the negative features of their characters, beliefs and behaviour onto scapegoats who are blamed for them and excluded, persecuted or attacked in order to preserve the 'good consciences' of Christians. In this book, I want to take this argument further and show how the Bible's description of the relationship between God and humanity, which frequently displays violent and abusive features, has been and continues to be replicated by Christians. *The violence of God becomes enacted by and used to justify the violence of Christians; and this is a direct outcome of the contents of the biblical text.*

This is a very serious conclusion with widespread implications, especially at a time in which religion is becoming more and more an active component of political conflict – in particular, in the Muslim response to Western economic and cultural domination and in the prosecution of the war on terror by the United States and its allies, an action endorsed by the conservative Christian theology of many members of the American political leadership. One contribution a theologian can make to the opposition movement against the militarism of the world's one remaining superpower is to point out the assumptions and errors in the theological bases used to justify its violence.

However, it would be one-sided and misleading simply to criticise the Americans and the 'coalition of the willing'; it will be much more illuminating to locate their beliefs and actions within the larger cycle of abuse within which much contemporary conflict is contained and by which it is fuelled. The United States is by no means the only country or interest group which behaves abusively. However, it is the most powerful by a very large margin and, therefore, inevitably attracts the most resentment, not to say rage. Even so, to demonise America is neither accurate nor helpful to the many Americans who also wish to resist the overweening actions of the current administration. The violence of other regimes, not least Muslim ones, and of terrorists of whatever hue needs also to be condemned and the perpetrators held to account; but first of all, it needs to be understood, and the interactions of the domination of one side with the responses of the other must be tracked. Only so will the larger picture be drawn and the contribution of the abusive dynamics contained within the Christian and other monotheistic religions to the current cycle of violence be recognised and confronted. It is my hope that this book will make a worthwhile contribution to this process.

We will explore the sources of violence in the monotheistic traditions and the implications of recognising them for our contemporary political situation, especially for those seeking to resist the war on terror. The first aim of this book is to identify the roots of violence in the Judaeo-Christian tradition. The second is to apply the insights gained to the present political situation. The third is to suggest how Christians and others may respond constructively to the current conflict in the light of those insights. The fourth is to reassess Christian theology in order to confront and change its tendency to produce or justify violence.

Along the way, we will also be examining the roots of violence in Judaism, since many of them are identical to those in Christianity. We will also look briefly at the roots of violence in Islam by way of comparison with the Judaeo-Christian tradition. However, since I am not an Islamic scholar, I will not be analysing Islamic theology in depth –

others who are far better qualified than I have already done so (e.g. Esposito, 2002; Lewis, 2004; Habeck, 2006). It is not my intention to do more than point out the similarities that derive from the common monotheistic tradition, both in the depiction of the believer's relationship to God and in the divine authorisation of violence. I include Judaism and Islam with some trepidation since I am neither a Jew nor a Muslim, and it is so easy to be misunderstood or to give offence without meaning to when commenting on other people's traditions. However, it is necessary to do so, since the war on terror is a complex phenomenon, involving conflict not only about politics, economics, land and resources, especially oil, but also about culture and religion. My argument would be incomplete if Muslim and Jewish attitudes to God and violence were not included.

Samuel Huntingdon, in his book *The Clash of Civilizations and the Remaking of the World Order* (2002), claims that there is an inevitable clash between different cultural blocs within the world – including between Islam and the West. This is a view I do not share. I do not believe that such monolithic cultural units exist. Rather, I believe that there is a remarkable diversity within as well as between cultures, and that there are many similarities which could be used to promote understanding and co-operation between different societies, and which are obscured by Huntingdon's thesis. My hope is that this book will help to make such oppositional thinking untenable by highlighting some of the similarities and promoting mutual recognition. Indeed, it is often the similarities which are divisive, especially the claim that one or another religion or race is chosen or specially favoured by God. Such 'chosen people theology' is central to each of the monotheisms, and it is one of the major causes of violence in the history of their interactions. The depressing fact is that all three of the major monotheistic religions have the capacity to produce inter-communal violence in the name of God. Contrary to popular prejudice, Christianity and Judaism have at least as much claim to be viewed as 'religions of violence' as Islam; and historically Christianity has often been more intolerant and persecutory of non-believers and dissidents than Islam, let alone Judaism. All three religions are highly complex, containing many different traditions of interpretation, and each has been subject to schisms, heresies and internal conflicts. Some of these traditions are more violent or aggressive than others; some are more pacific. These differences also need to be recognised. Above all we must beware of comparing the most distasteful aspects of the other two religions with the most exemplary of our own. In particular, as Christians, before we blame Islam or Judaism for promoting violence, we should take the beam out of our own eye.

THE VIOLENCE OF GOD IN THE HEBREW BIBLE

The violence of God is central to this enquiry or, at any rate, the violence attributed to God by the Bible which, contrary to the idea that God is a God of peace, is very considerable indeed. In this context, violence means primarily physical assault, including murder. However, the term 'violence' should not be limited to physical assault; it also includes any form of intimidation. In addition, violence may take the form of structural violence, a term referring to the imposition of social and economic inequalities within social groups by various forms of coercion, including the law, the police, the courts, imprisonment and economic exploitation.

Although the Christian and Jewish religions stress the love and mercy of God, God is frequently portrayed in the Bible as extremely violent, as often towards his chosen people as towards those who oppose them:

> Raymond Schwager points out that there are six hundred passages of explicit violence in the Hebrew Bible, one thousand verses where God's own violent actions of punishment are described, a hundred passages where Yahweh [the holiest name for God] expressly commands others to kill people, and several stories where God kills or tries to kill for no apparent reason (e.g. Exod. 4:24–26). Violence, Schwager concludes, is easily the most often mentioned activity and central theme in the Hebrew Bible.
>
> (Wink, 1992, p. 146; see Schwager, 2000)

The potential for divine violence is built into the covenant through which God chose the Hebrews as his people. According to its terms (Genesis 17; Exodus 24; Deuteronomy 29), God undertakes to be the God of the Hebrews and, in return, they undertake to obey his Law. The benefits of this agreement for the Hebrews include the gift of the Promised Land, but the tool God uses to bring this about is violence. Through violence God rescues Israel from Egypt, overturning the forces of Pharaoh, and through violence God enables the Hebrew tribes to conquer and annihilate the Canaanite peoples and to settle the Promised Land.

The disadvantage of the covenant is that the Hebrews will be punished if they break God's commandments. The speeches attributed to Moses in the Pentateuch (the first five books of the Bible) make this abundantly clear. For example, the following passage from Leviticus lists some of the punishments the Hebrews will face if they are disobedient:

> But if you will not listen to me and carry out all my commands, and if you reject my decrees and abhor my laws and fail to carry

out all my commands and so violate my covenant, then I will do this to you; I will bring upon you sudden terror, wasting diseases and fever that will destroy your sight and drain away your life. You will plant seed in vain, because your enemies will eat it. I will set my face against you so that you will be defeated by your enemies; those who hate you will rule over you, and you will flee even when no-one is pursuing you. (Lev. 26:14–17)

This quotation is followed by a long list of further threats, and is representative of many others (e.g. Exod. 33:3; Deut. 4:25–36; 6:13–14; 7:10; 8:19–20; 11:16–18, 26–28; 28:15–68; 30:11–20). In confirmation of God's domineering attitude towards Israel, the Hebrew Scriptures contain numerous examples of a wrathful God punishing his chosen people, as well as other nations and specific individuals, for their transgressions.

THE VIOLENCE OF GOD IN THE NEW TESTAMENT

Despite the common Christian claim that the 'loving' God of the New Testament is different from the 'angry' God of the Old, violence is also central to the New Testament: through violence God inaugurates the Christian dispensation. The primary Christian symbol, the crucifixion, which is the ineradicable centrepiece of the Christian message of redemption, is indubitably an act of extreme violence, as Mel Gibson's film *The Passion of the Christ* has made only too plain. The New Testament accounts frequently state that Jesus was sent to die, that his death was both intended and required by God (e.g. Matt. 17:21; 26:39; Mark 8:31; 14:36; Acts 2:23; Rom. 1:18–20; Col. 1:19–20; Heb. 8:26–28; 9:11—10:18; 1 Pet. 1:18–20). God's full involvement in the violence of the crucifixion is well illustrated in those medieval murals which show angels hammering the nails into Jesus' cross. However, we should note that, unlike Gibson's film, the passion narrative and the New Testament documents in general do not pay any particular attention to the violence of Jesus' death or to his suffering. This emphasis is a later development in Christian spirituality.

Violence is also prominent in the New Testament in those passages which are referred to as 'apocalyptic', especially the Little Apocalypse (Mark 13; Matt. 24; Luke 21:5–36) and the book of Revelation, which describe the calamities that will happen at the end of time when God comes to judge the world. Christians are promised that the final con-summation of history will take place through a great outbreak of divine violence, when the evil will be destroyed, before the revealing of a new heaven and a new earth.

But violence is by no means confined to apocalyptic passages. Despite its repeated claims that God is love, a constant refrain in the New Testament is the message, as St Matthew's Gospel puts it, 'Do not be afraid of those who kill the body, but cannot kill the soul. Rather, be afraid of the one who can destroy both soul and body in hell' (Matt. 10:28). These words, attributed to Jesus, are neither exceptional nor extreme; the message of judgement is constantly reiterated throughout the Gospels and Epistles (e.g. Matt. 7:1–2; 10:14–15; 17:27; 19:21–35; 23—24; Mark 8:34–38; 9:42–48; John 12:47–48; Rom. 1:18; 2:16; 1 Cor. 10:1–11; 2 Pet. 2:4–10; 3:7, 10). Indeed, it is absolutely central to traditional Christian teaching.

The prominence of violence in the New Testament should not be surprising, especially since the relationship between God and the Church, like that between God and the Hebrews, is described as a covenant. The covenant relationship between God and the Hebrews was appropriated by the early Christians and applied to themselves (Heb. 8; 13:20) and, from very early on, Christian teaching predicated God's favour towards the faithful upon the basis of belief in Christ and obedience to his commands, and threatened eternal punishment for those who do not conform. The abusive pattern of the covenant appears to have been replicated in the early Church. This pattern is found as early as the deaths of Ananias and Sapphira (Acts 5:1–11) in the Acts of the Apostles and in the practice of excluding sinners, advocated by Paul in the case of the incestuous man at Corinth (1 Cor. 5:1–13) and adopted generally in the early Church.

Even so, the early Church stood out against the use of violence to solve disputes, and Christians refused to join the army until after the conversion of the Emperor Constantine. However, from that point onwards, the Church moderated its teaching as it became more and more identified with the imperial establishment. Ultimately, *only* Christians were permitted to join the imperial army (Griffith, 2004, pp. 24–7)! Moreover, increasingly in subsequent centuries the Church subjected its deviant members and unbelievers to forms of restriction and violence which emulated, and even exceeded, those used by the God of the Hebrews.

THE VIOLENCE OF GOD AS THE INTERPRETATIVE KEY TO THE BIBLE

Of course, God is not always or only violent in the Bible. There are many passages which depict him as loving and merciful, and these have conventionally been taken as the Bible's central teaching about God. Nevertheless, since God is so often depicted as violent in the Bible and this aspect of his behaviour is so often minimised or ignored, in this book I am going to take the violence of God as the interpretative key to the Bible, and seek to elaborate a theology and religious psychology on that basis. This may seem a surprising, even scandalous method of proceeding, but it has the advantage of showing many familiar features of the biblical record in a fresh light and revealing much about the dark underside of the Christian religion, which has inspired so much violence in the name of its God.

In highlighting the importance of violence for the interpretation of the Bible, I am following several commentators who have been disturbed by the ways in which Christian faith has been associated with violence and oppression in many different forms, including militarism, colonialism, racism, sexism, physical and sexual abuse of women and children, and economic exploitation. These commentators have sought to argue either that these practices are a contradiction of Christianity properly understood or, more radically, that genuine Christianity advocates non-violence (e.g. Cone, 1969; Hauerwas, 1985; Girard, 1987; Brown & Bohn, 1989; Wink, 1992; Yoder, 1994; Weaver, 2001; Nelson-Pallmeyer, 2001). Some of these writers also argue that God is not violent and find ways of explaining away the biblical texts that suggest that he is. I am not convinced by such attempts. In my opinion, the violence of God in both Testaments in the Bible must be accepted as an irreducible part of the overall biblical picture of the divinity. As we shall see, if God is not violent, then the authority of large parts of the Bible is put into question. We shall examine this problem extensively.

For our purposes, the most significant fact is that, however one interprets these texts, the existence in the Hebrew Bible of numerous accounts of the God of Israel's bloody interventions in history, alongside the New Testament accounts of Jesus' crucifixion and of the punishments awaiting sinners in this present life and the world to come, creates the emotional context in which contemporary Christians engage with both the deity and contemporary world politics. This is the case, I believe, even when the violent side of the Christian story is watered down or ignored by church-goers or Christian ministers. I have often felt acutely uncomfortable sitting in church listening to stories of massacres commanded by God or expressing the vindictiveness of 'God's people', at the end of which I am expected to assent to the statement, 'This is the Word of the Lord', with the response, 'Thanks be to God' – for example, the end of Psalm 137: 'O Daughter of Babylon, doomed to destruction, happy is he who repays you, for what you have done to us – he who seizes your infants and dashes them against the rocks' (vv. 8–9).

The reality is that, however much we may wish that it were not so, the presentation of God as violent occurs very frequently in both the Bible

and much traditional Christian teaching. It is barely credible that
Christians, who proclaim a religion of universal peace, should for the
most part accept God's violence without demur. A major reason for this
is, I believe, that many of us have been brought up listening to the biblical stories in an uncritical manner: the behaviour of God was presented
to us as normal and commendable before we were old enough to make
an informed judgement. In my own case, I remember at the age of nine
or ten marching around a classroom acting out the destruction of
Jericho without considering the fate of the inhabitants who, apart from
the traitor Rahab and her family, were all massacred down to the
smallest baby. As the Bible says: 'They devoted the city to the Lord and
destroyed with the sword every living thing in it – men and women,
young and old, cattle, sheep and donkeys' (Josh. 6:21).

Whatever else may be happening in a church, the violence of God is
constantly being re-presented to the congregation through the reading
of the Bible, whose predominant depiction of God, in spite of the claim
that he is loving and peaceful, is of one who is violent to those who
disobey him. My experience is that once you allow yourself to notice the
parallels between the behaviour of abusive men and that of God, they
crop up ubiquitously. God's violence is so much a part of the Judaeo-
Christian tradition that most Christians barely notice it. Like people
who have watched too many violent videos, the sensibilities of the
majority of Christians appear to have been numbed by overexposure
from early childhood onwards. If we are to grasp the degree to which the
Bible depicts God as abusive, we need to recover a sense of shock and
horror at what it records, rather than reading such passages out blandly
in church week by week.

THE ABUSIVENESS OF GOD

I first became uneasily aware of the prevalence of divine violence in the
Bible when working as a family therapist with both the victims and the
perpetrators of domestic violence at a psychotherapy centre in inner-
city Dublin. My work opened my eyes to a disturbing parallel between
the behaviour of the biblical God and that of men who are abusive
towards their female partners or their children. In several places in the
Hebrew Bible Israel is portrayed as a woman, the wife of God, and the
behaviour of God towards Israel has a very great deal in common with
that of men who abuse their female partners. Strangely, as I have struggled with this insight, I have come to realise that, far from being a
perception to resist or reject, the recognition of the similarities between
the biblical presentation of God and abusive men provides an essential
clue to understanding not just the Bible, but the Christian tradition as a

whole. Indeed, the emotional reactions of many Christians to God and the Church, as well as their behaviour towards both their fellow believers and those outside their congregations, make little sense without this insight.

Before going further, it will be helpful to give a definition of abuse. I am using the term to refer to *the attempt by one person (or group) to impose his or her will on another in ways that are detrimental to the well-being or best interests of the other, even if the other has given express consent.* In essence, conformity to the will of the abuser is achieved by the making of some sort of threat, whether or not this is carried out, or by undermining the self-knowledge of the abused to such an extent that she or he comes to accept the point of view of the abuser. Abuse is not the same as violence, although violence may well be used by an abuser to intimidate and dominate his victim. The means used may include physical violence, sexual assault or seduction, verbal denigration or threat, neglect or emotional manipulation.

Of course, this definition begs the question of what is detrimental to the well-being or best interests of the other. For most people, there is no doubt that the sexual attentions of a paedophile are extremely damaging to a child, although a paedophile may think the opposite. Over the centuries men have often thought that to 'discipline' a wife was an acceptable or even necessary activity which was for her benefit as well as for her husband's. She would thereby become a better wife and, furthermore, gain in virtue before God. Nevertheless, wife-beating is now generally considered to be unacceptable and it is now illegal in the United Kingdom. In contrast, many people still consider smacking to be a normal, necessary and completely appropriate part of bringing up a child, even though it has now been made illegal in a number of European countries. Others disagree.

The reference to consent in the definition may surprise some readers. Surely, if someone agrees to an action, that action cannot then be called abusive? However, although the giving of informed consent is in most cases a necessary condition for an action to be considered not abusive, it is not a sufficient one. There are many circumstances in which individuals consent to remain in a situation which is detrimental to them because they have come to believe that they in some way or another deserve to be treated badly, or else because they have been confused by the person who is taking advantage of them and feel that they have made a free choice. A classic example of the latter is sexual abuse, in which a child may have been groomed by her abuser and may feel special because of his attentions. Likewise, a woman who has been on the receiving end of constant criticism may internalise a negative view of herself and begin to believe that she deserves to be beaten. The same can happen to oppressed groups who learn to view themselves with the eyes of their oppressors and to conform to their expectations – for instance, by becoming 'good slaves'. For this reason, the expression of consent does not automatically mean that an action is not abusive. If an action is actually damaging, even if the person on the receiving end has been educated or seduced or verbally bludgeoned into accepting it, it is still abuse. This conclusion raises many complex and contested ethical and philosophical, not to mention legal and political, issues which are beyond the scope of this study to explore. Suffice it to say that my own perspectives will emerge as this book progresses.

I have said that in most cases consent is necessary if an action is not to be considered abusive. This statement needs to be clarified: there are some actions to which the recipient does not consent which may be regarded as not abusive because they are genuinely for that person's good. Again, we are in contested territory. What actions are genuinely for someone's good and who is to decide? For example, while many people would think it acceptable to restrain or medicate someone forcibly in a psychotic episode, others would be suspicious of the infringement of the human rights of the individual, even in such circumstances.

One of the reasons why God's behaviour has not normally been considered as abusive is that in the Judaeo-Christian tradition God is believed always to have the best interests of human beings at heart, even when he behaves in ways that appear detrimental to us. Thus, even if we cannot reconcile his actions with our ideas of what is best for someone, we may be able to live with our perplexity because we can trust that God in his love and goodness is doing the right thing. For example, if we do not understand why some people suffer, that is our limitation and does not justify us in accusing God of acting harmfully towards them. In addition, the right of God to do whatever he likes with his creatures is assumed in this tradition. Put together, these two convictions produce the belief that because God is powerful and is good, whatever he does must be for our ultimate well-being, however incomprehensible his actions may seem to us. From this perspective, *the most disturbing implication of the idea that God is abusive is that he is not good and cannot be trusted, that his actions may actually damage us*, a concern that we will examine extensively as this study proceeds.

As well as noticing the similarities between God and abusive men, my interest has been drawn to the similarities between the emotional reactions of members of the family of an abusive man to his conduct and those of the Hebrews to the behaviour of God. In families, such behaviour is expressive of a pattern of abuse that is often passed down and replicated in each new generation. Such a pattern has a life of its own which the family both contributes to and is victimised by. The same is true, I suggest, of the persecution and marginalisation that the children of Israel have experienced.

The religion of the Israelites originated in the experience of a victimised people who, according to the Bible, experienced slavery in Egypt until they were rescued by their God. However, the psychological effects of slavery did not cease with the escape from Egypt, if indeed it was an historical event. The psychological reactions of victimised and abused people appear to have been incorporated into their religion, and are now evident in the Scriptures. All the more so because they subsequently suffered further serious experiences of oppression, especially the undoubtedly historical exile in Babylon. Indeed, since biblical scholars have raised many questions about the historicity of the Exodus from Egypt and the invasion of the Promised Land, it is likely that these later experiences had a highly formative influence upon how the earlier stories were told. In sum, what we seem to be dealing with in the Hebrew Scriptures is a presentation of God which has been filtered through the group psychology of the children of Israel, one formed by experiences of defeat and humiliation. This psychology has been inherited by Christianity, and has, consequently, been constitutive of the relations between Christians and the Jewish people over the centuries, as the history of anti-Semitism demonstrates. Those who have been victimised frequently become the persecutors or abusers of others. The cycles of abuse thus generated have been lived out repeatedly in the history of the Church, during which Christians have been both victims and persecutors, often of each other.

THE ABUSIVENESS OF GOD AS THE CORE TESTIMONY OF THE BIBLE

In his *Theology of the Old Testament*, Walter Brueggemann (1997) describes Israel as possessing both a 'core testimony' about God as righteous, steadfast, loving, merciful, faithful, just and so on, and a 'countertestimony' (*sic*) which questions God's love, consistency and faithfulness, recognising that he often does not live up to his promises and may behave in totally arbitrary, even abusive ways. In this book, I am inspired by Brueggemann's structure but, in contrast to his approach, want to suggest that the core and counter testimonies discerned by him are two parts of an overarching *implicit* testimony to the abusiveness of God's relationship with both Israel and the Church, the 'New Israel', within the Bible as a whole, not just the Old Testament. In other words, rather than seeing God's love and his abusiveness as core testimony and counter testimony, they are better understood as two aspects of the same relational dynamic: an abusive one in which God is the dominant and controlling partner who uses threats and violence as the means of imposing his will on his partner when she does not do what he requires, and sometimes is violent for no particular reason. What I am arguing is that *the Bible's core testimony is to the abusiveness of God*, even though this is not at all what the biblical writers intended to convey.

In seeking to justify this assertion, my starting point is the recognition that the combination of love and violence in abusive relationships has much in common with the biblical depiction of the relationship between Israel and God, especially when that is imagined as being like a marriage. Similar abusive dynamics are apparent in the depiction of God in the New Testament, where the father–son relationship is the primary analogy used (see Chapter 7). The main feature of men who abuse their female partners is their desire to control them, and the most important point of comparison between the deity and abusive men is that the God of the Bible is extremely controlling. Violence in family contexts is almost always related to the issue of control, and is usually part of a larger pattern of behaviours used by a man to dominate the woman with whom he lives. It may also be used by women against men or between partners of the same sex. However, I am going to concentrate on male-to-female violence because God is normatively imaged as male in the Judaeo-Christian tradition, and Israel, the Church and individual souls are often described as 'female' in relation to the 'male' God.

Abusive men need not necessarily be overtly violent, provided that the women they live with do what they wish. Thus, although some men are frequently physically abusive, many only use physical violence as a weapon of last resort. Instead, control of a woman may be achieved by constantly putting her down, telling her what to wear and how to behave in public, restricting her access to money, work, family or other people, or by verbal abuse. For much of the time, even though she may attempt to act independently, her knowledge of what he is capable of and her fear of her partner's anger may be enough to keep an abused woman under his thumb. In this respect there is a great deal in common between such relationships and that between God and Israel.

Furthermore, because of this similarity, even when the relationship between God and his people appears to be peaceful and loving, it is only because they are doing what they are told. This circumstance is why the claim that the core testimony of the Bible is to God's abusiveness is not contradicted by the frequent occasions when God does appear to be treating his followers in a loving manner. It is necessary to distinguish between those depictions of God's love and steadfastness which are merely descriptions of the 'loving phase' of an abusive relationship, and those which suggest that God does indeed care for Israel or the Church as herself and for her own sake, rather than merely for what she gives him in the way of obedience, praise and so on.

Having said this, it needs to be emphasised that the 'core testimony' to God's abusiveness is not at all what the biblical authors were intending to communicate or consciously advocated; rather, it is the implicit message of their presentation of God. Their failure to recognise God's relationship with Israel and the Church as fundamentally abusive is, I suggest, due to their ignorance of the connection between violence and 'love' in the dynamics of abusive relationships, and also because they were caught up in a patriarchal view of human relationships in which men's dominance over women was normative and taken for granted. Consequently, they have accepted God's declarations of love at face value, rather than enquiring sufficiently into the problematic inconsistencies in the character of God, who can be violent at one moment and soon afterwards be lamenting the suffering of Israel which he himself has brought about! Of course, there are some notable exceptions to this lack of recognition of God's abusive behaviour, most notably Job, and we will examine them at the appropriate point. For the moment, what I am proposing is to read the Bible through the lens of an awareness of the dynamics of abusive relationships, in order to open the reader's eyes to what the Bible is principally saying about the nature of God's relationship with humanity.

However, the Bible does not only witness to the abusiveness of God. There is most definitely a counter testimony to the abusive tradition in the Bible, one which challenges the idea that God is abusive and presents patterns of relationship between God and humans which are different from those contained in the core testimony. According to these portrayals, God is the bringer of peace, harmony and reconciliation, who redeems the world through *refusing to act violently* (e.g. Wink, 1992; Weaver, 2001; Griffith, 2002). Strangely, this testimony has been substantially obscured both in the Bible and in the history of the Church, even though it is central to the teaching of Jesus, who refused to fight to defend himself even when facing crucifixion. It may be discerned, even if vulnerably and fleetingly, in the pages of Scripture and in the lives of Christians who have refused the path of violence. It is my belief that this testimony offers us all the best hope for a way out of the never-ending cycles of violence that the followers of the God of Violence continue to inflict upon the suffering world in the name of the Christian God. This counter testimony also includes those occasions when individuals or communities stand up against abusive behaviour by God or, more generally, act in ways that do not conform to the pattern of abusive relationships. These exceptions are vitally important because they give us indications of how Jews and Christians may develop a relationship with God which is mutually respectful and loving, and in which true intimacy may develop.

A FAMILY THERAPIST MEETS THE FAMILY OF GOD

Even though I am writing about the biblical depiction of God and will draw upon the theories of biblical scholars, this book is not intended as a work of biblical scholarship. I am not a biblical scholar but an Anglican priest, pastoral theologian and systemic family therapist. My perspective is, therefore, one based in pastoral experience and in therapeutic work with families, couples and individuals struggling to improve their relationships and to incarnate something of the reality and mystery of love into their lives. A systemic therapist is one who regards problems not as the 'possession' of an individual, but as the product of the interactions of all involved in the networks of relationship which surround the problem. Thus, for example, a child who has temper tantrums is not most helpfully regarded as a 'naughty' child who disobeys her parents but, rather, as one whose behaviour exists within, and is in large part generated by, her interactions with her parents, siblings, extended family and other people. Her behaviour cannot be adequately understood without examining it in reference to that network, and any therapeutic treatment that ignores her wider system of relationships is very likely to fail or to have only short-lived success.

My method in this book is to survey the Jewish and Christian Scriptures and the histories of Jews and Christians as if I were a family therapist meeting a family who have come for therapy. In the case of this family there is only one parent, namely, God, who never turns up to give an account of himself. Indeed, the family tells me that he repeatedly says that he is not answerable to anyone. As a result, I have to rely on what his family reports about his behaviour, including many statements that its members claim that he has made. In practice, this means looking at what the Bible says about God. In doing so, however, I will not be assessing the Bible in the same way as a biblical scholar would. I will not be asking literary-critical or historical questions of its text. Rather, I will be reading it as a unified document, as if it were an extremely long and complex case history drawn from the accounts of many witnesses. As such, it is not always consistent and is sometimes clearly contradictory. Biblical scholars seek to make sense of these disparities by discovering the history of the writing, editing and transmission of these documents. In contrast, in this study the Bible will be taken, on the one hand, as evidence for the psychology of its Hebrew and Christian authors and the communities for which they wrote and, on the other hand, as an indicator of the psychology of contemporary Christians who have been inducted into their faith through exposure to these texts. The emotional world of modern believers is still in many respects a product of the emotional world of the ancient Hebrews and the early Church. One of the purposes of this book is to make clear what some of the major continuing influences of the biblical outlook are on both the psychology of today's Christians and their political commitments.

I fear that my method and conclusions may offend some believers and disconcert some scholars. It is as well at this stage to acknowledge that my emphasis on the violence of God may appear to give too little recognition to the ways in which both the religion of Israel and Christianity have promoted peace and justice, and my attention to the abusiveness of God may seem to underestimate the biblical witness to God's love and faithfulness. This is not because I do not accept that there are many elements in the texts which support these ideas, but because I believe that they have been given undue prominence and have consequently obscured what the Bible also says about the abusive and violent behaviour of God and, indeed, of the ancient Israelites. In order to compensate for this deficiency, I am quite deliberately highlighting the negative elements of the tradition so that they cannot be ignored or easily argued away. In the process, the more positive aspects may well appear to be neglected or minimised. This is an unavoidable consequence of this approach. It is also necessary to prevent readers from evading acknowledging the abusiveness of God, as depicted in the Bible, by imagining that the occasions when he is loving and attentive somehow cancel out his threats and violence. As I will describe in the next chapter, the alternation of violent and 'loving' phases is a characteristic of many abusive relationships.

This book is a sequel to *The Cost of Certainty: How Religious Belief Betrays the Human Psyche*. Although it can be read quite independently of that earlier work, it continues an exploration I began there into the connection between human emotional needs and the destructive effects of religion, especially the Christian religion. In that book I concentrated on how the desire to be loved by God, combined with the fear of rejection for not being good enough or not believing the right things, can lead individuals to deny or repress their doubts along with the less acceptable aspects of their characters in order to find acceptance from God and their religious communities. The consequence is often that those negative characteristics are projected and experienced as if they belong to others, giving birth to scapegoating in the form of shunning, exclusion, persecution or violence.

In this book I explore the religious origins of violence from the perspective of the psychology of abusive and violent relationships, and I include reference to these dynamics in the religion of ancient Israel, later Judaism and Islam. Even though I have indicated some of the more positive aspects of the biblical and theological traditions, this analysis may appear excessively negative. It has not been possible within the constraints of a volume of this length to include much in the way of a reconstruction of Christian belief in the light of my conclusions. However, I have outlined some possible ways forward in the final chapter and I intend to develop these ideas in the future. If I succeed in getting readers to recognise the existence of the biblical witness to the violence and abusiveness of God, and the significance of its continuing influence on the psychology and politics of Jews, Christians and Muslims, and thus on the peace of the world, I will regard my emphasis as justified.

In reading the biblical documents, I am trying to make sense of the interactions that happen in the family of God as a whole, both past and present, to recognise repetitive patterns of behaviour, and to identify the stories, assumptions, beliefs and rules which maintain these interactions and behaviours. My particular concern is with reports of God's actions which suggest to me that he is abusive towards both his family and others outside it, and with evidence provided by the behaviour of members of his family that indicates that the psychological dynamics of abusive relationships are widespread in this extended family network, including violent behaviour by several individuals and subgroups. From the systemic viewpoint, there are plenty of grounds to conclude that the parent does indeed behave abusively, and that the children show many signs of suffering from the emotional and relational effects of abuse. In the next chapter I shall present some of the case notes that have led me to the above conclusion.

A confusing factor is that it is often not clear whether the descriptions of God that the various members of his family give of him are accurate or not. Obviously, there are inconsistencies both between the different books of the Bible, and between the Hebrew Bible as a whole and the New Testament as a whole and, indeed, the Qur'an. But a more fundamental difficulty is knowing whether what they record is the product of 'divine revelation' and is thus a true depiction of the deity, or whether it is the product of human imagination and thus merely a reflection of the ideas of God produced by human minds. This is an issue which we will have several occasions to examine.

One problem in presenting these case notes is that the family of God is not like other families and the nature of the interaction of its members with God does not fit any one category of relationship. Sometimes God is described as their father, at other times as lover or husband, at still others as judge or lord or tribal leader. Another confusing factor is that the family of God is actually at least three different, though interrelated families – Jews, Christians and Muslims – and the connections between them over the centuries have been complex and myriad. In order to make some sense of this confusing mass of data, I shall begin by concentrating on the story of God and the Hebrews as found in the Hebrew Bible. In later chapters I shall consider God's other two families as well as two specific branches of his family tree in the contemporary world, the United States of America and the State of Israel.

Chapter 2

CASE NOTES OF A SUSPECTED ABUSER

ISRAEL'S JEALOUS HUSBAND

The primary justification for making a comparison between the behaviour of God and that of abusive men is that the Hebrew Bible actually uses this analogy to depict God's relationship to Israel. Of course, the passages concerned do not use the language of abuse – that is anachronistic – rather, they appeal to the rights of a cuckolded husband in their society in order to explain and justify the violence that God directs at Israel, and they portray God's actions in terms typical of the most destructive of abusive men.

A number of the prophets (Hos. 2:1–13; Jer. 2:1–3; 13:20–27; Ezek. 16; 23) employ the metaphor of marriage to describe the covenant relationship (Weems, 1995, p. 13). The use of this metaphor attributes to God all the rights belonging to a husband in a patriarchal society such as that of ancient Israel, including the right to chastise and beat his wife when she has been disobedient or unfaithful. These prophets present Israel as an unfaithful wife who is both disobedient and sexually promiscuous, running after 'other gods' with whom she has sexual relations, and God as an aggrieved husband who in his anger and humiliation repeatedly acts in controlling and abusive ways towards his wife, including extreme physical violence. According to these accounts, the violence in God's relationship with Israel begins with Israel's unfaithfulness as a wife, an unfaithfulness which the Hebrew Bible traces back to the period in the wilderness when the Israelites abandoned their God and worshipped the golden calf (Exod. 32).

A sure indication of a man's essential insecurity and of how much he relies on his female companion to boost his ego is the jealousy that he experiences when he believes that she does not love him or, worse, has directed her affections elsewhere. The greatest threat to an abusive man is that 'his' woman will turn her attention away from him and withdraw the many benefits he gets from her. A man may be insanely jealous and imagine all kinds of unfaithfulness on his partner's behalf, even when she is completely innocent, and may attempt to control her movements so that she has no opportunity to be unfaithful. If his partner does leave him, he may become extremely violent.

An important parallel between God's attitudes and behaviour and those of abusive men is that the latter are at their most dangerous at the point when a woman actually leaves. This is when such a man is most likely to assault his partner to the extent of causing serious injury and even death (Jacobson & Gottman, 1998, pp. 204, 236–7). The primary reason why God displays violence towards Israel is because of her unfaithfulness. The threat of punishment associated with the terms of the covenant was referred to in the previous chapter. The worst offence that Israel can commit against God is to be unfaithful by worshipping other gods. Above all else, God will allow his people, in the words of the second commandment, to have 'no other gods before me' (Exod. 20:3; Deut. 5:7), because he is 'a jealous God, punishing the children for the sin of the fathers to the third and the fourth generation of those who hate me, but showing love to thousands who love me and keep my commandments' (Exod. 20:5; Deut. 5:9).

Israel does not have the right to leave God or to pursue other gods. In the biblical narrative, when Israel worships other gods she is subjected to the severest punishments. As Renita Weems explains:

> Like a jealous husband who has been humiliated by his wife's affairs, God was capable of taking some unimaginably harsh measures against Israel his wife. God is described as an abusive husband who batters his wife, strips her naked, and leaves her to be raped by her lovers, only to take her back in the end, insisting that when all is said and done Israel the wife shall remain interminably the wife of an abusing husband, 'and I will take you my wife forever' (Hos. 2:19) … He is not simply hurt, desperate, or jealous of his wife's infidelities. He is outraged, menacing, and un-predictable in the measures he takes against her. Here the prophets admitted that Israel's history had shown repeatedly that God was as capable of being abusive as God was of being compassionate.
>
> (Weems, 1995, p. 72)

The kind of divine behaviour she is referring to is well illustrated by the following passage from Ezekiel:

> I will sentence you to the punishment of women who commit adultery and who shed blood; I will bring upon you the blood vengeance of my wrath and jealous anger. Then I will hand you over to your lovers, and they will tear down your mounds and destroy your lofty shrines. They will strip you of your clothes and

take your fine jewellery and leave you naked and bare. They will bring a mob against you, who will stone you and hack you to pieces with their swords. They will burn down your houses and inflict punishment on you in the sight of many women.

(Ezek. 16:38–41a)

Despite the ferocity of God's wrath, his 'love' for Israel is not obliterated. In re-reading the Bible in preparation for this book, I was forcefully struck, on the one hand, by the ease and frequency with which God gives vent to his rage, whether towards the Hebrews or other nations, and, on the other hand, by a number of passages in which God does movingly express his love for Israel, albeit a love which is injured by her disobedience or rejection and always teetering on the edge of violence. The alternation frequently found in abusive relationships between times when a couple appear to be getting on and when the man becomes violent has much in common with the biblical picture of God's interaction with Israel: times of closeness are followed by periods of estrangement when God is angry and punitive, and then by others when his anger has been exhausted and he promises to bind up Israel's wounds and to bring in a new era of permanent, loving intimacy (e.g. Isa. 9:1–7; 11:1–9; 40:1–31; Jer. 31:31–34; Ezek. 11:19–20).

The metaphor of Israel as the wife of Yahweh is particularly well suited for expressing his continuing, though injured, devotion to unfaithful Israel. For example, in Hosea 1—3, God is portrayed as the husband of an adulterous wife who is intent on winning her back. Indeed, Hosea is commanded to marry an 'adulterous wife' to advertise the Lord's predicament. God seems to be in turmoil, moving between fantasies of revenge and a desire to restore Israel to the faithfulness of her youth. He proclaims:

How can I give you up, Ephraim? How can I hand you over, Israel? How can I treat you like Admah? How can I make you like Zeboiim? My heart is changed within me; all my compassion is aroused. I will not carry out my fierce anger, nor devastate Ephraim again. For I am God, and not man – the Holy One among you. I will not come in wrath. (Hos. 11:8–9)

Nevertheless, his anger was subsequently enacted in the destruction of the kingdom of Israel, to which Hosea was prophesying.

BLAMING THE VICTIM

Most abusers blame their victims for their own abusive behaviour, seeing the woman's behaviour as the 'cause' of their violence. They may say that they love their partners and only get annoyed with them because they need correcting or because they behave badly – 'If only she would do what is right, I would not hit her' – but such a rationalisation denies that a man makes a choice about how to respond to his partner's 'wrong' actions. This is another respect in which the God of the Hebrew Bible is very similar to an abusive man. He is excessively emotionally aroused by Israel's 'disobedience'. He is unable to control her by persuasion, and so repeatedly seeks to bring her back into line through violent means. When he does so, he blames her for his own actions. He never accepts any blame for the violence that he inflicts on the Hebrews, justifying his violence as a just 'punishment'. Israel is guilty and is responsible for the punishment she receives. It is always the wife who is at fault, never the husband – a view frequently expressed by the prophets:

> In the prophetic descriptions, the husband repeatedly reminds his wife that he has fulfilled his side of the relationship – he has fed, clothed and protected her (Hos. 2:8; Ezek. 16:1–8). It is the wife's failures and indiscretions that are repeatedly elaborated upon: her false claims about her lover (Hos. 2:5, 12), her sexually extravagant and wanton behaviour (Ezek. 16:15–22), her flagrant failure to remain faithful to her husband (Jer. 3:3, 10; 4:30; Ezek. 16:25–52; 23). The implication is clear: the wife deserves to be punished …
>
> God, then, is not a harsh, cruel, vindictive husband who threatens and beats his wife simply because he has the power to do so. He is himself a victim, because he has been driven to extreme measures by a wife who has again and again dishonored him and has disregarded the norms governing marriage relations.
>
> (Weems, 1995, pp. 19–20)

Israel is always held by God to be responsible for the violence he inflicts upon her. In the Bible, God's aggression towards Israel is rationalised and justified by calling it 'justice'. God, being God, has the right to expect and to exact absolute obedience and faithfulness from his people and, because this is so, it is just if he punishes her for failing to give them to him. This applies even if the punishments are disproportionate and include massacres, plagues, fire from heaven and general devastation. Very often the treatment of his people by God resembles a tyranny more than the behaviour of a loving, if authoritarian, husband.

PATRIARCHY AND MEN'S VIOLENCE TOWARDS WOMEN

Even if God's violence towards Israel far exceeds that of any mere human male towards his partner, the violence of both God and abusive men is puzzling. One would expect a lover who genuinely cares about his mate to be tender towards her rather than violent or controlling. Why, if men genuinely love their partners, would they wish to impose their wills violently upon them? Many commentators regard patriarchy as one of the most important, if not the primary, causes of men's violence towards women. Amongst the common characteristics of men who abuse women is a belief in what is known as patriarchal privilege (Jenkins, 1990, p. 30) – in other words, in the right of men to control the actions of their women and to expect certain services from them, such as domestic work, child-rearing and sex. The feminist theologian Elizabeth Johnson defines patriarchy as 'a form of social organisation in which power is always in the hand of the dominant man or men, with others ranked below in a series of graded subordinations reaching down to the least powerful who form a large base' (Johnson, 1992, p. 23). Others, especially women, are regarded as inferior because they fail to meet the standard set by the male norm. Their experience is not regarded as important and they are denied the opportunity to take a leadership role in society.

A man raised with patriarchal values is likely to view 'his woman' as precisely that: his own possession, who exists to provide him with the emotional support, sexual activity and domestic services that he requires. His ability to control her is used by an abuser to make his partner into what he wants her to be (de Zulueta, 1993, p. 242). He ensures the meeting of these expectations by the threat or enactment of violence. Thus, part of the answer to our question why men who love their partners are violent towards them is that *patriarchal males tend to treat their partners as their possessions or extensions of themselves, rather than as independent people in their own right* and, furthermore, that in patriarchal societies men have traditionally had the right to make their female partners conform to their wishes. But even though they have had the right, why have so many patriarchal males chosen to exercise it? In order to answer this question it is necessary to understand something of the nature of patriarchal masculinity.

Societies described as patriarchal have in common the belief that men and masculinity are superior to women and femininity, and that men should have authority over women, including control of financial resources. Generally, women in these cultures are expected to con- centrate on domestic matters and the raising of children, whereas men are the providers and the ones who participate in the world of public affairs and government. A central aspect of patriarchal masculinity is the ability to be violent. For Sam Keen, this is its primary characteristic:

> The male psyche is, first and foremost, the warrior psyche. Nothing shapes, informs, and molds us so much as society's demand that

we become specialists in the use of power and violence, or as we euphemistically say, 'defense.' Historically, the major difference between men and women is that men have always been expected to be able to resort to violence when necessary. The capacity and willingness for violence has been central to our self-definition. The male psyche has not been built upon the rational 'I think; therefore I am' but upon the irrational 'I conquer; therefore I am.'

(Sam Keen, 1992, p. 37)

The ability to fight has always been central to the notion of masculinity in patriarchal cultures and, even today, the conviction that the army will 'make a man' out of a callow youth is widespread. The warrior is an ambivalent figure: although he may be violent and destructive, his violence and destructiveness is not necessarily negative; it can be regarded in a positive light since he fights to protect his family and community and puts his own life at risk in doing so.

Of course, masculinity is not only about violence. Keen's emphasis on violence may seem somewhat outmoded now that compulsory military service has been abolished in most Western countries. However, I believe that the idea that men should be strong and able to protect their families remains central to most men's idea of what it means to be a man, whether or not they have engaged in military service. Certainly, this is what I observe in my clinical practice, along with the belief, despite the rise of feminism, that a man should be the provider for his family. Of course, masculinity has many other aspects – Keen points out the importance and value of men's activities as workers, loyal members of a group, lovers and fathers – but the ability to fight, whether physically or verbally, including standing up for oneself and protecting one's family, remains central to the definition of patriarchal masculinity.

However, masculinity is not simply about being able to fight; its essence is the exercise of power. 'Male power, especially over females, appears to be central to many men's definitions of themselves. With power they are men; without they are no better than women' (Kahn, 1984, p. 238; quoted by Meth, 1990, p. 13). A major consequence of this system of power is that males in patriarchal societies are brought up to believe in their superiority over women and to expect women to attend to their needs. However, the experience of power for men within patriarchal society is highly ambiguous: although they have power over women, the world of men is structured in an hierarchical manner which actually disadvantages most men with respect to other higher-status males. The consequence is that many men experience themselves as disempowered within society and subject to the control of their superiors. In the modern corporation this sense of insecurity is exaggerated by the frequent 'restructuring' and 'downsizing' that takes place, and which can so easily result in individuals losing their livelihoods and status (Kaufman, 1994; Faludi, 1999).

THE COST OF MASCULINITY

Men's assumptions of superiority over and entitlement from women are encouraged by the manner in which boys are socialised into masculinity. As the family therapist Terence Real says:

> For most boys, the achievement of masculine identity is not an acquisition so much as a disavowal. When researchers asked girls and women to define what it means to be feminine, the girls answered with positive language: to be compassionate, to be connected, to care about others. Boys and men, on the other hand, when asked to describe masculinity, predominantly responded with double negatives. Boys and men did not talk about being strong so much as about not being weak. They did not list independence so much as not being dependent. They did not speak about being close to their fathers so much as about pulling away from their mothers. In short, being a man generally means not being a woman. As a result, boys' acquisition of gender is a negative achievement. Their developing sense of their own masculinity is not, as in most other forms of identity development, a steady movement towards something valued so much as a repulsion from something devalued. Masculine identity development turns out to be not a process of development at all but rather a process of elimination, a succession of unfolding loss. Along with whatever genetic proclivities one might inherit, it is this loss that lays the foundation of depression later in men's lives.
>
> (Real, 1997, p. 130)

Because it is defined over and against femininity, rather than being something positive in itself, masculinity is a negative and oppositional identity: a man is only a man if he is not a woman and does not share characteristics which are regarded as feminine. Since masculine identity is based on success, achievement, superiority over women, and the possession of power, it excludes qualities considered feminine such as feeling, vulnerability, relatedness and weakness. Gender socialisation begins very early; young boys learn to repress their emotions, to be assertive, competitive, hard, and able to cope in all circumstances, and above all to be different from women and effeminate men, fearing especially any suggestion of homosexuality (Meth & Pasick, 1990; Kimmel, 1994). Such male socialisation produces an emotional wound, the loss of the relational, which gives rise to considerable psychological and relational difficulties amongst men. The cost to men of pursuing this form of masculinity is enormous: they are cut off from their feelings; fear intimacy or loss of control; become isolated; and ignore or abuse their own emotional and physical well-being, and that of the environment and planet as a whole (Easlea, 1983; Lee, 1991; Keen, 1992; Farrell, 1994).

Often men are subject to a tendency towards depression as a result of their boyhood experiences (Real, 1997, pp. 113–14). Many men compensate for this depression, or for a more general sense of inadequacy, whether conscious or not, by striving for power or success in one form or another. However, not all men can be successful; many men feel disempowered over and against other men (Kaufmann, 1994, p. 145). Men have constantly to struggle for their place in the male hierarchy and many, indeed the majority, are permanently excluded from positions of power and privilege. The consequence is a sense of inferiority accompanied by shame. According to the forensic psychiatrist James Gilligan, shame is one of the main motivating forces in the generation of violence, which acts as a compensatory means of asserting the self (Gilligan, 2000). Consequently, one way through which men who have been forced into subordinate positions in the male pecking order may compensate for their social inferiority and 'prove themselves men' is by resorting to violence against other, weaker, men or the women they live with. This is an important dynamic through which general economic and class differences reinforce the mistreatment of women in patriarchal societies.

Given the secret emotional fragility of male social identity, a fragility often hidden even from men themselves, the role of women in their emotional lives becomes of paramount importance, but ambiguously so. Although men have learned to deny in themselves, and look down upon, characteristics which are labelled as 'feminine', they are human beings who need closeness and warmth just as much as women do. However, because they have been taught not to behave like women, they cannot behave intimately without losing their 'masculine' identity. They frequently resolve this contradiction by getting women to live out their 'feminine' qualities on their behalf. Thus, it is usual for women to take the major responsibility for family relationships and the social life of a couple.

One consequence of men's ambivalence towards women is that they may experience a need to reassert their dominance when they begin to feel uncomfortably dependent upon a woman. This is a major reason why men are violent towards their partners. Virginia Goldner, a leading clinician and theoretician, and her associates regard battering as 'a man's attempt to reassert gender difference and gender dominance, when his terror of not being different enough from "his" woman threatens to overtake him' (Goldner et al., 1990, p. 348). They have identified what they describe as a 'violence/redemption' cycle in these relationships. For a time the man displays 'feminised devotion' towards his partner, but then when his masculine identity begins to feel threatened by this devotion, he shifts and attempts to assert 'macho domination' through violence (Goldner et al., 1990, p. 353). Similarly, Olivia Carr describes a 'cycle of violence' marked by the alternation of calm periods after a violent episode, often referred to by abused women as the 'honeymoon period', and a gradual build-up to another violent episode marked by an escalation of tension (Carr, 2005, pp. 2–3; cf. Walker, 1984).

NARCISSISTIC RAGE AND VIOLENT MEN

A theory which contributes to our understanding of the interaction of patriarchy and violence, and which also illuminates the behaviour of God as reported in the Hebrew Bible, is the self psychology of the psychoanalyst Heinz Kohut, who studied the phenomenon of narcissism. Drawing on the myth of Narcissus, who fell in love with his own reflection, narcissism refers to the love of self. Kohut believed that an infant needs to experience sufficient love from others to feel good about herself. We may describe this as having her narcissistic needs met. This does not mean that the child is being 'selfish'. Paradoxically, a child needs to have received sufficient love and affirmation of herself, if she is to be able to love others unselfishly. In particular, Kohut spoke about the need for a carer to give the child a positive experience of 'mirroring' – in other words, to reflect back her behaviour in a positive way and to affirm her worth. Such good experiences help a child to internalise and build up a good sense of self.

When these experiences are lacking, individuals will continue to look for a source of narcissistic recognition as adults. They will form relationships in which the other acts as a 'good mirror', giving them positive feedback without criticism. Alternatively, they will seek to gain a sense of value through identification or 'merger' with a figure who appears positive, even idealised. If they can maintain a connection with such a person or group, they can feel good by association. When this happens they require the idealised person, referred to by Kohut as a 'selfobject', to be constantly available, and they tend to imitate his or her characteristics and behaviour. If this figure is a group, they need to feel that they are fully accepted by the other members and that they are the same as them in all essentials. The use of merger to meet narcissistic needs is an important reason why couples may spend all their time together and may find it difficult to express disagreement with each other. When there is no one available to act as a positive mirror or as an idealised selfobject, a person who has had insufficient narcissistic reinforcement will experience low self-esteem, including a sense of loss and shame. The normal reaction to the threatened loss of one who provides narcissistic affirmation is either 'shame-faced withdrawal' or extreme anger, which Kohut refers to as 'narcissistic rage' (Kohut, 1978, p. 637). He explains that:

> Narcissistic rage occurs in many forms; they all share, however, a specific psychological flavour which gives them a distinct position within the wide realm of human aggressions. The need for revenge, for righting a wrong, for undoing a hurt by whatever means, and a deeply anchored, unrelenting compulsion in the pursuit of these aims, which gives no rest to those who have suffered narcissistic injury – these are the characteristic features of narcissistic rage in all its forms and which set it apart from other kinds of aggression ...
>
> [Furthermore,] although everybody tends to react to narcissistic injuries with embarrassment and anger, the most intense experiences of shame and the most violent forms of narcissistic rage arise in those individuals for whom a sense of absolute control over an archaic environment is indispensable because the maintenance of self-esteem – and indeed of the self – depends on the unconditional availability of the approving-mirroring selfobject or of the merger-permitting idealized one.
>
> (Kohut, 1978, pp. 637–8, 644–5)

Many violent men exhibit narcissistic vulnerability to an extreme degree: the partner is used to provide narcissistic affirmation and hence any degree of separation or independent will is intolerable. Aggression and rage are connected with the need for power and control over the selfobject (partner) to ensure that she continues to give him the sort of narcissistic mirroring or merger that he requires.

We are now in a position to recognise how narcissistic deprivation may combine with patriarchy to create violent men. As we have seen, male socialisation entails the systematic emotional deprivation of boys during childhood, and their initiation into patriarchal masculinity involves an attack upon their narcissistic needs through shaming and through separation from their primary narcissistic selfobject – that is, their mother. The subsequent wound to their self-esteem is a source of vulnerability which can easily turn into narcissistic rage.

One way in which individuals compensate for low self-esteem is by grandiosity – in other words, they claim for themselves an importance out of proportion to their true significance. Grandiosity is often an aspect of men's attempts to use achievement to reimburse themselves for the emotional deprivation involved in male socialisation, but the fact that masculinity is an achieved identity means that when they fail, they are liable to feel both narcissistically depleted and lacking in manhood. Many have no inner sense of a good, valuable self. Hence, men are very vulnerable to falling into shame, low self-esteem and depression when deprived of an external source of validation (whether the male group or the adoring female). In my opinion, the privileges of patriarchy act as a compensation for the narcissistic wounding of boys and men which is itself an essential part of the process of male socialisation and initiation into masculine gender roles. This fact accounts for many men's sense of powerlessness and sensitivity to insult, neither of which makes sense if patriarchy is simply an expression of power and superiority.

All in all, patriarchal masculinity is an ambivalent achievement: it endows men with privileges over women but at the cost of having constantly to reaffirm their masculinity and compete for their position in the male hierarchy, and also of bearing the legacy of a traumatic initiation which has injured them emotionally and resulted in insecurity and incipient depression. In addition, when men fail to meet the demand to perform well and compete successfully with other males, they are left with few, if any, emotional resources to cope with their humiliation, and many compensate through violence.

GOD'S NARCISSISM AND NARCISSISTIC RAGE

Wounded narcissism in the context of the ambiguous mix of privilege and emotional insecurity that is patriarchal masculinity appears to me to be a good explanation of the behaviour of God towards Israel, whom he seeks to control absolutely so that she is always available as 'the approving-mirroring selfobject' who praises and glorifies him. In the biblical narrative, God is very insistent upon his glory, so much so that he appears to be unduly reliant upon others to give him a sense of self-esteem, and this requirement seems to be the chief motivation of his conduct towards Israel. From a theological perspective, interpreting God's insistence on his glory as a symptom of narcissism may seem inappropriate, even outrageous, because theologically giving God glory is essentially about acknowledging the true difference in status between human beings and their creator. However, in the context of this book, in which the character of God, as it is depicted in the Bible, is being interpreted *as if* he were a human being, narcissism is what God's desire for glory most closely resembles.

At times God shows compassion for the Israelites' difficulties. For example, he sent them manna and quails to eat after they had grumbled about their hunger, but even so, his chief concern in doing so was not their well-being but, rather, that 'they will know that I am the Lord your God' (Exod. 16:12). At other times, he showed little understanding or tolerance of the Israelites' natural human weakness or discouragement; rather, he was driven to an outburst of narcissistic rage by their complaints and exacted revenge for them. For instance, 'fire from the Lord' 'consumed some of the outskirts of the camp' when they 'complained about their hardships in the hearing of the Lord' (Num. 11:1). Even his gift of quails turned out not to be an act of genuine generosity; instead, it became an occasion to vent his anger: as the Israelites began to eat it, 'he struck them with a severe plague' (Num. 11:33). In addition, God condemned the generation who left Egypt to die in the desert before they reached the Promised Land, because they lost heart and did not trust him after hearing a false report of the strength of the people of the land (Num. 14:1–35). Indeed, at that time, God even threatened to wipe out the Hebrews and to make a nation instead from Moses, and only relented because of Moses' intercession on their behalf (Num. 14:11–12). Other complaints by the people were also met with draconian punishments (e.g. Num. 16:1–35, 41–50; 20:12; 21:4–9). In sum, *the Hebrew Bible depicts the God of Israel as a narcissistic character who requires constant adoration, or else he flies into a rage.* An indication that God's reactions towards Israel's 'offences' are an expression of his narcissistic rage rather than of his justice is the fact that his 'punishments' are often totally disproportionate to the offences committed. The numerous massacres of the Israelites during the wilderness period are good examples; to send a plague or fire from heaven because the people complain is excessive by any standards!

God not only expects to be honoured by Israel, but by other nations as well. There are many examples of him using Israel and other nations to 'give him glory', which essentially means to recognise his dominance, usually through victory in warfare. Even though doubts and dissatisfaction may be expressed at other times, the Israelites' general response to God's great deeds – for example, after the crossing of the Reed Sea – is to 'fear the Lord' because of his 'great power' (Exod. 14:31). However, his chosen people's fear does not eradicate God's need for reassurance, and he repeatedly calls on Israel and the nations to witness his power and might.

This demand is characteristic of God throughout the history of Israel. At its beginning, he commands Moses to tell Pharaoh, 'I have raised you up for this very purpose, that I might show you my power and that my name might be proclaimed in all the earth' (Exod. 9:16). Centuries later, after using the Babylonians to destroy the kingdom of Judah, nothing has changed: he is still wanting to be acknowledged by all peoples, as can be seen in the manner in which he calls Cyrus, king of Persia, to release the Jewish exiles in Babylon:

> I am the Lord, and there is no other; apart from me there is no God. I will strengthen you, though you have not acknowledged me, so that from the rising of the sun to the place of its setting men may know there is none besides me. I am the Lord, and there is no other. (Isa. 45:5–6)

God's concern for his public image is not limited to Israel and the nations. He sometimes displays considerable insecurity about how he is regarded by particular individuals whom he favours. For example, he commands Abraham to sacrifice his son Isaac in order to prove to himself that Abraham truly fears him. Thus, at the point when Abraham is about to kill the boy, the angel of the Lord says, 'Do not lay a hand on the boy ... Now I know that you fear God, because you have not withheld from me your son, your only son' (Gen. 22:12). It seems that only by pushing Abraham to such an extreme is God able to reassure himself of his devotion. Similarly, the insinuations of Satan that Job is only worshipping God for his blessings expose a deep-seated doubt in God's mind about the genuineness of Job's loyalty, and so he allows Satan to destroy everything that he possesses, including his children (Job 1:9–12). One can only wonder why the creator of the universe should require such reassurance if it is not because he is secretly insecure and lacking in self-esteem.

OTHER MAJOR METAPHORS FOR GOD'S RELATION-SHIP TO ISRAEL

The interpretation of God's relationship to Israel as abusive does not depend solely on the marriage metaphor. The marriage metaphor is actually used relatively rarely in the Hebrew Scriptures. Even so, I have based my argument upon it because it makes very clear the conditional nature of God's 'love' for Israel and his readiness to bring her into line by the use of violence. Men who abuse their partners generally treat them as inferior – the pattern of their interactions is one of domination and subordination – and this is precisely the way in which God relates to Israel. Indeed, *the most significant similarity between God and an abusive man is not his violence, but his determination to control and dominate his partner.*

Of course, God is God and is, therefore, infinitely superior to Israel.

The Hebrews are innately unequal and, it must be conceded, this inequality does not necessarily prevent genuine love existing between themselves and God, any more than the inequality between a parent and a child precludes the possibility of real love. However, a person can only be described as loving if he has a true regard for the well-being of the object of his love. Although the Bible claims that God is loving in this way, as we have seen, his behaviour very frequently puts this claim in question. Rather than being concerned about Israel, he seems primarily to want Israel to be what he requires her to be for his own peace of mind, and to be willing to impose the most terrible 'punishments' on her when she does not conform to his wishes.

The other major metaphors used about God's interactions with Israel also support the idea that he is abusive towards her by exercising his power to control her and to force her to conform to his wishes. Weems notes that: 'The prophets used five human relationships as metaphors of the relationship between God and Israel: (1) judge and litigant, (2) parent and child, (3) master and slave, (4) king and vassal, and (5) husband and wife' (Weems, 1995, p. 17), and that, although each of these metaphors entails 'mutual obligations and mutual responsibilities', they all indicate that the subordinate must be careful to fulfil his obligations to the superior or expect retribution: 'judges punished defendants; kings banished or executed servants; masters beat slaves; parents disciplined children; and husbands divorced or assaulted wives' (Weems, 1995, p. 18).

Similarly, Brueggemann says: 'The metaphors that appear to dominate Israel's speech about Yahweh may be termed images of governance, wherein Israel witnesses to Yahweh's capacity to govern and order in ways that assert sovereign authority and that assure a coherent ordering of life in the world.' These include 'judge, king, warrior, and father', each of which 'pertains to the use of power' (Brueggemann, 1997, p. 233). As such, these metaphors do have many positive aspects, not least their capacity to speak of God's concern for justice, especially for those of his people who are poor and oppressed by the rich and powerful. There is a very strong tradition in the prophets asserting God's outrage at such exploitation, for instance: 'Woe to those who make unjust laws, to those who issue oppressive decrees, to deprive the poor of their rights and rob my oppressed people of justice, making widows their prey and robbing the fatherless' (Isa. 10:1–2). The requirements of justice are of more importance than ritual propriety, as Hosea puts it: 'I desire mercy, not sacrifice, and acknowledgement of God rather than burnt offerings' (Hos. 6:6).

These requirements do not in any way dispense with the prohibition of idolatry or with God's demand for absolute commitment to him and no other. However, they do show God's concern for his people in a much more positive light than the one that I have cast upon it hitherto. He intends the society that his people creates to be ordered with justice and compassion for the needy and even the alien, and he is quite prepared to use coercive force to ensure that this happens (Deut. 26:12; 15:4). In other words, God's violence is not only an expression of his anger at being rejected in favour of other gods; it often has the constructive function of righting injustice and restoring social order.

Each of these metaphors is also, although Brueggemann does not say this, an example of the pattern of domination and subordination enforced by actual or potential violence which is characteristic of abusive relationships. Even though they do include elements indicative of God's justice, mercy and love, all of these metaphors may be used to support the description of his relationship with Israel as abusive because, whichever of them is being used to describe it, *the association of God with Israel is one which always takes place in a context of threat: if Israel does not do what God wants, she will be on the receiving end of his rage or 'punishment'.* Indeed, like a woman living with an abusive man, it is precisely the fact that she is the one chosen by God that puts Israel in this position of jeopardy, as God says: 'You only have I chosen of all the families of the earth; therefore I will punish you for all your sins' (Amos 3:2).

Furthermore, as Brueggemann does observe, although these metaphors of governance witness to God's mercy and love as well as to his awesome power and, in addition, are often positive and affirmative of God's actions, they are also capable of pointing to his severity and to internal contradictions in his character, and they each have an ominous quality (Brueggemann, 1997, pp. 247–50):

> One has the sense that a violent potential is always present where Yahweh is. Most of the time that violence can be accepted and justified in terms of the justice through which Israel comes to understand Yahweh. And yet, an undomesticated quality of Yahweh allows a play of violence, on occasion, that cannot be contained in any sense of justice. That potential violence can break out at any time, because Yahweh is not fully accountable to any other agent, not even Yahweh's partner Israel to whom fidelity has been pledged. This is indeed the God who is gracious and merciful. But in this testimony, the danger intrinsic to the character of Yahweh is never fully or finally banished. (Brueggemann, 1997, pp. 249–50)

DOMINATION AND SUBORDINATION AND THE GOD OF ISRAEL

The Hebrew Scriptures almost always portray relationships between humans in terms of domination and subordination. Ancient Israel was a patriarchal civilisation, along with its neighbours and the empires which dominated the then-known world. It appears that the terms in which God is portrayed in the Hebrew Bible are representative of the manner in which the biblical writers thought of human relationships in general. The story of the Hebrews is centred on the theme of the land that God will give to them and the promise of greatness. When God calls Abraham, he says: 'I will make you into a great nation and I will bless you; I will make your name great, and you will be a blessing. I will bless those who bless you, and whoever curses you I will curse; and all peoples on earth will be blessed through you' (Gen. 12:2–3). Part of this blessing is the promise that Abraham's 'descendants will take possession of the cities of their enemies' (Gen. 22:17).

The Scriptures also depict Israel's interaction with other nations in terms of domination and subordination, victory or defeat, whether with the Canaanites whom she conquers or the foreign nations who surround or invade her (e.g. Deut. 15:6; Josh. 1:27–36; 31; Judg. 1:27–36; 2 Sam. 22:44–49; 1 Kings 9:20–21; Esth. 9). Moreover, there are very few examples of Israel working co-operatively with other nations or of genuine reconciliation between different tribes or communities in the Bible. One of the few exceptions is the treaty made between Isaac and Ahimelech to do each other no harm (Gen. 26:26–30); and the reconciliation of Jacob and Esau is a rare example of a conflict being resolved without violence (Gen. 33).

In the hierarchy of males God is, of course, the dominant male and the one who is responsible for the hierarchy amongst Jewish males. Those men whom he favours become the leaders of Israel, whether as patriarchs, judges or kings. The family of Israel is itself organised hierarchically: each family has its head under whom all the other male members have a recognised order of seniority, though inconsistently God rather delights to subvert this order by, for example, favouring younger sons over their elder brothers – for instance, Abel, Jacob and Joseph.

God shares in the restricted emotionality of the patriarchal male. He seems to have little awareness of the negative aspects of his character and behaviour. Although he repeatedly gives vent to his wrath, often with hardly any provocation and in total disproportion to the offence, God's self-image is positive:

> The Lord, the Lord, compassionate and gracious, *slow to anger*, abounding in love and faithfulness, maintaining love to thousands, and *forgiving* wickedness, rebellion and sin. Yet he does not leave the guilty unpunished; he punishes the children and their children for the sin of the fathers to the third and fourth generation. (Exod. 34:6–7, italics added; cf. Num. 14:18–19)

If he is unaware of the impulsiveness and mercilessness of his own character, the Lord has just as limited an ability to understand or empathise with human emotions. All in all, he shows little or no appreciation of what human beings mean to each other, riding roughshod over normal family affections in pursuit of his aims. Thus, he allows Satan (in Hebrew thought, not the Devil but the one who accuses people before God) to kill Job's children, and seems to believe that giving him new children at the end of the story will make up for Job's multiple bereavement (Job 1; 42). It is barely conceivable that a father who experienced such a loss would ever recover from such a trauma; and the feelings of Job's wife are never taken into account. God's command to Abraham to sacrifice Isaac is equally callous (Gen. 22:1–18). One wonders what the reaction of Sarah was when she heard what had happened!

The people whom God favours often display a similar lack of human solidarity and a lack of empathy equal to that of their divine master. Astonishingly, Noah displays absolutely no emotion or protest when God announces that he is going to destroy all the people on earth. Noah simply obeys as if he had no concern for his extended family, his neighbours or humanity in general; but at least he knows that his wife, sons and daughters-in-law will accompany him (Gen. 7:9–22). Other 'friends of God' extend their lack of compassion to members of their own immediate families. For example, Lot offers his own daughters to the men of Sodom to be raped in place of his two male guests (Gen. 19:8; cf. Judg. 19 & Gen. 42:37), Jephthah sacrifices his daughter (Judges II), and, of course, Abraham is willing to sacrifice Isaac at God's command.

CONCLUSION

The case notes on the suspected abuser, Yahweh, the God of Israel, presented in this chapter contain very extensive evidence for his abusive behaviour towards his family, the children of Israel. As portrayed in the Hebrew Bible, God is a being who is violent above all other characteristics, and his violence often extends beyond Israel to include other nations as well. He treats Israel as an extension of himself from whom he expects and demands absolute faithfulness, worship and obedience, and he appears only to care for her to the extent that she meets his needs, attempting to coerce her into compliance with threats, and quickly turning nasty when she shows any signs of non-compliance.

He appears to be motivated by a belief in patriarchal privilege, includ-ing proprietary rights over Israel, for whose misdemeanours he has the right to exact punishment of the most draconian variety. His treatment of her also displays symptoms of narcissism, which result in angry attacks upon Israel when she disappoints his expectations of constant adoration, obedience, availability and faithfulness. In all of this, he acknowledges no fault or responsibility but, rather, blames Israel for any difficulties in their relationship. In the light of this survey, Israel's rela-tionship with God is justly compared with that of a woman who lives with a violent and controlling partner, ever aware that, even if he is peaceful for the time being, he can turn vicious at any moment and at the slightest provocation, and may do so for no particular reason at all. In short, the Hebrew Bible depicts God as a patriarchal male who is abusive towards his wife Israel.

This conclusion gives weight to the very important question that was mentioned at the end of the last chapter and that will recur as this study proceeds: Is the biblical portrayal of God really a picture of the nature of God or is it, rather, a result of the projection onto God of characteristics that actually belong to the biblical authors or their communities? The remarkable similarity between those aspects of the image of God in the Hebrew Bible that we have been examining and the psychology and behaviour of abusive patriarchal men is in itself a ground for suspicion that we are dealing here with a human creation rather than a product of revelation. In other words, the biblical text may give us a great deal of information about the psychology and social organisation of the ancient Israelites but little about the nature of God. This is a question to which we will return.

Chapter 3

THE CYCLE OF ABUSE IN ANCIENT ISRAEL

THE CYCLE OF ABUSE

We have seen that the relationship of God to Israel, as represented in the Hebrew Bible, has much in common with that between an abusive man and his female partner, but why would the ancient Israelites choose to portray their God in such terms? One possible answer is that their God is a projection of their own psychology and that it was formed through experiences of abuse. If this were so, we would expect to find evidence of the psychology of abuse amongst them. However, unhelpfully, this would also be the case if God were an abuser. To exist in an abusive relationship for any length of time has severe psychological consequences which we would expect Israel to exhibit if this were so. In this and the next chapter, therefore, we will be looking for evidence of the psychology of abuse in Israelite history and thinking.

Many women are systematically undermined by their male partners, so that they cease to believe in themselves and come to internalise the negative messages about themselves that their partners use – for example, that they are selfish, stupid or sluttish. An abused woman may suffer from self-blame, self-loathing and guilt, and may even feel that she is going out of her mind (Jacobson & Gottman, 1998, pp. 76–9). Children who have been abused or neglected by their parents have similar reactions. We have already examined some of the psychological reasons why men become abusive towards their partners. Many commentators have noted that the experience of being abused as a child is widespread, possibly universal, amongst adult abusers. Indeed, some claim that experiences of abuse or neglect are necessary to turn infants into abusive adults. For example, Alice Miller says: 'Those children who are beaten will in turn give beatings, those who are intimidated will be intimidating, those who are humiliated will impose humiliation, and those whose souls are murdered will murder' (Miller, 1987, p. 232; cf. Gilligan, 2000).

According to the psychoanalytic school known as 'attachment theory', children tend to internalise patterns of relationships from their earliest years and, consequently, when they grow up they are able to live out either side of a relationship pattern (de Zulueta, 1993, pp. 66, 87). In other words, *those who have been abused as children have the potential later to become either victims or abusers as adults.* This does not mean that everyone who has been abused is doomed to enter abusive relationships in adult life, whether as abuser or abused, but that there is a strong tendency to do so. Psychologists speak about a 'repetition compulsion', and it is quite common to come across couples in psychotherapy who are behaving in very similar ways to their parents. Indeed, the repetition of family patterns of behaviour down the generations is a major observation of family therapy.

Abusive behaviour appears usually to be passed down the generations in an ongoing 'cycle of abuse', in which abused children become abusing adults or their victims, whose abused children become abusers or their victims, and so on. This cycle of abuse should be distinguished from the 'cycle of violence' within a particular relationship. The former refers to the pattern of interaction through which abusive behaviour is passed down the generations. The latter refers to the alternation of violent and peaceful periods within a relationship. Fortunately, there is, third option: to break the pattern and escape from the cycle of abuse. Many people are determined not to pass on their childhood experiences to their own children and work very hard to create a different environment for them and to behave differently from their own parents. Even so, ancestral patterns may continue to influence them in subtle ways of which they are unaware. For example, a man may succeed in not being physically violent like his father, but may still end up being very controlling or critical.

THE REVERSAL OF VICTIMHOOD

The 'reversal of victimhood' that takes place in the cycle of abuse, when someone who is abused subsequently becomes an abuser, is a feature not only of familial relationships but also of the interaction of social and ethnic groups. Communities who are oppressed by other communities have typical psychological reactions which are very similar to those of individuals who are abused (Ruth, 1988; Moane, 1994). Sean Ruth points out that one of the reactions of a group to oppression is that 'They may seek relief from oppression by oppressing some other group rather than trying to change the system' (Ruth, 1988, p. 437). This response is important because it points towards a link between individual and communal patterns of abuse. One oppressed group may find relief through oppressing another, but so too may oppressed individuals.

There is often an hierarchical pattern of victimisation in communities. Those who are abused by those who are more powerful than themselves may compensate for their sense of inferiority by discharging their anger onto those who are weaker and less powerful than themselves. For instance, high-status males may abuse low-status males, who abuse women and/or children; women may abuse children; older children may abuse younger children. The reaction of abusing others in your own group when your group is oppressed is referred to as 'horizontal violence'.

'Identification with victimhood' is as much a part of the psychology of group oppression, whether enslavement, colonisation, persecution or class disadvantage, as it is a part of the psychology of domestic abuse. We may, therefore, expect to find signs among oppressed groups, including the ancient Israelites, of the reversal of victimhood and the repetition compulsion associated with the cycle of abuse. An extremely good example of the reversal of victimhood is the behaviour of former Afro-American slaves when they were set free by the philanthropic American Colonization Society in that part of Africa which later became the Republic of Liberia. Instead of turning their backs on slavery and all its ills, they set about establishing a society that replicated that of the Southern states of the USA. They set clear boundaries between themselves and the indigenous peoples, introducing laws against intermarriage and creating a highly oppressive state. They even practised slavery! As the Polish journalist Ryszard Kapuściński notes:

> Liberia is the voluntary continuation of slave society by slaves who did not wish to abolish an unjust social order, but wanted to preserve it, develop it, and exploit it for their own benefit. Clearly, an enslaved mind, tainted by the experience of slavery, a mind born into slavery, fettered in infancy, cannot conceive or conjure a world in which they are born free. (Kapuściński, 2002, pp. 238–9)

THE 'CHOSEN PEOPLE DEFENCE' AND THE CONQUEST OF CANAAN

According to the biblical account, the descendants of Jacob, also known as Israel, settled in the land of Goshen in Egypt, where they flourished until a Pharaoh came to power who oppressed them, reducing them to slavery. God took compassion on their distress and sent Moses to call on Pharaoh to release his people. Pharaoh refused but, after suffering ten plagues culminating in the Passover, the death of all the first-born sons of the Egyptians, he agreed to let them go. Subsequently, he changed his mind and pursued the Israelites, but his army was drowned when they followed the Israelites across the dry bed of the Reed Sea and God, who had held back the waters so that the Israelites could cross over, let them fall back on the Egyptians.

Biblical scholars have raised questions about the historicity of this account. From the historian's perspective, the origins of the Israelite tribes are obscure. Opinion is divided between two main theories, one of which, 'the immigration model', postulates that the tribes were originally nomadic shepherds who eventually settled in Canaan; the other of which, 'the revolt model', proposes that the tribes were originally *hapiru*, exploited slaves, whose designation may be the origin of the name 'Hebrew', who fled from the cities of Canaan and then joined up with a group who believed in Yahweh and possessed a tradition of having escaped from Egypt under Moses. The numbering of the tribes as 12 is a later systematisation from the time of the early monarchy (Gerstenberger, 2002, pp. 111–20). What is notable in both these scholarly accounts, as well as the biblical one, is that the ancestors of the Jewish people were oppressed or marginalised in one way or another, either as slaves or nomads. In other words, they were originally victims in the economic and political cycle of abuse of their era.

However, instead of simply internalising a negative view of themselves in a similar manner to other oppressed races, the Hebrews came to believe that God had chosen them to be his special people: 'Now if you obey me fully and keep my covenant, then out of all nations you will be my treasured possession. Although the whole earth is mine, you will be for me a kingdom of priests and a holy nation' (Exod. 19:5–6a). I call this reaction of the Israelites to their oppression 'the chosen people defence'. From a psychological point of view this defence functions as a compensation for experiences of inferiority, enslavement, abuse, defeat, and so on. Over the centuries the belief that they have been chosen by God has acted as a very powerful defence for the children of Israel against the loss of self-esteem which accompanies the experience of marginalisation and domination. It has given them a source of significance and reassurance even when, as often, their fortunes have been eclipsed.

The chosen people defence is a form of 'the spirituality of identification'. This spirituality is based on the identification of a particular social or ethnic group with the favour of God or a god. Usually the group claims both to be chosen for a special relationship with, and a particular role in the purposes of, God, and also to possess some special revelation or authority from God. This may take the form of a scripture, a law or a priesthood or some other authoritative institution. Although this spirituality is found in ancient Israel, it is very common in other religions and is foundational of both Christianity and Islam as well as Judaism.

Since it afflicts all three of the major monotheistic religions, it is profoundly significant in their interactions and is one of the major contributory causes of conflicts between them. The spirituality of identification is particularly dangerous when adherents of a religion go beyond identifying their foundational documents and ruling institutions with the truth and authority of God, to identifying themselves with the favour of God over and against some other group who disagrees with them or is competing with them for some resource. The result is likely to be intolerance, persecution or war, as will be seen when we come to examine the war on terror.

According to the Hebrew Bible, God chose one people arbitrarily, or at least for no stated reason, out of all the others and favoured them. What is more, he rescued them from slavery in Egypt and gave them the Promised Land, and at his command they invaded, conquered and slaughtered the inhabitants of Canaan. The Israelites' claim to the land of Canaan was based solely on the idea that God had given it to them because they were his chosen people. Indeed, God's choice of Abraham was from the first associated with the gift of the land to his descendants. *There is absolutely no consideration given to the rights of the Canaanites in the Hebrew Bible.* At best, they are simply occupants of the land who must be removed if the Israelites are to take possession of it. At worst, they are described as sinners because of their idolatry, and thus their extinction is justified as a punishment for their sins (Deut. 9:4–6). The biblical account of the invasion displays one of the most destructive aspects of the spirituality of identification: the treatment of other people as non- or sub-human because they are different and do not share the same religious identity. This feature of this spirituality, especially when associated with the chosen people defence, has produced untold conflict and suffering over the centuries, especially in the forms of enslavement, ethnic cleansing and genocide.

Let us be clear: the invasion and conquest of Canaan is a story of unprovoked aggression and genocide, both of which are attributed to the direct command and intervention of God. The actions of the ancient Hebrews represent the kind of behaviour that, in the contemporary world, would call down the strongest condemnation. If God were a human being, he would be tried and found guilty of war crimes. We do not normally recognise that *the God of the invasion of Canaan is the moral equivalent of any of the great perpetrators of genocide in the twentieth century, such as, Hitler, Stalin, Mao, Pol Pot and Saddam Hussein.* Startlingly, this story of the dispossession and genocide of the Canaanites is central to both the Jewish and Christian religions and to their respective beliefs in the active intervention of God on behalf of his chosen or elect people. I have been deeply disturbed by allowing myself to recognise that the fulfilment of the terms of the covenant relationship between God and the Hebrews (the gift of the Promised Land) is to be found in the genocide of the Canaanites, and that, consequently, *the foundation-stone of both the Jewish and Christian religions is the divinely assisted transformation of the victimhood of the slaves who escaped Egypt into the inhuman violence of genocidal invaders.*

To add to my dismay, the Bible has in successive generations frequently been used to support readings by particular nations, races or sects who have identified themselves with those chosen by God and who have, on this basis, claimed his support for the promotion of their own political interests over and against other people whose rights they have denied, especially if they have been heretical or of a different religion or race. It is all too easy for specific groups to perceive themselves as those who are chosen and favoured by God and their enemies as those whom he rejects and condemns. This perception then becomes the basis of a reversal of victimhood whereby the 'chosen' group attack and dominate another 'Canaanite' group; or, it may simply be a rationale for a tribe or nation that is already strong to conquer another. In this way 'the violence of God' very easily becomes converted into a rationale for the violence of human beings towards other human beings, something which we shall see is a feature of the history of the United States of America and of the war on terror.

THE THEOLOGICAL IMPORTANCE OF THE EXILE

The reversal of victimhood often results in the ex-victim-turned-victimiser attributing the favourable position he is now in to the favour of God. In the case of ancient Israel, the reversal of victimhood, which began at the Exodus and was completed with the Conquest leading Israel to assume a position of dominance in the Promised Land, was attributed to the favour of God. The Israelites' reversal reinforced their pre-existing spirituality of identification associated with being the chosen people, and contributed to the development of a religious attitude which took the favour of God for granted. However, this presumption of divine favour was radically undermined by the experience of the Exile in the sixth century BCE.

After the death of Solomon (c. 922 BCE), the kingdom which had been ruled over by Saul, David and Solomon was divided. The northern tribes deserted the house of David and chose Jeroboam as their king, whilst the tribe of Judah remained loyal to Rehoboam, the son of Solomon (1 Kings 12:1–24). Thereafter, the two kingdoms remained separated, the northern one known as Israel and the southern as Judah.

The former was ruled by a succession of dynasties, each short-lasting, until its conquest by the Assyrian Empire in 721 BCE; the latter by the Davidic dynasty until its conquest by the Babylonian Empire in 587 BCE. The conquest of the northern kingdom by Assyria and, more particularly, of the southern kingdom by Babylon, along with the subsequent deportation of the leaders of Judah to Babylon, resulted in a radical undermining of the spirituality of identification. No longer could God's favour be taken for granted. The Exile was the biggest challenge to their existence that the Hebrew people had ever faced. Their belief in their chosenness was hard to sustain in the face of defeat and deportation.

Nevertheless, the period immediately preceding and during the Exile was used by certain theological thinkers to fashion an understanding of the nature of God and of the Israelites' relationship to him which proved capable of withstanding the destruction of the two kingdoms. The principal problem that these theologians faced was to make sense of the failure of God's many promises to maintain the Israelites in the land which he had given them. The answer they produced was centred on the covenant made with God at Sinai, according to the terms of which the commitment made to them by God was conditional upon their obedience. Since his people had broken this condition by frequent and flagrant breaches over many centuries, God had withdrawn his protection and abandoned them to destruction. This is the central import of the biblical passages that speak of Israel as the unfaithful wife of Yahweh. In short, according to this theological perspective, which is particularly associated with the book of Deuteronomy, God had allowed Israel and Judah to be conquered as a punishment for breaking the covenant. Thus, in one of his speeches in the wilderness, Moses refers explicitly to the possible future judgement of Israel and its subsequent desolation, saying:

> All the nations will ask: 'Why has the Lord done this to this land? Why this fierce, burning anger?' And the answer will be: 'It is because this people abandoned the covenant of the Lord, the God of their fathers, the covenant he made with them when he brought them out of Egypt. They went off and worshipped other gods and bowed down to them, gods they did not know, gods he had not given them. Therefore the Lord's anger burned against this land, so that he brought on it all the curses written in this book. In furious anger and in great wrath the Lord uprooted them from their land and thrust them into another land, as it is now.'
>
> (Deut. 29:24–28; cf. 2 Kings 24:20; re. the fall of Israel, cf. 2 Kings 17:7–8)

This theology clearly incorporates the psychology of the abused into its conception of God and, in particular, what is known as 'the moral defence'.

THE MORAL DEFENCE

The psychoanalyst Ronald Fairbairn recognised a common reaction to parental neglect or abuse which he called 'the moral defence'. It arises from the fact that, if children are not adequately cared for by their parents, whether through neglect, abuse or inconsistency, they are unable to replace their parents and are forced to find an emotional means of coping with the reality of their behaviour. As Fairbairn puts it: 'If a child's parents are bad objects, he cannot reject them, even if they do not force themselves upon him; for he cannot do without them. Even if they neglect him, he cannot reject them; for if they neglect him, his need for them is increased' (Fairbairn, 1952, p. 67). The child is thus in a conundrum: if he recognises the 'badness' of his parents, he is left alone in the world without a sufficient source of attention, affirmation and protection. In order to feel secure, the child has to 'imagine' that his parents are 'good'. The solution to this problem is *to blame himself for his parents' failures* (Fairbairn, 1952, p. 65). Fairbairn expresses the child's attitude graphically in religious terms, which are very apt for our purposes:

> It is better to be a sinner in a world ruled by God than to live in a world ruled by the Devil. A sinner in a world ruled by God may be bad; but there is always a certain sense of security to be derived from the fact that the world around is good – 'God's in His heaven – All's right with the world!'; and in any case there is always a hope of redemption. In a world ruled by the Devil the individual may escape the badness of being a sinner; but he is bad because the world around him is bad. Further, he can have no sense of security and no hope of redemption. The only prospect is one of death and destruction. (Fairbairn, 1952, pp. 66–7)

The reaction of Israelite theologians to the Exile follows these lines exactly and for the same reasons. The explanation that they give for the conquests of Israel and Judah lies entirely in the actions of the people of Israel: because they sinned, God punished them by summoning the Assyrians and the Babylonians to overrun their kingdoms and carry off their leaders. The advantage of this position is that the Hebrew people could do something about their predicament; they could repent and pray that God would forgive them, help them to defeat their enemies and restore the land to Hebrew rule. The conviction that God was the only God and that he was in charge of the fates of all peoples reinforced this hope.

This theology is startling in its unprecedented and radical divergence from the general view in the ancient world of the interaction of a people and its gods. Although, on the one hand, human beings existed to serve the gods – in the Babylonian mythology humans were explicitly created so that the gods could take their ease (Wink, 1992, p. 15) – on the other hand, people judged the power of their gods by their effectiveness in providing practical, this-worldly benefits for those who worshipped them. Of course, they could be offended and exact punishments, but if they were worshipped in the right ways, they could be relied upon to come to the aid of their followers. Thus, in the Bible the conflict between Yahweh, the God of Israel, and the Canaanite gods, especially Baal, is marked by the scorn which Yahweh ladles onto the heads of the other gods, who are 'no gods' because they can do nothing. In contrast, Yahweh claims to be the Lord of everything and to be able to do anything he chooses, a claim which makes his failure to deliver Israel and Judah from the hands of their enemies all the more perplexing. The Deuteronomist turns the old way of thinking on its head: instead of God's power being demonstrated by his protection of Israel, it is shown by his ability to summon her enemies to destroy her for her sins.

The Babylonian occupation of Judah, the destruction of Jerusalem and its temple and the associated deportation of the leaders of Judah to Babylon is the defining moment in Jewish history, and the emotional and theological fulcrum of the Hebrew Bible. Although, according to these Scriptures, the Exodus from Egypt, the giving of the Law at Sinai and the Conquest of Canaan are the foundational events of the Israelite nation, the books which were selected for the Hebrew Bible were all either given their final editing or else were written during or after the Exile. As a consequence, they all reflect the theological impact of the Exile in one way or another. Indeed, it is reasonable to assume that they were selected for inclusion precisely because they were consonant with the theology of covenant and judgement.

Even though there are many ancient traditions of varying ages contained within the biblical text, many much older than the Exile, those responsible for the exilic and post-exilic writing, editing and collation of the biblical texts viewed the whole of Hebrew history through the lens of the Exile and the theology based on the moral defence which had been developed to account for it. It is probable, therefore, that they read this perspective into the documents which they had inherited from their forebears. If so, it is not surprising that these narratives are expressive of the psychology of oppression or abuse which would inevitably have developed amongst the Hebrew people after the trauma of national defeat and occupation. Indeed, the scriptural accounts of the early history of the people of Israel, especially of the Exodus and Conquest, may well be more a reflection of the hopes of the exiles for a 'reversal of victimhood' in the form of a 'new exodus' and a restoration of Hebrew rule in Israel, than an historical record of Jewish origins.

The idea that God had punished Israel for her sins enabled those Hebrews who accepted it to keep alive their conviction that their God was in charge of the universe, but at the cost of blaming Israel herself for the dire suffering that she had undergone. It was her own fault; if she had been faithful and obedient, God would not have allowed her to be conquered. This belief has much in common with the reactions of an abused woman who comes to internalise and believe the accusations of her abuser, who repeatedly tells her that she is to blame for the mistreatment that she receives. She may come to be convinced that she has brought her partner's violence upon herself because of her own failures and, therefore, excuse her partner's abuse and regard it as her own fault, believing that if she behaves better, her man will treat her well (Jenkins, 1990, p. 36) – a form of the moral defence. Although he treats her badly much of the time, the occasions when he is good to her keep alive her belief or hope that he does really love her. This attitude is often associated with an extreme reluctance to leave him despite his behaviour. She holds on to the hope that he may change and that his protestations of reform or his good intentions may be borne out in experience (Goldner, 1998, pp. 265–6). She will put up with almost anything as long as she is not abandoned, and may repeatedly forgive her abusive partner and take him back. For many such women being alone is a more threatening prospect than being put down or assaulted.

There are a number of similarities between the psychology of abused women and that of the ancient Israelites. In particular, they, or at least their religious leaders, could not contemplate the idea that God is arbitrary or unjust, and so they clung onto the possibility that if *they* were faithful, God would treat them better and their lives would improve. This attitude was expressed in the pre-exilic prophets' appeals for repentance in the hope that God would not destroy Israel and Judah, and in the post-exilic prophets' emphasis on the continuing need for holiness in order to encourage God to bring about a new exodus and a full restoration of the Israelite kingdom.

Chapter 4

THE CYCLE OF ABUSE IN POST-EXILIC ISRAEL

THE RENEWAL OF THE 'CHOSEN PEOPLE DEFENCE'

After the fall of Jerusalem, the threat inherent in the Mosaic covenant had been carried out; the Israelites had been returned to the status of victims of oppression. In these circumstances, the 'chosen people defence' came to be used as a basis for the hope of a future reversal of their fortunes, through which they would be returned to Israel and once again be established as God's favoured people. The Israelites' suffering was mitigated by their continuing belief in the covenant and their identification of themselves with the chosen people of God. Even if they were once again victims, they were victims who were chosen by God and whom God would eventually redeem after their punishment had ended.

Even in the midst of disaster, the prophets began to emphasise God's great love for Israel and his inability to let her be completely destroyed. There are several passages in which God proclaims his devotion to Israel and his distress at her indigent state after he himself has punished her with defeat and exile, saying that he cannot let Israel go because of his great love for her and promising to restore her fortunes. This expectation is often associated with the idea that a remnant of Israel will return to their land. This is only a small rump of the original people who were scattered but, nevertheless, it is a group who will act as the foundation of the restoration of the people and the fulfilment of God's promises to their ancestors (e.g. Isa. 10:20–22; Jer. 23:3–8; 31:1–14; Ezek. 11:16–20; Joel 2:32; Amos 9:14–15; Mic. 2:12; 4:6–7; 5:7–9; Zeph. 3:12–13; Zech. 8:7–13).

The recovery of the idea that the covenant was conditional made it possible to speak about this coming restoration. However, this hope ran up against the fact of Israel's constitutional sinfulness. Jeremiah located the basis of Israel's fault in her lack of the knowledge of God. He regarded it as something that was part of Israel's nature: 'Can the Ethiopian change his skin or the leopard its spots? Neither can you do good who are accustomed to doing evil' (Jer. 13:23). This was a serious problem because, if God could punish Israel once for her sins, he was quite capable of leaving her to languish in exile or punishing her again if she continued sinning. Jeremiah and Ezekiel both advanced the idea of a 'new covenant' initiated by God as a solution to this problem. According to the terms of this covenant, God would change Israel's 'heart' so that she would know him and be able to obey him perfectly:

> 'The time is coming,' declares the Lord, 'when I will make a new covenant with the house of Israel and with the house of Judah. It will not be like the covenant I made with their forefathers when I took them by the hand to lead them out of Egypt, because they broke my covenant, though I was husband to them,' declares the Lord. 'This is the covenant that I will make with the house of Israel after that time,' declares the Lord. 'I will put my law in their minds and write it on their hearts. I will be their God, and they will be my people. No longer will a man teach his neighbour, or a man his brother, saying, "Know the Lord," because they will all know me, from the least of them to the greatest,' declares the Lord. 'For I will forgive their wickedness and will remember their sins no more.'
>
> (Jer. 31:31–34)

This is a very beautiful vision of renewed intimacy with God in an idealised future in which the conditions allowing for both corporate and individual holiness will have been changed. Each person will know God and each person will, therefore, be obedient so that the whole nation will also be sinless and know God. Ezekiel's vision is similar:

> I will give you a new heart and put a new spirit in you; I will remove from you your heart of stone and give you a heart of flesh. And I will put my Spirit in you and move you to follow my decrees and be careful to keep my laws. You will live in the land I gave your forefathers; you will be my people, and I will be your God.
>
> (Ezek. 36:26–28)

These visions of Jeremiah and Ezekiel both develop the implications of the moral defence at the core of the Deuteronomistic theology to their logical outcome: *because the Hebrews are inherently sinful and thus incapable of winning God's favour, God has to take the initiative to change Israel so that she can obey him. If the Hebrews cannot help themselves, God must act.*

On the face of it, these inspiring prophecies of God's intervention are benign and uplifting. However, there is a sinister side to them which is easily overlooked: God does not want simply to win back Israel's love, he intends to remake her into the object that he truly desires her to be. The prophecies of the future state of a purified and restored Israel represent the transformation of Israel into the idealised and totally obedient object of God's affections. What this means is that God does not accept or love Israel as herself in all her very human imperfections; he intends to change her into the person he wants her to be to fulfil his own desires. In this respect, he once again behaves like an abusive man, one who tries to turn his partner into a source of his own narcissistic gratification without regard to her own wishes. Israel will become a partner who will always 'do as she is told' because she has been 'reprogrammed' to be obedient – the ultimate male fantasy!

Furthermore, although God 'forgives' her, it is only *after* he has v-ented his rage upon her in a most terrible manner. Indeed, Deutero-Isaiah (Isaiah 40—55) admits that 'she has received from the Lord's hand double for all her sins' (Isa. 40:2). Here God resembles an abusive man at the point when he enters the 'honeymoon stage' of the cycle of violence after a violent outburst and starts to be 'loving' towards his mate, whom he has forcefully put in her place and whom he now wishes to keep close to him as the one who will be available to fulfil his narcissistic needs. Thus, after she has completed the 'purification' of punishment, God promises to recreate Israel as his ideal lover, one who will be unable to 'sin'.

PURITY AND EXCLUSIVENESS IN THE JEWISH RELIGION

The idea that, once Israel had propitiated the wrath of God, the people would be redeemed out of exile by him was a major cause of hope for the exiles. All the more so after Cyrus of Persia (ruled 559–530 BCE) launched a successful coup and took over the Babylonian Empire. He initiated a policy of allowing exiles to return to their homes, an opportunity taken up by a significant number of the Jewish exiles in Babylon. In the event, the return was a rather miserable affair, nothing like the prophecies of a glorious new exodus (e.g. Isa. 40:35; 43:18–19). Israel and Judah remained ruinous, depopulated and under foreign rule. The Davidic kingship was not restored.

The failure of reality to match the idealised conditions of the prophecies of renewal raised the question why God had not brought about a full restoration, a question answered by a renewal of the moral defence: God had not yet fulfilled these prophecies because the Jewish people were not sufficiently righteous (e.g. Hag. 2:9–11; Zech. 5:1–11). This approach resulted in an emphasis on the observance of the Law to ensure that God would fulfil his promises, and was expressed in additions to the Pentateuch made by priestly editors at this time:

> If you follow my decrees and are careful to obey my commands, I
> will send rain in its season and the ground will yield its crops and
> the trees of the field their fruit: Your threshing will continue until
> grape harvest and the grape harvest will continue until planting,
> and you will eat all the food you want and live in safety in the land.
> (Lev. 26:3–5)

Alongside this promise went an insistence on the observance of the Law
as a sign of the separateness or distinctiveness of the Jewish people (as it
now becomes legitimate to call them, since this is the period during
which the distinctive characteristics of the Jewish religion were developed). Practices such as the observance of the Sabbath, circumcision
and food regulations became more important because other national
and cultic distinguishing marks had disappeared (e.g. Isa. 58:13b–14).

In essence, in the post-exilic period, *the chosen people defence was
combined with the moral defence to produce an exclusive religion of purity designed to gain the approval of God* and, thereby, to encourage him to
bring about the fulfilment of his promises and the inauguration of the
new age. However, the consequence was that the returned exiles were
hostile to any amongst the people of Judah who did not meet their strict
standards for membership of the chosen people and, especially, any who
had any connections with idolatry. In effect, this meant anyone of
foreign or mixed-race origin.

IDOLATRY AND BIBLICAL RACISM

The Hebrew fear of idolatry was associated with foreigners because they
worshipped other gods and it was from other nations that such idolatry
had been introduced into Israel, calling down the judgement of God
upon the Israelites. The first commandment is: 'You shall have no other
gods before me' (Exod. 20:2; Deut. 5:7), and the worst sin for the
Hebrews was idolatry, the worship of other gods. Far from being an
inclusive document, the Hebrew Bible is trenchantly intolerant of any
deviations from belief in the one true God. Other peoples do not have
the right to choose to worship other gods and their 'sin' in doing so
entitles the Hebrews to destroy them. This attitude is foundational to the
narrative of the conquest of Canaan. In the Hebrew Scriptures, again and
again, those who worship other gods are treated with contempt, and the
central project of the prophets was to cleanse the Israelite religion from
the influences of paganism. Thus, for example, Elijah slaughtered the
prophets of Baal because they promoted the worship of this 'false god' (1
Kings 18:40). For the same reason, the prophets were particularly
antagonistic to the foreign wives of their kings. Hence, the very bad press
that, for example, Ahab and Jezebel received because they promoted the

worship of Baal and persecuted the prophets of the Lord, including Elijah (1 Kings 16—22; 2 Kings 9).

Such xenophobia is explicit in the book of Ezra, in which Ezra returns from Babylon in order to rebuild the temple in Jerusalem. He is informed that:

> The people of Israel, including the priests and the Levites, have not kept themselves separate from the neighbouring peoples with their detestable practices ... They have taken some of their daughters as wives for themselves and their sons, and have mingled the holy race with peoples around them. And the leaders and officials have led the way in this unfaithfulness. (Ezra 9:1–2)

Consequently, all the foreign wives that the Jews had taken were sent away in order to avert 'the fierce anger of our God in this matter' (Ezra 10:14; cf. Neh. 13:23–28), and Ezra refused to let the people of Judah, whom he did not regard as proper Jews, help in the rebuilding of the temple – an attitude which antagonised these people and led to the Samaritan schism (Ezra 4:1–4; cf. Neh. 13:1–3).

In the Hebrew Bible the foreigner is often seen as a source of potential pollution, and the exclusion or annihilation of the foreigner is frequently advocated by biblical writers or commanded by God. To the degree that such exclusion is advocated, we need to recognise that *the Hebrew Bible is a racist document.* This racism is an unavoidable concomitant of covenant theology, and especially of the idea that the children of Israel are the chosen people, but it feels like breaking a taboo to say so. The Bible is, after all, supposed to be revelation, 'the word of God'. If the Bible is racist, then God too must be racist, and this is an idea that seems quite blasphemous!

SCAPEGOATING IN ISRAEL

Usually, this racism is associated with scapegoating. Scapegoating is one of the quickest and most effective means of creating a strong sense of group belonging: the differences and conflicts which may exist within a group can be ignored and projected onto another community or onto its own deviant members, thereby producing the illusion of unity. This device is one that groups who are under pressure in one way or another almost always resort to. The Jewish exiles who returned to Israel from Babylon certainly used it to create a sense of belonging and specialness by projecting out their religious inadequacies onto foreigners and those of mixed blood.

My understanding of scapegoating is very much influenced by that of the Jungian analyst, Erich Neumann. Neumann based his hypothesis on the fundamental psychological defence mechanisms which have been recognised by Freud, Klein, Jung and numerous others in the broad church of psychodynamic psychology. Neumann was a Jew who shortly after the Second World War wrote a book, *Depth Psychology and a New Ethic* (Neumann, 1973), in which he sought to account for the rise of Nazism, the War, and the Holocaust. He asked why the Judaeo-Christian tradition had been unable to prevent this catastrophe. His answer was that it had failed because it advocated what he called the 'old ethic'. The aim of this ethic is to live according to an ideal of perfection – in other words, always to do what is considered to be good. In practice this means living according to a religious law or set of moral rules which lays down what ideal behaviour is.

This aim can in part be achieved by 'suppression', the conscious refusal to act out any impulse which contradicts the ideal but, more often than not, rather than genuinely meeting the demands of the ideal, the illusion of compliance is created by 'repression' – in other words, by forgetting that any contradictory tendencies exist. These unconscious aspects of the personality Neumann, following Jung, refers to as 'the shadow'. Repression does not actually get rid of these tendencies; it merely makes them invisible or unconscious and thus much more dangerous. They are subsequently 'projected' – in other words, experienced as if they belonged to someone else, who is then held responsible for them and is blamed for their existence – that is, scapegoated. Scapegoating also occurs in groups, in which case the psychological process is identical to that in individuals. However, the injury that can be inflicted by a group is on a larger scale, and can be very destructive indeed. The Nazi persecution of the Jews is an example of such scapegoating. In wars there is usually a process of mutual scapegoating whereby each side sees its own 'evil' in its opponents, and thereby justifies fighting against them.

Following Neumann, I perceive the myths and laws which a religion uses to create group conformity as the origin of much of the scapegoating associated with religious communities. This process I have traced in my previous book, *The Cost of Certainty* (Young, 2004). Unfortunately, religious affiliation is often the means whereby both individuals and communities defend themselves from having to know the real truth about themselves and so, in the manner described by Neumann, they find scapegoats either within or outside their boundaries who are blamed for whatever the community cannot accept about itself. Scapegoating is the easiest way for a religious group to give itself a sense of righteousness. It is hardly surprising, therefore, that the returning exiles scapegoated the people who had remained in Judah as religiously inadequate in order to achieve a sense of their own purity, thereby giving themselves the impression that they had gained God's favour. The religion of the post-exilic Israelites, which was a form of the old ethic, generated a tendency to scapegoat foreigners and those regarded as 'sinners' within their own community.

Religion often creates conflict between religious groups and outsiders, on to whom their members project negative characteristics and whom they scapegoat. This is particularly the case when inter-group conflict is fuelled by religious differences, which often include an element of rivalry about who is the one chosen by God and who is the one who possesses the true revelation. This is a dynamic which is evident in the war on terror, in which both conservative evangelicals in the American administration and fundamentalist Islamists claim to possess the truth and favour of God. Indeed, as we shall see, mutual scapegoating in the war on terror is fuelled by these religious differences. The Bush administration regards itself as 'good' and those who oppose it as 'evil', including 'terrorists' and the group of countries which it has named the 'Axis of Evil'. In a mirror image of this attitude, Osama bin Laden and other opponents of the United States locate the evil in America and its allies, or in Western civilisation itself. This mutual scapegoating is one of the most disturbing and dangerous features of the present political situation because it is accompanied by the closing of minds on both sides, resulting in an inability to listen to each other or to comprehend each other's motives.

THE MYTH OF REDEMPTIVE VIOLENCE

The work of the American theologian Walter Wink gives us a further perspective on the connection between violence and religion, and why religions tend to promote scapegoating. Wink (1992) has identified a myth which appears to be highly influential upon the Judaeo-Christian tradition and which continues to make its mark on contemporary politics and religion. Following Paul Ricoeur, he calls it 'the myth of redemptive violence'. According to Wink, the true God of this myth is not love, but violence; and its prototypical expression is found in the Babylonian creation myth contained in the *Enuma Elish* (c. 1250 BCE). This myth concerns the replacement of an older generation of gods, Apsu and Tiamat, by a younger one headed by Marduk. As Wink explains:

> In the beginning, according to this myth, Apsu and Tiamat (the sweet- and the saltwater oceans) bear Mummu (the mist). From them also issue the younger gods, whose frolicking makes so much noise that the elder gods cannot sleep and so resolve to kill them.

This plot of the elder gods is discovered, Ea kills Apsu, and his wife Tiamat pledges revenge. Ea and the younger gods in terror turn for salvation to their youngest, Marduk. He exacts a steep price: if he succeeds, he must be given chief and undisputed power in the assembly of the gods. Having extorted this promise, he catches Tiamat in a net, drives an evil wind down her throat, shoots an arrow that bursts her distended belly and pierces her heart; he then splits her skull with a club, and scatters her blood in out-of-the-way places. He stretches her corpse full length, and from it creates the cosmos. (Wink, 1992, p. 14)

It is important to note that, because the cosmos is made from the body of Tiamat, who represents chaos, in the world represented by the myth chaos is prior to order. This means that the potential for chaos has not actually been eliminated by the act of creation; instead, it has been incorporated into the foundations of the created order and is always threatening to break out again. Consequently, chaos needs repeatedly to be controlled by force and intimidation, and this applies as much to the social order as to the natural world. In the annual Babylonian New Year Festival, during which the battle with Tiamat was ceremonially re-enacted, the king represented Marduk to the nation and played the part of Marduk in the ritual. In this way the myth and its accompanying ritual both mirrored and justified the structures of Babylonian society: social order was created by violence and the threat of violence.

When you think about it, it is obvious that violence or the threat of violence is fundamental to the creation of the peace of most communities. This is clear in the case of the armed forces, who are trained in the use of violence to defend a country against both external threat and internal revolution or terrorism, and of the police, who have the powers of arrest. The courts, the judiciary and the prison system are all systems of legal violence. No one would allow themselves to be locked away unless they were compelled to go to prison, nor would they pay fines unless they faced a worse sanction for failing to do so. The military and legal systems underlie all of our communal interactions, but violence is not confined to them; if violence is defined as any form of coercion, it can be seen to be endemic within all human groups.

With the possible exception of some isolated and 'undeveloped' tribes, all social groups defend their boundaries and apply sanctions to non-conformist members and threatening outsiders. This can be seen not only in the existence of prisons and immigration laws, but more subtly in the possibilities of being sacked in the workplace, of being expelled or sanctioned by clubs, societies and all manner of groups, and of being disowned even by one's own family. All groups also create hierarchies within themselves that are defined and defended by rules or legal structures and the forces of law and order, and these hierarchies are often unjust and disadvantage many people considerably, whilst advantaging a small minority. The reality that many people live in poverty whilst others enjoy extreme wealth could not be sustained were it not for the formalised violence of our legal system which supports the property rights which exclude many from a fair share of the world's resources. The same can be said for the differences between rich and poor nations and the compulsion that is exercised over many poorer countries by the structures of international capital. These are systemic forms of violence.

The establishment of a system of social differentiation with its entailments, exclusion and hierarchy, is necessarily an act of violence and can only be maintained by the threat or actual use of some kind of violence: the forces that could result in disruption of the system have to be kept in order. From this perspective, there is a positive side to the myth of redemptive violence: the victorious god creates social order for the benefit of all, not just the ruling class. However, the cost is oppression and, furthermore, this oppression is justified by scapegoating the oppressed groups as a source of chaos or evil. As Wink concludes:

> The distinctive feature of the myth is the victory of order over chaos by means of violence. This myth is the original religion of the status quo, the first articulation of 'might makes right.' ... The gods favor those who conquer. Conversely, whoever conquers must have the favor of the gods. The mass of people exists to perpetuate that power and privilege which the gods have conferred upon the king, the aristocracy, and the priesthood. Religion exists to legitimate power and privilege. Life is combat. Any form of order is preferable to chaos, according to this myth. Ours is neither a perfect nor a perfectible world; it is a theater of perpetual conflict in which the prize goes to the strong. Peace through war, security through strength: these are the core convictions that arise from this ancient historical religion. (Wink, 1992, pp. 16-17)

Although the official names given to the gods and the dominant mythologies have changed since Babylonian times, according to Wink, the myth of redemptive violence has continued to exist and to exert its influence on subsequent societies down to our own day. Indeed, he sees it as 'one of the world's oldest, continuously surviving religions' (Wink, 1992, p. 13). This is possible because this myth has the peculiar capacity to drape itself in the clothes of a multitude of other mythologies, including Christianity, and covertly to dominate the religious and political life of societies and nations who overtly are committed to quite different values. Whenever the myth of redemptive violence is determinative of a social structure, the result is an authoritarian, hierarchical form of social order in which the privileged few at the top benefit from the labour of the disadvantaged many, who have been subdued so that they conform to the requirements of their superiors. The disempowered masses represent a form of chaos which is always threatening to destabilise the social hierarchy and which has to be controlled by force.

THE GOD OF ISRAEL AND THE MYTH OF REDEMPTIVE VIOLENCE

One important reason why God is so often depicted as violent in the Bible is that the myth of redemptive violence has been influential upon the biblical view of God (Wink, 1992, p. 28). This is hardly surprising, since the Israelites were conquered by the Babylonians, their leaders were taken into exile in Babylon, and much of the Hebrew Bible was written or edited during the time of the Babylonian captivity or shortly thereafter. Furthermore, the Israelites were in contact with various forms of the myth of redemptive violence long before the Babylonian invasion, especially through Canaanite mythology, which includes the exploits of the god Baal, against the worship of whom the prophets of Yahweh, God of Israel, campaigned. Although there is no creation story in this cycle of myths, there are accounts of Baal the storm god's battles with two chaos monsters: one, Yam, who represents the sea; the other, Mot, who represents the dry season (Cross, 1973).

The imagery associated with the battle against chaos, normally depicted as some sort of monster or dragon, in such myths has directly influenced the depiction of God in the Hebrew Scriptures. The figures representative of chaos in the Bible go under various names drawn from various sources. Leo Perdue identifies six: Rahab, Leviathan, Tannin, Yam, Mot and Behemoth (Perdue, 1991, p. 54). An important feature of these descriptions of God's battle with chaos is that, even though the process is not complete and some mythic elements remain, the battle tends to be historicised. In other words, instead of God doing battle with the forces of nature depicted mythologically as gods, the enemies of Israel are portrayed metaphorically as chaos threatening to engulf her, a chaos held at bay by the violent intervention of God. The chief instance of this historicisation is the narrative of the Exodus and the Conquest (Cross, 1973, p. 163).

The story of the Exodus and the Conquest is undeniably a myth of redemptive violence: Israel's God is very much like Marduk, the god who will bring order and prosperity to his followers, provided that they acknowledge his absolute authority over them and give him complete obedience. In addition, the myth of redemptive violence appears to play an important part in determining the nature of the covenant relationship. God seems to hold the belief that violence is the solution to any problem that he may have with Israel. His usual response to disobedience or even complaints is extreme violence; the problem is dealt with by annihilating the miscreants as if they were some form of chaos which has to be destroyed in order for him to exercise complete control over Israel.

The myth of redemptive violence also lies behind the instructions God gives to the Hebrews concerning the invasion of Canaan, and biblical racism in general. He commands them to destroy completely the people whose land they are conquering:

> However, in the cities of the nations the Lord your God is giving you as an inheritance, do not leave alive anything that breathes. Completely destroy them – the Hittites, Amorites, Canaanites, Perizzites, Hivites and Jebusites – as the Lord your God has commanded you. Otherwise, they will teach you to follow all the detestable things they do in worshipping their gods, and you will sin against the Lord your God.
>
> (Deut. 20:16–18; cf. Num. 33:50–53, 55–56; Deut. 7:1–6; Josh. 23:12–13; Ezra 9—10)

In this passage, the annihilation of the peoples of Canaan is justified on the grounds that they will lead the Hebrews astray – in other words, that they are a source of pollution and sin, of religious chaos, which needs to be eliminated to protect the Israelites from their corrupting influence. This attitude is typical of the book of Deuteronomy and the books known as the Deuteronomistic History – that is, Joshua to 2 Kings – which form a connected narrative of Hebrew history from the time of Moses to the conquest of Judah by the Babylonians. A similar outlook is found in the later history books, 1 and 2 Chronicles, Ezra and Nehemiah, and in many of the prophets, especially Jeremiah and Ezekiel. We may conclude that the myth of redemptive violence is absolutely central to the depiction of God in the Hebrew Bible.

THE MYTH OF REDEMPTIVE VIOLENCE AND THE DAY OF THE LORD

We have seen that in several places the Hebrew Bible portrays the God of Israel as a warrior god fighting against an oppressor (represented as chaos) on behalf of the Israelites. This presentation became particularly important after the Exile. As well as looking forward to a new Exodus, this time from Babylon to Israel, the prophets used two other themes to support the hope of a restoration. God's promise to David that he would never lack a descendant on the throne became the basis of a hope for the restoration of one of his descendants to rule as king (e.g. Isa. 55:3; Jer. 30:8–9), and Ezekiel foresaw the return of the glory of God to a rebuilt temple in the midst of a rebuilt city (Ezekiel 40—48).

In addition, the idea of a forthcoming Day of the Lord (which before the Exile had been used by the prophets to refer to the approaching judgement) was rehabilitated as the Day when God would bring about Israel's restoration and remake the world order to her advantage. The prophecies about this Day are very much an expression of the basic philosophy expressed by the myth of redemptive violence: violence is the means by which redemption will be achieved; in this case, the violence of God directed against Israel's enemies. For example:

> 'In that day,' declares the Lord Almighty, 'I will break the yoke off their necks, and will tear off their bonds; no longer will foreigners enslave them. Instead, they will serve the Lord their God and David their king, whom I will raise up for them.' (Jer. 30:8–9)

In the new world order the chosen people will dominate other nations under the overarching rule of God. The defeated Israelites' reversal of victimhood will be complete:

> The products of Egypt and the merchandise of Cush, and those tall Sabeans – they will come over to you and will be yours; they will trudge behind you, coming over to you in chains. They will bow down before you and plead with you, saying, 'Surely God is with you, and there is no other; there is no other god.' (Isa. 45:14)

In other prophecies the nations are not in chains; they come freely to worship God in Jerusalem: 'My house will be called a house of prayer for all nations' (Isa. 56:7), and Israel has a positive role in communicating the knowledge of God to them. Even so, there is no doubt that the Hebrews will be the dominant nation whose progression from victim to ruler, if not victimiser, will be permanent under the protection of their God.

Some of these prophetic visions were extremely violent indeed. Zechariah includes one of the coming of the Day of the Lord, which he sees as a day of judgement, including a universal bloodbath, through which God will bring about the end of history and set up his everlasting kingdom (Zech. 14). It is notable that this ideal state would only come about as the result of a further outpouring of God's violence onto the whole of creation. In Zechariah's view, the destruction of Israel and Judah had not exhausted God's capacity for violence; he would exact revenge on the nations who had oppressed his people and impose his rule on the whole world. Even Jerusalem and Judah would suffer in the conflagration. God promises to create a perfect world of peace for Israel to live in, but that world is peaceful only because everyone in it acknowledges God's sovereignty and obeys him. One wonders how much this vision of the future encapsulates Zechariah's rage at his community's continuing humiliation and failure to prosper.

It seems clear that the controlling and abusive features of the God of Israel continued to be influential after the Exile, even in the vision of the ideal future for Israel that God would bring to pass. Fantasies of a vicious and bloody revenge on their enemies are a frequent feature of these oracles which give full vent to the anger generated by the Jewish people's defeat and enslavement. They are a very clear example of the influence of both the cycle of abuse and the myth of redemptive violence on the formation of the biblical text and of the spirituality of the people who wrote it, and they prefigure similar visions of a universal outpouring of the violence of God contained in later extra-biblical literature as well as in the New Testament, especially the book of Revelation. The spirituality which anticipates and celebrates the redemptive violence of God has continued to flourish ever since and, not surprisingly, is extremely significant in the war on terror.

Chapter 5

COUNTER-ABUSIVE TESTIMONY IN THE HEBREW BIBLE

THE DOUBLE OPPRESSION OF THE ISRAELITES

The biblical descriptions of God that we have been considering are the products of the minds of the people of Israel. As such, they reflect their psychology and, therefore, the psychological effects of their communal victimisation. This realisation helps to account for the ambiguity in the image of God contained in the Hebrew Bible, and recognised by Brueggemann in his distinction between its core and counter testimonies to the nature of the deity. The God of the Hebrews has a double aspect: on the one hand, he is loving, faithful and gracious, fighting for his people in times of trouble and giving them the great blessing of the land of Canaan; on the other hand, he is demanding, controlling, easily roused to anger and excessively violent. The Israelites coped with this duality by emphasising the beneficent aspects of God's character and using the moral defence to justify his violence as an expression of his 'justice'. Thus, when God behaved destructively it was 'their fault' and not his. In this way, their God was preserved from both fault and blame. This strategy was assisted by the existence of actual historical oppressors who could be blamed for the dire condition into which the Israelites had fallen, conveniently overlooking the fact that, according to the Deuteronomistic theology, it was God who had summoned these powers to 'punish' Israel for her sins and so, logically, it was God who was ultimately responsible for their actions.

When this strategy is recognised, it becomes evident that, despite the many positive aspects of God's behaviour towards them, as a result of his abusiveness, to which the biblical text also bears witness, the Israelites actually suffered a 'double oppression': one by the colonial power of the time; the other by God. However, the oppression by God was disguised and made invisible by the oppression of the colonial power. The Israelites split the two apart and regarded the earthly overlord as the source of their sufferings and God as the source of their potential liberation, a hope encouraged and nurtured by their belief in their chosenness – the chosen people defence. This psychological division into good God and evil ruler has sustained their descendants through centuries of persecution and prejudice, and has been adopted by many Christians who have also been social, economic or political underdogs, and who have looked to God for salvation from their oppression.

In the last two chapters, I have been describing how the Hebrew view of God appears to have been influenced by the cycle of abuse, and have highlighted the violent and abusive behaviour of both God and the ancient Hebrews. However, this is by no means the whole story. As I pointed out in Chapter 1, this book is concentrating on the negative aspects of the biblical witness so that they are given their due weight and, in the process, the positive may appear to be given short shrift. In proceeding in this manner, I do not mean to suggest that the positive elements are not genuinely positive when read at face value. Even so, I am suggesting that they should not be read apart from an awareness of the psychology of abuse and the abusive traditions within the Bible. This is essential precisely because, only when the existence of positive phases within the cycle of violence within an abusive relationship is recognised, is it possible to assess accurately whether or not a relationship is abusive. This applies just as much to the relationship between God and his chosen people as to that between a man and a woman.

Having said that, it is now time to look at the counter-abusive testimony in the Hebrew Bible. What I am particularly concerned to note are those of its traditions which challenge, transcend or exist outside the cycle of abuse. We can expect to find counter-abusive traditions in the Hebrew Bible in three distinct forms. First, there will be those which express attitudes towards God, creation, other people and the self which are at least relatively free from the implication that God is abusive, and which do not display the psychology of abuse. Second, there will be those which speak of opposition to the oppressive rule or actions of human agents, whether foreign occupiers or native rulers or the wicked in general. Third, there will be those which confront the abusive behaviour or culpable neglect of God himself.

THE THEOLOGY OF CREATION IN THE HEBREW BIBLE

The theology of creation in the Hebrew Bible is one of the most positive and potentially counter-abusive aspects of its teaching, and this theology is central to what is known as the Wisdom tradition. The Wisdom books (Job, Proverbs and Ecclesiastes in the Bible, and the Wisdom of Solomon and Ecclesiasticus in the Apocrypha) reflect on the relationship between God and his creation and on the right ordering of society. The sage is one who is able to recognise the rule of God in the ordering of the cosmos and knows how to adapt his behaviour to the realities of God's righteousness and the practicalities of everyday life. The Wisdom books contain much practical advice for the 'young man' on how to conduct himself which is both worldly and religious. They also have a very high view of Wisdom herself, who in the great hymn to Wisdom in Proverbs 8:22–31 is viewed as the primordial companion of God in the act of creation: 'The Lord possessed me at the beginning of his work, before his deeds of old; I was appointed from eternity, from the beginning, before the world began' (Prov. 8:22–23). Because of their emphasis on creation, the Wisdom books do not often refer to the history of God's saving actions on behalf of Israel. Thus, with the exception of Job and some of the Psalms, there is much less occasion for the reader to be made aware of the abusive side of God's nature in the Wisdom literature than in the rest of the Hebrew Bible.

The Priestly theology that was developed during and after the Exile also contains a positive affirmation of the goodness of creation in the creation narrative of Genesis 1:1—2:4. According to Wink, the biblical myth of creation is fundamentally different from and opposed to the myth of an original struggle with chaos (the myth of redemptive violence) contained in the Babylonian, Canaanite and many other ancient Near Eastern mythologies, and it has a totally different meaning (Wink, 1992, p. 14). Although it does contain some residual elements of the battle with chaos, the first chapter of Genesis describes how creation took place out of nothing, not through conflict, but simply through the activity of the Word of God: God said ... and it was so. There is nothing to oppose the creative Word. In addition, God's creation is good and God acknowledges it as such: 'God saw all that he had made, and it was very good' (Gen. 1:31). Furthermore, this narrative expresses a very positive view of humanity, whom he created 'in the image of God' to rule over the earth (Gen. 1:26–28). Although this passage has been extensively misused to justify human domination and exploitation of the world's natural resources, it is actually positive in intention: human beings are to share in God's benign ordering of the earth.

A chief theme of exilic theology was that 'Yahweh is Lord'. He is the Lord of history who created the world and sustains it to work out his purposes in history. The omnipotence of God and the powerlessness of the idols are two themes which support each other, and are especially prominent in Deutero-Isaiah: 'I am God, and there is no other; I am God, and there is none like me' (Isa. 46:9a). God is definitely in control of creation: 'I am he; I am the first and I am the last. My own hand laid the foundation of the earth, and my right hand spread out the heavens; when I summon them, they all stand up together' (Isa. 48:12b–13).

In contrast, in the Babylonian creation myth, the world is made from chaos and chaos is always threatening to re-emerge. It can only be kept under control by violence. This results in a fundamentally different attitude to the world from that in the Genesis tradition: the world is not good but evil, and good can only be created and protected through constant vigilance and violent coercion. In addition, far from being created in the image of God, human beings are created from the blood of a murdered god. They originate from violence and are all too prone to resort to violence and, so, have to be kept under control by the exercise of violence. In the myth of redemptive violence evil can only be overcome by force – in other words, evil cannot be redeemed but must be destroyed. This is a further fundamental difference from the biblical myth. The Jewish and Christian traditions have always maintained the belief that the world is fundamentally good, even though evil exists, and that it will be redeemed. The difference of outcome in the world of practical politics between a belief in the possibility of redemption and a belief in the myth of redemptive violence is highly significant and of great relevance to the prosecution of the war on terror.

INCLUSIVENESS IN THE RELIGION OF ISRAEL

The positive theology of creation in the Hebrew Bible was associated with a positive view of all races and nations as the creation of God. Despite the xenophobia of the returned exiles in Jerusalem, there are many inclusive elements in the religion of Israel. Although this did not apply universally, it seems clear that even after the settlement of Canaan it was possible for foreigners of particular races to become members of Israel, provided that they were attached to an Israelite household and were in the third generation or later of those who had settled with the people of Israel (Deut. 23:1–8). Furthermore, the Hebrew Bible is remarkable in the degree to which it acknowledges the rights of foreigners who are living within Israel to considerate and just treatment, often on the basis that the Israelites were themselves exiles in a foreign land. For example: 'When an alien lives with you in your land, do not ill-treat him. The alien living with you must be treated as one of your native-born. Love him as yourself, for you were aliens in Egypt. I am the Lord your God' (Lev. 20:33).

However, this toleration was never extended to their religious beliefs. Rather, other peoples might come to know the true God through the people of Israel. Indeed, a number of the prophets present this as a primary role of Israel and, at the time of Jesus, many Jews were engaged in evangelism. In addition, there is a strong tradition emphasising the universality of God's rule over the nations. Because he is the creator of everything, all peoples owe him worship and he is their king and their judge. This theme is found especially in some of the Psalms (e.g. Pss. 96; 148) and in Deutero-Isaiah (Isaiah 40—55), and the possibility of foreigners being virtuous is demonstrated by the exemplary righteousness of Job, a foreigner about whom God himself boasts.

Two books of the Hebrew Bible are of particular significance in promoting inclusivity: Ruth and Jonah. Ruth is the story of a Moabitess who was married to an Israelite who died; it tells how she was so devoted to her mother-in-law Naomi that she decided to leave her own country and return with her to Judah and to adopt her religion. In Naomi's home town Ruth won the favour of Boaz, a relative of her husband, who married her. As a result, she became the great grandmother of King David. Scholars are divided about whether to date Ruth to the pre-exilic period when relations between the Israelites and the surrounding nations were more relaxed than in the post-exilic period, or to place it in the latter and interpret it as a direct challenge to the exclusiveness of the priestly establishment in Jerusalem (Emmerson, 2001; West, 2003). Whichever is the case, its inclusion in the Bible provides a welcome counterweight to the xenophobic tendencies of Ezra and Nehemiah. It is also one of the few books in the Hebrew Scriptures from which the cycle of abuse is entirely absent, unless one is pedantic and takes the general subordination of women in the patriarchal structure of Israelite society, which sets the context for the story of Ruth, as an expression of the cycle.

Jonah is generally regarded as a post-exilic composition (fifth to second centuries BCE) written precisely to counter xenophobic tendencies (Southwell, 2001; Gunn, 2003). It purports to be the story of the prophet Jonah, whose historical original flourished in the northern kingdom when it was still independent. God commands Jonah to preach a message of judgement to the Assyrians in Nineveh. Jonah resists and sets sail in the opposite direction until a storm arises and he is cast into the sea where, famously, he is swallowed by a giant fish, in whose belly he remains for three days. At length the fish spews him up on the coast of Nineveh, where he announces God's judgement. The people of Nineveh, from the king to the poorest, immediately repent. God sees their penitence and forgives them. At this point Jonah's motive in running away from God becomes clear: he was afraid that God would relent: 'I knew that you are a gracious and compassionate God, slow to anger and abounding in love, a God who relents from sending calamity' (Jonah 4:2). Jonah could not live with the fact that God might not punish the Assyrians, who were the dominant imperial power of the time, if they repented; his hatred was opposed to God's mercy. The book was written a considerable time after the conquest of the northern kingdom by Assyria. It is an eloquent plea for a recognition of the universality of the Lord's compassion, even on Israel's greatest enemies.

Even though the story implicitly accepts the idea of a potentially violent God who imposes retribution on those who disobey him, the will to violence is found more in the heart of Jonah than in his God. Consequently, this book stands in opposition both to the cycle of internecine violence which is fuelled by the desire for revenge and also to the reversal of victimhood. Its message is that there is an alternative to the interminable switching between the roles of victim and victimiser in the cycle of abuse – namely, a mutual acceptance of the grace and mercy of God to all who repent. Implicitly, the story also holds out the possibility of reconciliation between enemies on the basis of a common submission to God. It is representative of the most pacific and universalistic elements in the Hebrew tradition which, despite the long history of Israelite defeat and oppression, witness to the humanity of foreigners and enemies, alongside God's concern for their well-being and the possibility for all peoples to enter into a benign relationship with him.

COUNTER-ABUSIVE THEMES IN THE PSALMS

One place where all three counter-abusive themes are to be found is in the Psalms, which are the biblical context where the human experience of God is most fully explored in all its paradoxical complexity. Most of the Bible is written from the perspective of God, whether in the form of oracles spoken in the name of God or that of narratives presenting theological positions implicitly purporting to present the truth about God. In the Psalms and the Wisdom literature the human perspective has much more prominence, including the questions that people raise when they cannot make sense of the ways of God.

In the vast majority of the Psalms, though not in all, the issue of justice is raised. These psalms may contain an affirmation of the justice of God, or a plea for help to God by the innocent against the oppression of the wicked, or a pondering of the paradox that the wicked prosper when God is just, or a complaint against God for having failed to protect either his people or the individual complainant, or an admission of guilt, followed by repentance and a plea for forgiveness. They explore the issues of injustice, violence, oppression, exploitation and abuse in many varied and suggestive ways.

Brueggemann suggests three main general themes in the Psalms which he describes as orientation, disorientation and new orientation (Brueggemann, 1984, p. 19). The 'psalms of orientation' represent a time when life is going well and God is accepted as the powerful and righteous orderer of the cosmos and human society. In the world of these psalms there is a direct correlation between the behaviour of individuals and groups and their standing in the world: the just are rewarded and the wicked are punished. These are poems affirming the *status quo* as a condition willed and blessed by God. Such psalms include those celebrating the goodness of creation (e.g. Pss. 8; 33; 104; 145), the goodness of the Torah, God's Law (e.g. Pss. 1; 119), the just and beneficial ordering of society by God (e.g. Pss. 14; 37; 111; 112; 131), and one may add, although Bruggemann does not, royal psalms which celebrate the king of the ruling Davidic dynasty, the Lord's anointed (e.g. Pss. 2; 45; 72; 110). For example:

> Let Israel rejoice in their Maker;
>> let the people of Zion be glad in their King.
> Let them praise his name with dancing
>> and make music to him with tambourine and harp.
> For the Lord takes delight in his people;
>> he crowns the humble with salvation.
> Let the saints rejoice in his honour
>> and sing for joy on their beds.
>
> (Ps. 149:2–5)

Brueggemann says that the psalms of orientation express 'a consensus about theodicy' in a society in which the social order is regarded as expressive of the justice of God (Brueggemann, 1984, p. 171). In terms of the cycle of abuse, the psalms of orientation represent an identification of God with goodness. They do not question but proclaim the righteousness of things as they are. In these psalms the secular ruler or the current social order are identified with the just ordering of the world by this good God. These psalms do not challenge the cycle of abuse in the realm of politics, let alone the abusiveness of God. If God is violent, they regard his violence as an expression of his justice, which is not questioned. Rather, they point towards positive aspects of creation and of God's governance which the awareness of the dark side of the biblical witness to God's character may obscure. It is all too easy to see everything through this negative lens and to forget that there is much about the world that is good and which faith may rightly attribute to the grace of God. These psalms are counter-abusive insofar as they point out the non-abusive, loving and just side of God's character.

THE GOD OF RULERS AND THE GOD OF VICTIMS

Paradoxically, because of their reliance on a positive theology of creation and their view that the present ordering of the community reflects God's will, there is a potentially abusive side to the psalms of orientation. They run the risk of encouraging internalised oppression by celebrating the power of God as good, without acknowledging the negative consequences of the violence that he uses to guarantee his rule. This is a particular danger because they represent an attitude to the relation between God and the present social order which can all too easily be hijacked by secular leaders to provide a religious rationale for their authority. Whenever, as has happened so often in Christian history, a secular ruler is identified with God's anointed – that is, as a new David – he can claim the right to govern for and on behalf of God. Since God's governance is seen as good and for the common good, the ruler's governance in the name of God is promoted as part of the divinely ordered structure of society. Thus, resistance to the secular authority is equated with resistance to God, and obedience to the ruler is commended as a form of obedience to God, however oppressive or unjust he may be. This is the theology of all established churches. We will examine it further in Chapter 9.

In Christian history this identification was first advanced by the Emperor Constantine, and it has been very widely copied by Christian monarchs and commonwealths since. It lies behind Erastian views of the Church, which hold that the Church should be under the authority of the secular ruler or the state, a belief promoted by many Protestant churches. In the war on terror such an identification is the covert assumption behind American 'civic religion' which, although not established, is the dominant ideology of the governing class. The American *status quo* is assumed to be divinely ordained and guided by God. Indeed, President George W. Bush and many of his supporters are convinced that he has been chosen as president by God (Wallis, 2005, pp. 138–41).

In opposition to this ideology, at the heart of the biblical outlook is a considerable scepticism towards worldly power. Millard Lind associates this viewpoint with the Exodus tradition which emphasises that the Israelites do not rely upon human forms of power, but 'solely upon Yahweh's miraculous power'. He points out that:

> In the thought of the Song of the Sea [Exod. 15:1–18] Yahweh is involved in Israel's history by the fact he *alone* is warrior. This experience was institutionalized in that Yahweh *alone* is king. The experience of Yahweh as the sole warrior at the sea results in the experience of Yahweh as the sole king at Sinai.
>
> (Lind, 1980, p.51, italics in original)

This tradition leads the Deuteronomic History to include an indictment of the rule of human kings. Specifically, its account of the choice of Saul as a king for Israel makes it very clear that the Israelites had rejected God as their king. As Lind explains: 'This demand for human kingship was recognized by the tradition as a rejection of the kingship of Yahweh and was connected with the people's choice of other gods' (Lind, 1980, p. 52). As Yahweh tells Samuel: 'it is not you they have rejected as their king, but me. As they have done from the day I brought them up out of Egypt until this day, forsaking me and serving other gods, so they are doing to you' (1 Sam. 8:7b–8). Furthermore, Samuel forsees that the king will exploit them. At Yahweh's command he warns the people:

> This is what the king who will reign over you will do: He will take your sons and make them serve with his chariots and horses, and they will run in front of his chariots. Some he will assign to be commanders of fifties, and others to plough his ground and reap his harvest, and still others to make weapons of war and equipment for his chariots. He will take your daughters to be perfumers and cooks and bakers. He will take the best of your fields and vineyards and olive groves and give them to his attendants … He will take a tenth of your flocks, and you yourselves will become slaves. When that day comes, you will cry out for relief from the king you have chosen, and the Lord will not answer you in that day. (1 Sam. 8:11–18)

There are many passages in the Hebrew Bible which do unambiguously present God as concerned for justice and righteousness and opposed to any who wish to exploit those who are weaker, especially the poor, the widow and the orphan. The prophets are full of denunciations of such behaviour. For example:

> For three sins of Israel, even for four, I will not turn back [my wrath]. They sell the righteous for silver, and the needy for a pair of sandals. They trample the heads of the poor as upon the dust of the ground and deny justice to the oppressed. (Amos 2:6–7)

The books of the Law include many regulations designed to protect the poor from exploitation, in particular, the provision for 'a year of Jubilee' every fiftieth year, when land which had been sold was to be returned to the family from whom it had originally been bought, and Israelites who had become slaves were to be set free (Lev. 25:8–55). The Law includes provisions for the support and protection of the poor. For example:

> If one of your countrymen becomes poor and is unable to support himself among you, help him as you would an alien or a temporary resident, so that he can continue to live among you … You may not lend him money at interest or sell him food at a profit.
> (Lev. 25:35, 37)

It is not clear how far these rules were followed by the ancient Israelites. Undoubtedly, injustice and exploitation continued to occur, alongside prophetic denunciations of them. The situation of those who suffered as a result also finds expression in the Hebrew Scriptures, especially in the Psalms.

PSALMS OF DISORIENTATION AND NEW ORIENTATION

In contrast to the psalms of orientation are the 'psalms of disorientation' which, as the designation suggests, give voice to the opposite experience – that is, of the current order appearing to be at odds with God's justice. Brueggemann describes the situation from which the psalms of disorientation arise as a 'crisis of theodicy'. In other words, they question the justice of God. This scepticism involves a challenge both to the 'doctrine of God' that supports the social order and to the 'social system of authority' that relies on that theological legitimation (Brueggemann, 1984, p. 171). The issues of justice and righteousness may be handled in one of two ways by these psalms.

> On the one hand, in a few texts God, *along with the social system*, seems to be rejected. In these harsh statements, the critique is made not only of 'the enemy' but also of God who has been unjust or absent. In those extreme cases, the issue of theodicy is acute and painful, because in fact the psalmist has no other court of appeal and so must come back in appeal to the very one who has been accused. In these cases, the prayer questions whether God is just, without even speaking of the social system God legitimates.
>
> On the other hand, more often, appeal is made to God, *against the system*. In those cases God is assumed to be just and faithful, but it is 'the enemy' who has perverted God's way and so must be judged. In that case the appeal to God makes sense, for it is against one who has violated God's known will.
>
> (Brueggemann, 1984, p. 171, italics in the original)

Amongst the latter category, Bruggemann distinguishes between: those which find fault with Yahweh, many of which complain about the actions of an 'enemy', including personal laments (e.g. Pss. 13; 35; 86), communal laments (e.g. Pss. 74; 79; 137) and Psalms 88 and 109 (Bruggemann, 1984, pp. 51–88); those in which Yahweh finds fault with Israel and 'calls Israel to repent' (e.g. Pss. 50; 81); those which acknowledge Yahweh's charge and ask for forgiveness or 'take a posture of submission', collectively referred to as 'The Seven Psalms' or, elsewhere, as the penitential psalms (Pss. 6; 32; 38; 51; 102; 130; 143); and those which affirm that Yahweh is ultimately going to 'override all the negative realities which may now seem decisive' (e.g. Pss. 49; 73; 90) (Brueggemann, 1984, pp. 88–121).

The last subgroup prepares the way for the 'psalms of new orientation' which, as the name suggests, 'bear witness to the surprising gift of new life just when none has been expected' (Bruggemann, 1984, pp. 122–3), and which recognise how God has proved his trustworthiness and power. These include: personal (e.g. Pss. 30; 34; 40; 138) and communal (e.g. Pss. 65; 66; 124) thanksgivings when God has rescued the psalmist or Israel from a disorientating situation; songs of the victory and enthronement of Yahweh who has triumphed over his enemies (e.g. Pss. 29; 47; 93; 96—99; 114); songs of thanksgiving which affirm confidence in God (e.g. Pss. 23; 27; 91); and hymns of praise (e.g. Pss. 100; 103; 113; 117; 135; 146—150) (Brueggemann, 1984, pp. 123–67). For example: 'The righteous cry out, and the Lord hears them; he delivers them from all their troubles. The Lord is close to the brokenhearted and saves those who are crushed in spirit' (Ps. 34:17–18).

Brueggemann discerns a paradigmatic spiritual development in the Psalms which gives a positive theological meaning to the experience of disorientation. He refers to a movement from orientation through disorientation to new orientation which, basing himself on Philippians 2:5–11, he compares to that from Christ's original glory in heaven through his incarnation and passion to his glorification after the resurrection (Brueggemann, 1984, pp. 10–11). Thus the Psalms, taken as a whole, complete a cycle from orientation through disorientation to new orientation.

A similar witness to God's help in trouble, and the restoration to peace and prosperity of those who trust in him, is found in many other places in the Hebrew Scriptures. It is well represented by the numerous accounts of God's assistance to his people in resisting both foreign oppressors and those amongst the Israelites themselves who sought to exploit their kindred. The paradigmatic instance is, of course, the Exodus from Egypt. However, this example indicates an ambiguity in the texts celebrating God's help – namely, the aid that God gives to his people as a whole or an individual Israelite may well involve a reversal of victimhood resulting in the oppression of someone else.

'THE ESCHATOLOGICAL DEFENCE'

Even though such narratives, along with the psalms of new orientation, are encouraging, they do not address the condition of those who are *still* in danger or despair, and they give no direct defence of God's justice and love. Indeed, those which celebrate his assistance or which praise his control of creation only serve to emphasise the dire straits of those who complain and whom God has *not* helped *despite his power to do so*. The problem of the failure of God's redemption to arrive in the lifetime of those who had been faithful to him, even to death as martyrs, was a considerable theological difficulty for the Israelites. As we shall discover below, some of them became highly dubious about the justice or reliability of God. Others, however, developed an approach to the problem that I call 'the eschatological defence'.

In theology, the *eschaton* refers to the end of the age, the Day of the Lord, when God will remake the world. The eschatological defence is, therefore, a resort to a future state outside the normal boundaries of historical existence to make good the apparent deficiencies of God's justice in the world as it currently exists. For example, the prophet Malachi describes a situation in which the prosperity of the wicked has led to despondency amongst the Jewish people, and defends the justice of God by proclaiming that the day of the coming of the Lord draws near, and that the judgement of the wicked has only been delayed (Mal. 2:17—3:2).

A variation on the eschatological defence is to make life after death the opportunity for God to make right the injustices of the present age. However, belief in the resurrection of the dead is extremely uncharacteristic of the Hebrew Scriptures as a whole. It only became widespread amongst the Jewish people after most of the Hebrew Bible had been written, and it was still controversial in the time of Jesus. The only undisputed reference to the resurrection of the dead is Daniel 12:2, which is extremely late, dated in the second century BCE at a time when the Jews were experiencing persecution by the Seleucid Emperor, Antiochus IV Epiphanes, who was trying to eradicate the Jewish religion. This attempt led to the Maccabean revolt in which many devout Jews perished and which ultimately led to Jewish independence.

The experience of persecution and martyrdom encouraged the conviction that there must be an afterlife. This was necessary if those who had been martyred out of loyalty to God were to be rewarded by him. Without this possibility, God would prove to be unjust. The expectation of a future life could take the form of either bodily resurrection or immortality. The former, which is more common, is found in the Apocrypha in 2 Maccabees 7, the story of a mother and her seven sons who were all martyred. It includes an avowal of faith in a resurrection and judgement by God followed by reward for the martyred. Belief in immortality is expressed by the Wisdom of Solomon in a passage which also looks forward to a reversal of victimhood:

> But the souls of the virtuous are in the hand of God,
> no torment shall ever touch them.

In the eyes of the unwise, they did appear to die,
their going looked like disaster,
their leaving us like annihilation; but they are in peace.
If they experienced punishment as men see it,
their hope was rich in immortality;
slight was their affliction, great will their blessing be ...
They shall judge nations, rule over peoples,
and the Lord will be their king forever.

(Wisdom 3:1-4, 8, Jerusalem Bible)

Other possible references to life after death include: Psalms 49:15; 73:24; Isaiah 25:8; 26:19; Job 19:25-27.

The eschatological defence rescues the justice of God from the contradictory experience of his present failure to defend his faithful followers. However, it does so at the cost of implicitly conceding that the behaviour of God in this world does not make sense and cannot be regarded as just without a life after death to set things right. It also tends to reinforce the idea that God has favourites and, thus, encourages the exclusivity and scapegoating which are so often coupled with such a conviction. Furthermore, the belief in a resurrection is linked to the expectation of a judgement including the punishment of the wicked as well as the reward of the righteous. In other words, it anticipates a final reversal of victimhood and, as we observed in the last chapter in the visions of Zechariah, is usually associated with both an expectation that the people of Israel will rule over the other nations and an outbreak of horrific divine violence. The eschatological defence cannot, therefore, really be considered counter-abusive, even though it grew out of a desire to defend the justice of God. Even so, it is absolutely central to the New Testament witness to the resurrection of Jesus. We shall find that the double-sidedness of this defence is very much in evidence in the Christian religion.

The eschatological defence suffers from the ambiguity of many of the positive affirmations in the Hebrew Bible about the goodness of God and his ordering of the world and society, an ambiguity witnessed to by Brueggemann's distinction between its core and counter testimonies. Even though these scriptures are very strongly opposed to exploitation of one human by another, they rarely recognise the controlling and abusive actions of God as such, even when they are describing them in repulsive detail, nor do they apply their concern for justice to the victims of Israel's aggression. However, there are some texts, which do confront this problem head on and call God to account for his behaviour, which we must now examine.

Chapter 6

CALLING THE GOD OF ISRAEL
TO ACCOUNT

Questioning the righteousness of God arises from the combination of two beliefs: one, that God is the Lord of creation and in ultimate control of everything that happens; the other, that he is just and will, therefore, reward the good and punish the wicked. In Hebrew thinking God's justice was believed to be retributive. In other words, there was deemed to be a direct correlation between the degree of a man's righteousness or wickedness and the rewards or punishments God bestowed on him. This belief was a prominent theme of the Wisdom literature, especially the book of Proverbs (e.g. Prov. 5:21–23; 21:12, 21). In theology, the problem that what happens in the world does not always reflect God's justice, understood in this way, is known as theodicy. Brueggemann refers to a crisis in theodicy in the psalms of disorientation. That crisis focuses on two questions: Why do the innocent suffer? and, Why do the wicked prosper?

WHY DO THE INNOCENT SUFFER?

Although in the traditional way of thinking God rewarded righteousness and punished sin, during the period before the Babylonian conquest there was a problem for many of the inhabitants of Jerusalem with the manner in which he did this. The ancient Israelite view of the relationship between God and his people put a great emphasis upon the Israelite community as a corporate personality. The modern idea of individuality had not yet developed. People were identified with their families and tribes in a much more intimate manner than is usually the case now. In other words, the Israelites were not seen simply as individuals in their own right, but as sharing in the deeds and fate of the community as a whole, whether or not they had had any personal responsibility for them. Thus, individuals might not only receive the reward or punishment for their own actions, but also for those of their families and the wider groups to which they belonged. Hence, a person might be punished for the deeds of his father or more distant ancestors, or for the misdeeds of a ruler or of the people as a whole. God's wrath could fall on anyone associated with an offender. For example, Achan's family were executed with him (Josh. 7), and the families of three Levites named Korah, Dathan and Abiram were swallowed with them by the earth (Num. 16). More generally, any Israelite might be punished when some others amongst the people or a leader sinned.

Even worse, God's 'justice' might be stored up and then unleashed upon the children or more distant descendants of those who had offended 'to the third and the fourth generation', and even after that. A good example is the case of the Amalekites. During the wilderness period the Amalekites attacked the Israelites for no apparent reason and were defeated (Exod. 17:8–16). Following this, Moses said, 'The Lord will be at war with the Amalekites from generation to generation' (v. 16). After several hundred years, he decided to take his revenge on the Amalekites and commanded Saul to annihilate them (1 Sam. 15:2–3). Such 'justice' was not reserved by God for the enemies of his people; he treated the Israelites in a similar manner. Their ancestral sins were stored up by him and eventually visited on the generations who experienced the conquests of Israel and Judah.

Amongst the people of Judah, the threatening events leading up to the fall of Jerusalem (587 BCE) resulted in a growing awareness of the inadequacy of the communal understanding of punishment. If the blame for a present-day disaster is that of the ancestors, there is nothing that the descendants can do to rectify the situation. So discouraging was the belief that God punishes the children for the sins of the fathers that in the pre-exilic period the prophets recorded an attitude of fatalism amongst the people of Judah, an attitude challenged by Ezekiel:

> What do you people mean by quoting this proverb about the land of Israel:
>   'The fathers eat sour grapes, and the children's teeth are set on edge'?
>   As surely as I live, declares the sovereign Lord, you will no longer quote this proverb in Israel. For every living soul belongs to me, the father as well as the son – both alike belong to me. The soul that sins is the one who will die. (Ezek. 18:2–4)

Ezekiel attempted to defend God's justice and to reassert individual responsibility by recounting a story of three generations – a righteous one, a sinful one and a righteous one – each of which received the reward or punishment due to his own actions, and he added this reassurance:

> If a righteous man turns from his righteousness and commits sin, he will die for it; because of the sin he has committed he will die.

But if a wicked man turns away from the wickedness he has committed and does what is just and right, he will save his life … Yet the house of Israel says, 'The way of the Lord is not just.' Are my ways unjust, O house of Israel? Is it not your ways that are unjust? (Ezek. 18:26–27, 29; cf. 33:17–20 & Deut. 24:16)

Even so, Ezekiel was inconsistent: he continued to use the idea of communal retribution in his denunciations of Israel and in prophecies of the destruction of the land: 'This is what the Lord says: I am against you. I will draw my sword from its scabbard and cut off from you *both the righteous and the wicked*' (Ezek. 21:3, italics added). This is a clear contradiction of the assertion of individual culpability.

In my opinion, the questioning of God's justice displayed by the people of Judah is one of the counter-abusive traditions in the Hebrew Bible. This is because they exhibited an attitude of independence and made their own judgements. They were not content simply to accept the teaching of a religious authority if it contradicted their own experience. Instead, they began to establish their own point of view. This is the first stage in the recovery of a woman who has been in an abusive relationship: the recognition of her right to hold her own opinions and to challenge the ideas of her oppressor. Likewise, the beginning of the process of liberation for oppressed peoples is the positive re-evaluation of their own traditions and insights as they struggle to free themselves from internalised oppression.

WHY DO THE WICKED PROSPER?

Amongst others, the prophet Jeremiah asked: 'Why does the way of the wicked prosper?' (Jer. 12:1). This is the opposite of what was supposed to happen. In contrast to this expectation, Jeremiah struggled with his experience of persecution by his countrymen and a sense of rejection by God. He complained that his people did not listen to him and that they persecuted him for proclaiming God's message of judgement. He was unable to account for the fact that he, who had been given the word of God, had not also been defended by him (Jer. 20:7–9). His despair became so great that he cursed his birth (20:14), and yet, he also expressed trust in God and appealed for revenge on his enemies (17:17–18). In other words, he did not doubt the fundamental connection between human actions and God's reward or punishment, but asked, 'How long?' (12:4).

Jeremiah's protest is very similar to that found in many of the Psalms. The Psalms are full of complaints about God's inexplicable failure to intervene according to his promises, even when the petitioner has been faithful. Collectively the complaining psalms are referred to as individual or communal laments. The individual laments (Brueggemann, 1984, pp. 54–7; Prinsloo, 2003, pp. 366–73) begin with an address to God, followed by a complaint telling God how desperate the situation is, and a petition asking God to act decisively. In order to encourage him, the psalmist adds various motivations for God to do so, which may include: the speaker's innocence; his repentance; God's goodness to an earlier generation; the value to God of his praise; or, the damage to God's own power, prestige and reputation if the speaker is not rescued (Brueggemann, 1984, p. 55). It is noteworthy how prominent amongst these reasons is the appeal to God's self-interest or narcissism. It seems that the psalmists were well aware of his need to have his ego massaged!

After the motivation comes the imprecation in which, in a manner reminiscent of Jeremiah, the speaker gives vent to his resentment and desire for vengeance, without restraint or compassion for his 'enemy' – that is, the person who is persecuting him or putting him in peril in some way. The most extreme example is found in Psalm 109:

> Appoint an evil man to oppose him;
>> let an accuser stand at his right hand.
> When he is tried, let him be found guilty,
>> and may his prayers condemn him.
> May his days be few;
>> may another take his place of leadership.
> May his children be fatherless
>> and his wife a widow.
> May his children be wandering beggars;
>> may they be driven from their ruined homes.
>> (Ps. 109:6–10)

Normally, after the imprecation, the individual lament then moves into praise, expressing an assurance of being heard, promising to make some payment as an act of thanksgiving, and concluding with a doxology and praise. The communal laments contain similar elements, but instead of concentrating on an individual's trials, they concentrate on a disaster that has befallen Israel, particularly the Babylonian conquest. The same pattern is found in the Lamentations of Jeremiah.

The laments have a complex relationship to the cycle of abuse. On the one hand, they recognise the abusiveness of God's actions or inactions:

> In a reproachful way the petitioner holds the Lord responsible for the crisis which he is experiencing: 'for it is you who have done it ... I am worn down by the blow of your hand' (Ps. 39:9b–10; see also Ps. 88:6–7). He accuses God of shooting arrows at him like an archer and of wounding him (Ps. 38:2).

The petitioner accuses the Lord by way of rhetorical questions that he has forgotten him (Ps. 42:9), forsaken him (Ps. 22:1), cast him off (Ps. 43:2), and is hiding his face from him (Ps. 88:14). He accuses God of being a passive onlooker and of not helping him (Ps. 35:17; cf. also Ps. 6:3). He thus blames God for the situation that has arisen because of God's inattentiveness [e.g. Ps. 13:1–2].

(Prinsloo, 2003, p. 367)

These psalms represent the counter-abusive movement from a victim finding fault in herself and accepting the outlook of her victimiser, to a victim finding fault in her victimiser for his abusive or neglectful behaviour. Furthermore, the victim does not simply change her perspective, she confronts her persecutor and demands that he change. This is a major step towards the transformation of an abusive relationship, or, if the abuser will not change, towards ending it.

Paradoxically, in spite of their venom, the psalms that call for vengeance may also be seen in a positive light. This is because they give expression to the rage of the suffering psalmist. It is anger at being treated so badly which may move a woman to stand up to her abuser or to leave him. The fury of the psalmist is a healthy, if disturbing, response to oppression. However, the danger is that these psalms, especially the communal laments about Israel's sufferings, could equally well be the beginning of a reversal of victimhood. For instance, Psalm 137 proclaims against Babylon the happiness of 'he who seizes your infants and dashes them against the rocks' (v. 9). One who is so angry is unlikely to restrain his wrath until the enemy has been completely subordinated, if not totally destroyed.

Strangely, despite the extremity of their distress, the complaining psalmists hold back from drawing the logical conclusion from their apparent abandonment – that God is either powerless or callous. Instead, they frequently finish with a renewed statement of trust in his protection and expectation that he will quickly come to their assistance. For instance, in Psalm 73 the speaker, like Jeremiah, laments over 'the prosperity of the wicked' and his own sufferings but, nevertheless, he concludes with a reassertion that God will bring down the wicked: 'Those who are far from you will perish; you destroy all who are unfaithful to you' (Ps. 73:27). These psalms look to a future in which God will indeed act to right the current woeful situation.

Those psalms which express the greatest disorientation and alienation from God confront him candidly with *his* failings and *do not acknowledge fault* in the psalmist or in Israel. The most direct challenges to faith in the justice of the God of Israel come from virtuous psalmists who are stuck in the darkness of danger and loss and whose God is nowhere to be found or is experienced as *actively hostile*. The most extreme example of these is Psalm 88. Notoriously, although it begins with an address to 'the God who saves me' (v. 1), it proceeds through a catalogue of disasters, all blamed on God, and concludes in darkness:

> Why, O Lord, do you reject me
> and hide your face from me?
> From my youth I have been
> afflicted and close to death;
> I have suffered your terrors
> and am in despair.
> Your wrath has swept over me;
> your terrors have destroyed me.
> All day long they surround me like a flood;
> they have completely engulfed me.
> You have taken my companions and loved ones from me;
> the darkness is my closest friend.

(Ps. 88:14–18)

This psalm gives no comfort and no way out of the gloom. It contains the most negative view of God in all the Psalms, if not the Bible as a whole, and as a consequence, has been a source of much discomfort and scandal amongst commentators. It embodies a complete breakdown in the moral defence: God is held to be accountable for the psalmist's ills, and he is not let off the hook; the psalmist does not blame himself, neither does he resort to a facile affirmation of faith in God's goodness and good intentions against the evidence. Psalm 88 is the purest form of protest against the abusiveness of God in the Bible and, as such, it is an undiluted example of the counter-abusive tradition of calling God to account. The psalmist receives no reply.

JOB: A FAILED ATTEMPT TO CALL GOD TO ACCOUNT?

However, someone else who called God to account did receive a reply of sorts – namely, Job. In the book of Job there is a systematic enquiry into the relationship between an individual's suffering and the righteousness of both himself and God. The book presents the reader with the artificial situation of a man who was sinless and, therefore, could not be undergoing suffering as a punishment for his own wickedness. Nowhere does the book resort to the idea of communal responsibility in trying to account for Job's plight, not even in the speeches of his friends. Instead, the book focuses its full attention on the inadequacy of the belief that God punishes the wicked and rewards the righteous according to their deeds. Neither does it resort to life after death as an explanation, but explicitly denies that possibility (Job 14:11–12).

The Prologue gives a picture of the heavenly council in which God himself points Job out as an example of exemplary virtue (Job 1:8). Nevertheless, Satan challenges the integrity of Job, declaring, firstly, that his piety is the result of still having his prosperity and, secondly, that it is the result of still having his own skin untouched by calamity. God allows Job to be tormented to demonstrate to Satan that it is possible for men to worship him without thought of reward. This dialogue makes the traditional arguments in favour of retributive justice completely untenable.

At first Job accepts the will of God for him. In reply to his wife telling him to 'Curse God and die!' he says: 'Shall we accept good from God, and not trouble?' (Job 2:9–10). He acts like the 'good slave', submitting obediently and without complaint to the will of his master. His response seems like a too-perfect example of internalised oppression. Could anyone really behave like this after the deaths of all his children, the destruction of all his property, and in the midst of suffering extreme physical pain, without resorting to a massive degree of self-deception or repression? Not surprisingly, there is soon a radical change in Job as the poetic section of the book takes over from the prose Prologue. So great is the shift that commentators have often concluded that the prose and verse sections of the book of Job are from different hands and even from different historical periods. Be that as it may, taking the book as a unitary work of literature as it now stands, Job's submission to God is short-lived. He begins to protest at his fate and, like Jeremiah, curses the day of his birth (Job 3:1–19).

Leo Perdue has identified a number of mythological metaphors which structure the dialogues of Job with his three 'comforters', Elihu, and God. One is that of 'humanity as slaves of the gods'. Perdue says: 'in his disputations with the friends (chs. 3–27), Job … [uses this metaphor] to describe the drudgery and oppression of all human life, tormented by the unrelenting God' (Perdue, 1991, p. 263). In addition, the friends use the slave metaphor to support their belief in retributive justice (Perdue, 1991, p. 264). Even though Job recognises his impotence, he cannot accept the reasoning of his friends. Instead, he questions the justice of God:

> If he snatches away, who can stop him? …
> Even if I summoned him and he responded,
>   I do not believe he would give me a hearing.
> He would crush me with a storm
>   and multiply my wounds for no reason.

> He would not let me regain my breath
> but would overwhelm me with misery.
> If it is a matter of strength, he is mighty!
> And if it is a matter of justice, who will summon him? ...
> *'He destroys both the blameless and the wicked.'* ...
> *If it is not he, then who is it?*
>
> (Job 9:12, 16–19, 22b, 24b, italics added)

This passage has much in common with the complaint of a battered woman who is aware that whatever she does, she is likely to be on the receiving end of her partner's violence, and that whatever she says will make no difference. Job has no one to rescue him and so, paradoxically, like some of the psalmists, he appeals to his persecutor against his persecutor – in other words, to God against God:

> I know that my Redeemer lives,
> and that in the end he will stand upon the earth.
> And after my skin has been destroyed,
> yet in my flesh I shall see God;
> I myself will see him with my own eyes – I, and not another.
> How my heart yearns within me!
>
> (Job 19:25–27)

Rather than being a reference to life after death, this is probably one to a future vindication of Job's name when he will be shown to have been innocent – and somehow he will know this, possibly even in Sheol (Dell, 2003, p. 354; Crenshaw, 2001, pp. 342–3).

The contest between Job and God is structured on the mythic pattern of 'the battle with Chaos'. This makes its first appearance in chapter 3 when Job wants to summon sleeping Leviathan and Yam, the sea, to unmake God's creation and 'return the world to nothingness' (Perdue, 1991, p. 266), and reaches its fullest expression in Job's challenge to God:

> Choosing the metaphor of the battle of chaos from the mythic tradition, Job moves to depict God as the Warrior who has irrationally turned against his own creation. As destructive tyrant, the ground for his rule over creation is now removed. God has been identified with the chaotic forces he had formerly controlled. As such, he must be removed from heaven's throne.
>
> (Perdue, 1991, p. 270)

At length, Job refuses to continue as an obedient, if complaining, slave and indicts God as a criminal. In chapters 29—31, 'Job envisions himself in the role of a just and god-like Primal Man whose own judgment and dispensations of justice contrast dramatically with those of the corrupt God. Now Job becomes the man who would be god' (Perdue, 1991, p. 264). Job's confrontation with God can be seen as an example of the mythic pattern of 'the revolt against the gods'. In terms of the cycle of abuse, it is an example of an attempted reversal of victimhood. However, it fails.

In chapters 38—41, when God eventually comes to answer Job, he does so as the Divine Warrior setting out to battle against chaos, ironically now represented by Job. When he speaks to Job out of the whirlwind, fulfilling Job's prediction that he would 'crush me with a storm', his reply is full of irony and reminiscent of prophetic denunciations of the powerlessness of idols (e.g. Isa. 41:22–24):

> Who is this that darkens my counsel
>   with words without knowledge?
> Brace yourself like a man;
>   I will question you, and you shall answer me.
> 'Where were you when I laid the earth's foundation?
>   Tell me, if you understand.
> Who marked off its dimensions? ...
> Surely you know, for you were already born!
>   You have lived so many years!'
>
> (Job 38:2–5b, 21)

God boasts about his creation to Job, indicating with particular pride his creatures, Leviathan and Behemoth, monsters representative of chaos, whom he controls. God points out that, if he is to rule, Job must be able to do the same: 'Kingship is not grasped, it is won through victory over chaos' (Perdue, 1991, p. 267). But God does not simply defeat these monsters, he delights in them. Paradoxically, God's ordering of the world includes nurturing the creatures representative of chaos, as well as keeping them within their legitimate bounds (Perdue, 1991, p. 271).

Faced with the overwhelming power and transcendence of God, there is only one possible response open to Job – renewed submission: 'My ears had heard of you but now my eyes have seen you. Therefore I despise myself and repent in dust and ashes' (Job 42:5–6). This looks like a total defeat of Job's rebellion. He has been pushed back into the role of slave of God. However, in a paradoxical twist, God says to Eliphaz the Temanite: 'I am angry with you and your two friends, because you have not spoken of me what is right, as my servant Job has' (Job 42:7). In other words, Job is right about the arbitrary behaviour of God and they are wrong about retributive justice! Why then did Job repent? To add further paradox, in the Epilogue (Job 42:7–17) Job is rewarded for his faithfulness with ten children to replace the ten who had been killed and twice the wealth which had been destroyed, a recompense which suggests the correctness of the view that the righteous are rewarded.

There is a sense in which God's ordering of the world is confirmed by the speeches from the whirlwind that push Job back into a proper recognition of his own limits and, thereby, redeem the justice of God (Perdue, 1991, p. 267). Nevertheless, Job's protest is necessary for his sanity, and he only achieves his new orientation towards God through making it. For, as Perdue points out, 'the struggle for justice' against 'the caprice of an unjust judge' is 'the proper way of being human in the world. And in the restoration of Job, there is the redemption of God' (Perdue, 1991, p. 272). Put differently, it is not clear who was redeemed by their struggle. Who won: Job or God?

There is no definitive interpretation of the book of Job and commentators have come to wildly varying conclusions about its meaning. I have made extensive use of Perdue's ideas because they are highly relevant to the cycle of abuse. He relates Job to the myths of the battle with chaos (i.e. the myth of redemptive violence), the slavery of human beings to the gods and their revolt against their divine overlords. In addition, Perdue's recognition of the necessity for humans to hold God, the unjust judge, to account for his ordering of the world is most helpful. If we puny humans are to have any sort of honest and psychologically healthy relationship with God, we must follow the example of Job in seeking to confront him with what his creation does to us. If we shirk this, we can only fall into a fake engagement with God in which we are hiding our true feelings. Our experience of the world is the primary means through which we experience divine providence. If the world appears arbitrary or hostile, then God will seem so as well, and we will either be forced to give up believing in a loving God or else be tempted to find some illegitimate way, such as the moral defence, to preserve our conviction of his beneficence. To do so will inevitably give rise to a fake spirituality. Such mealy-mouthed religion is all too common.

Job, of course, submitted after giving vent to his misery and sense of injustice and, perhaps, that is what we all need to do in the end, but it can only legitimately be *in the end*. If we give in too soon, we will remain trapped in the psychology of abuse which is so implicated in the biblical witness to God and has given rise to so much noxious religion, including many of the theological attitudes which underpin the war on terror. Only if we resist such theologies of abuse can a proper theological resistance to these distortions of religious conviction be adequately articulated.

QOHELETH'S FAITHFUL SCEPTICISM

One biblical writer, Ecclesiastes, provides a clear example of how it is possible to develop a spirituality of submission to God which is not an expression of the psychology of abuse. The book's protagonist, often referred to as the Preacher or Qoheleth, presents a confusingly mixed perspective on the justice of God. Commentators have often been puzzled by this book and many have questioned why such a sceptical document was included in the Bible. However, I think that it is extremely helpful for our purposes. Qoheleth appears to have given up the moral defence along with a belief in retributive justice and any attempt to make sense of the actions of God, and yet to have maintained a belief and trust in God and the goodness of life.

John Jarick (2003) handles the ambiguity of the text by discerning in the words of Qoheleth a thesis and an antithesis. The thesis is that the quest for wisdom is futile (Eccles. 1:17; 2:15; 8:17). So distant and impenetrable is God that it is impossible to find him in nature. Life is toil and vanity, in other words, a puff of breath which passes away, and there is no correlation between people's behaviour and their fate:

> So I reflected on all this and concluded that the righteous and the wise and what they do are in God's hands, but no man knows whether love or hate awaits him. All share a common destiny – the righteous and the wicked, the good and the bad, the clean and the unclean, those who offer sacrifices and those who do not.
>
> (Eccles. 9:1–2)

However, rather than drawing the conclusion that God is not just and that life is meaningless, Qoheleth also advances an antithesis: that life is to be enjoyed and that the pleasures of life come from God (e.g. Eccles. 2:24; 3:13, 22; 5:18; 8:15):

> Enjoy life with your wife, whom you love, all the days of this meaningless life that God has given you under the sun – all your meaningless days. For this is your lot in life and in your toilsome labour under the sun. Whatever your hand finds to do, do it with all your might, for in the grave, where you are going, there is neither working nor planning nor knowledge nor wisdom.
>
> (Eccles. 9:9–10)

The synthesis of these two outlooks is to live life moderately, avoiding extremes and being content with the simple pleasures of life, but knowing that you cannot fathom the ways of God. This is an alternative to Job's protest that is not based on repression. Qoheleth looked fully at the ambiguity of life and passed from seeking to make sense of it to attempting to live a life appropriate to human limitations. There is nothing grandiose in his attitude. He neither challenges God nor denigrates humanity. He does not resort to the moral defence to defend the righteousness of God, nor to the chosen people defence to boost his own sense of importance, nor does he avoid the problem by using the eschatological defence to project a solution into the future.

REVELATION OR PROJECTION?

Our investigation of Yahweh, the God of Israel, has definitely confirmed the accusations of abuse made against him and, furthermore, the attitudes and actions of his partner, Israel, support this conclusion. They demonstrate that historically she has suffered from the psychology of those who have been abused or oppressed and that the development of her character has been profoundly influenced by her participation in the cycle of abuse. The recognition that *according to the biblical record* the God of Israel behaves abusively or oppressively towards his people is an insight of primary importance for understanding the role of the Judaeo-Christian tradition in the creation of violence in both the past and the present, as well as the continuing influence of the psychology and dynamics of abusive relationships on the Jewish, Christian and Muslim religions in the contemporary world.

We have identified three different attitudes in the Hebrew Bible towards the involvement of God in the world. Two of them – that God is the beneficent ruler of a good world or the protector of his people who fights for them against their enemies – are conventionally given prominence in theological thinking. The third – that God is the abuser or oppressor of his people (and other peoples) who keeps them subjected through using violence and intimidation – is not normally acknowledged at all or else is explained away. However, it is, I contend, absolutely essential to face this central, if ignored, part of the biblical witness to God. The divine threat is the background to everything that happens in the Bible and in the life of the Christian Church. To acknowledge this is all the more important when we turn to the New Testament in which the crucifixion is central to the Christian conception of God; an event which the New Testament authors interpret as the means by which the divine threat of damnation is removed from those who believe in Christ.

However, if Job and Qoheleth are correct in rejecting the reality of retributive justice, much of the rest of the Hebrew Bible and, indeed, the New Testament must be wrong in advancing the idea that God behaves towards human beings according to this principle, including many rationales for the violence of God. How can we make sense of this contradiction? I have already mentioned the possibility that this view of the character and behaviour of God is derived from the experience of the people of Israel. To the extent that this is the case, their picture of God is actually a mirror of their own psychology derived from their own experiences of oppression, and may have little to do with God him-, her- or itself. Rather than seeing God as an abuser, it may be more accurate to consider the Hebrews as a victimised people who created an image of God for themselves which compensated their feelings of humiliation and low self-esteem, but which also covertly reproduced the victimisation that they were trying to escape. In other words, from a psychological perspective, it seems clear that the roots of religious violence in the Judaeo-Christian tradition grow out of the violence attributed to God by the Bible, and that this violence is itself a product of the cycle of abuse in which the ancient Israelites were both victims and victimisers.

When the testimony of the Bible to the abusiveness of God is taken seriously, the question of whether or not the Bible is recording a true picture of the Godhead or merely a projection of the human personalities of its writers onto the heavens becomes an essential one to address. Of course, if the latter is true, the problem of theodicy is solved at a stroke: God is not like the God of the Bible and so he did not do or fail to do what the Bible records. He is not to blame. However, in that case, neither is he revealed nor known through the biblical text or the history of the Hebrews or of Jesus. *We have arrived at a very distressing dilemma: if we take the Bible as revelatory, we have to cope with a God who is abusive, violent and arbitrary; but, if we take it as projection, we have no means of knowing God; the Bible is merely evidence for the communal psychology of Jews and Christians.* Whichever position we adopt, and even if we can find some middle ground, we have to face the further problem that belief in the abusive God to which the Bible witnesses has severe emotional, relational and political consequences for those who accept that belief. Living with an abusive God promotes the psychology of abuse amongst his people and encourages the cycle of abuse to replicate itself unabated down the generations of the devout. This is a process which is clearly evident in the war on terror.

Questions that we need to consider concerning both the violence attributed to God in the Bible and the violence committed 'in the name of God' by human beings include: Whose violence is it? Is it human or divine? Does it arise from a religious necessity or is religion an excuse for all-too-human aggression? These questions obviously apply to the war on terror but they are also of great importance in considering the violence at the heart of the Christian religion, especially the crucifixion of Jesus. So now we will turn to God's Christian family to see whether and in what ways the cycle of abuse is evident in its members' conceptions of God and in their attitudes and actions.

Chapter 7

GOD THE ABUSIVE FATHER

The central image in Christianity is, of course, the crucifixion. This is the absolutely distinctive feature of the Christian religion, which claims that the death and resurrection of Jesus of Nazareth reveal the nature of the Godhead. For Christians, these events are the interpretative key to all of life and the human relationship to God. Strangely, however, the Christian Church has never been able to agree on a definitive statement of how the cross brings about reconciliation between God and humanity, a process known in theological language as 'the atonement'. This failure is astonishing given the extraordinary lengths to which the Church went to debate and define the fundamental doctrines of the faith contained in the Creeds and promulgated by the Ecumenical Councils.

In this chapter we will examine the principal ideas about the atonement that have been advocated by mainstream Christian churches. At the centre of this investigation is the question of the relationship of theories of the atonement to the cycle of abuse. The crucifixion of Jesus is the story of the cruel death of a young man at the hands of an imperial occupying power, the Romans. As such, it has obvious relevance to the themes of abuse and oppression; all the more so, since in Christian history the cross has all too often been the inspiration and justification for both self-sacrificial, not to say self-hating, forms of spirituality and the abusive treatment of others in the name of Christ. The cross can be taken either as an event which overcomes the cycle of abuse or as one that participates in and reinvigorates it. In what follows, we will explore both possibilities.

The history of the interpretation of the cross in the New Testament and in the Church is a huge subject well beyond the scope of this study. I shall, therefore, limit myself to pointing out some of the psychological consequences of different interpretations. In other words, I shall assess the story of Christ and its effect on the Christian family from the point of view of a family therapist, looking especially at evidence for the psychology of abuse amongst believers and at the vicissitudes of the cycle of abuse in the history of the Church. This investigation will not be concerned with debating the 'truth' of any particular interpretation or

application of scriptural texts or with assessing Christian doctrine theologically; rather, it will be focusing on the psychological influences
which produced them and their psychological effects. In the final
chapter we will examine these matters from a theological perspective.

THE TRIPLE OPPRESSION OF CHRISTIANS

We have seen that the Israelites suffered from a double oppression: by
secular powers or 'enemies' and by God. In the New Testament a third
oppressor is added to the other two, namely, sin or the Devil. The central
message of Jesus is the coming of the kingdom of God (or heaven). The
kingdom represents the fulfilment of the eschatological hopes of the
Israelites which focused on the expectation that God would come to
redeem them from the oppression of foreign pagan rulers and to re-
establish the kingdom of Israel as an independent nation under the rule
of God and, usually, a restored Davidic king, the Messiah. As we noted,
this was more than a this-worldly transformation in the status of Israel;
at the Day of the Lord there would be a great outpouring of divine wrath,
a disruption of the cosmos and a recreation of the earth. Accompanying
this change would be a transformation in the people of Israel whose
hearts, according to the visions of Jeremiah and Ezekiel, would be
changed from hearts of stone to hearts of flesh so that they would obey
God. Nevertheless, at a popular level this expectation was probably associated primarily with a this-worldly reversal of the fortunes of the Jewish
people.

Jesus' teaching about the kingdom of God picks up these themes but
alters them significantly, so much so that most Jews from that time until
this have denied that Jesus fulfilled those prophesies at all. Despite the
Christian claim that he was the Messiah, he did not fulfil the messianic
expectation of freeing God's people from foreign rule and establishing
the reign of God in Israel. Indeed, according to John's Gospel, he explicitly declined the role of military revolutionary against the Romans
(John 6:15). Rather than the Day of the Lord being initiated by Jesus, he
talked about the coming of the kingdom of God in gradualist terms and
postponed the universal disruption until a later unspecified time when
'the Son of Man' would return in judgement (Mark 13). In the meantime,
Jesus called all people to repent and believe because the kingdom of God
was at hand (Mark 1:15), and spoke extensively, often in parables, about
the manner in which the kingdom was growing in this present world
(e.g. the parable of the mustard seed, Mark 4:30–32).

The kingdom of God has an uncertain relationship with this present
world. It has been inaugurated but is not yet fully present. However, this
does not mean that it is merely a question of time before it comes to

Rather, because the kingdom is an eschatological reality – in .ords, it represents the ultimate end towards which the world is .eading when it will be transformed totally into what God intends it to be – *the kingdom cannot be fully realised in this aeon.* Consequently, it exists in a dialectical relationship, with the current order as its antithesis, as both a divine potential and a divine initiative for change. Paradoxically, it is always both already within and yet outside and continuously entering the present reality. This confusing situation I describe as 'the dialectic of the kingdom of God' (Young, 2004, pp. 163–5). Jesus embodies the coming of the kingdom in his time and, therefore, he describes the reaction of people to himself as equivalent to their response to God and to the kingdom. In other words, Jesus' presence is a form of judgement revealing what is in the hearts of men and women (John 9:39). People have a choice either to respond and enter the kingdom or to stay outside and suffer condemnation for resisting God.

There is no third option. This observation is extremely important. In contemporary culture there is a very strong emphasis upon individual autonomy, self-determination and individual human rights. In discussing the triple oppression of humankind, we should, therefore, add a fourth possibility: in addition to being under the domination of God, or a secular ruler or enemy, or sin, individuals may seek to rule themselves. In New Testament terms this is an impossibility because it is the same as being ruled by sin. New Testament thought is dualistic: humans have no choice but to be ruled by God or by the forces opposed to God, whether 'spiritual' or human. Redemption consists in being transferred from the domination of the latter to the protection of the former.

In the Bible and in traditional Christian teaching, people are of value because they are created in the image of God, are loved by God and are called into a relationship of love by him. However, *from the biblical perspective, human autonomy is equivalent to sin.* This is the import of the story of Adam and Eve who were expelled from the Garden of Eden for eating of the fruit of the tree of the knowledge of good and evil (Gen. 3). Both their disobedience and their newly acquired knowledge represent a sinful contravention of proper human limitations.

In the Hebrew Bible, obedience is the chief requirement of God and, as we have witnessed, his punishment of any infringements by his chosen people was normally draconian. His gravest condemnation was directed at those who put anything else in a place of greater importance than himself, either by turning towards other gods or by asserting that their personal achievements were the outcome of their own powers rather than those of God. St Paul builds on this fundamental outlook; he argues that humans are either 'slaves to sin' or 'slaves to God' and that death is the consequence of human sin (Rom. 5:12). However, the good news is that through Christ believers have been transferred from one kind of slavery to the other: 'though you used to be slaves to sin … You have been set free from sin and have become slaves to righteousness' (Rom. 6:17–18). Paradoxically, this new slavery is actually freedom. Paul says that those who have faith are God's children and co-heirs with Christ, and he refers to 'the glorious freedom of the children of God' (Rom. 8:21).

In addition, contrary to the Jewish belief that obedience to the Law is the means through which his people are found pleasing by God, Paul speaks about being delivered from bondage to the Law. In his view, although the Law is itself good and God-given, the Law cannot deliver from sin: 'Before this faith [i.e. in Christ] came, we were held prisoners by the law, locked up until faith should be revealed' (Gal. 3:23). Rather, the Law becomes the means through which sin rules in humans hearts: 'The sting of death is sin, and the power of sin is the law' (1 Cor. 15:56). Paul's teaching about the Law is highly nuanced and paradoxical. For our purposes it is sufficient to note that the Law is yet another repressive influence on human lives from which we have to be released. However, release from the power of the Law does not mean that Christians are permitted to do anything that they please. They are not to sin because they have died with Christ and now share in his risen life (Rom. 6:11). The alternative is to return to being controlled by sin.

In sum, from the point of view of the early Christians, humans only have a choice between being under the rule of sin or of God. From this perspective, self-rule is equivalent to being under the rule of sin. Human autonomy does not have a positive value. The mission of Jesus is about breaking the power of sin so that the human race may be free to love and serve God. He sets individuals free not for independence or to follow their own desires, but to fulfil their essential destiny of loving, obeying and living for God, in whom is their ultimate satisfaction.

Even if this outlook is acceptable from a theological point of view, it creates considerable psychological problems. Two central values of most forms of contemporary psychotherapy are personal autonomy and the ability to relate to others. To function healthily individuals need both to be sufficiently differentiated from their parents and families of origin so that they are able to stand on their own feet, and also to be able to interact, share and live harmoniously with others. Both these abilities are inhibited or actually damaged by being in a relationship of subordination with another who is controlling or violent. The New Testament picture of God and its dualistic thinking about the rule of sin or of God considerable obstacles to healthy psychological functioning.

ar as individual Christians believe in a God who is at least implicitly abusive, they are likely to develop symptoms of the psychology of the abused, including the internalisation of the negative view of themselves held by their abuser. In other words, they are liable to think of themselves as sinners and to feel dependent on their abuser's approval for any sense of value. They are also likely to live out the dynamics of abusive relationships within their own families or within their ecclesial communities.

Only if obedience to God truly represents the means to liberate the self from all that distorts its true identity and integrity, as traditional Christian spirituality asserts, can Christian faith be regarded as psychologically healthy. When Christian belief enables such liberation to take place, it has a constructive role in the psychological development of those who accept it; but so often it has the opposite effect. Even so and despite what I have written about the abusive potential contained within Christian theology, I am convinced that the claim that our true freedom and fulfilment comes through surrender to God is correct. But this is only the case when that surrender is the free decision of a mature person, rather than the constrained action of someone conditioned by the psychology of abuse. It is vital that Christianity is purged as far as possible from the distorting influence of this psychological configuration. My desire that this should happen is a major motivation for writing this book. Failing this, belief in God is just as likely to fuel the cycle of abuse in Christianity as it was in the religion of Israel. This is a potential which is reinforced by traditional interpretations of the atonement, which we will now examine.

THE CROSS AND DIVINE CHILD ABUSE

Traditional theories of the atonement explain how the life, death and resurrection of Jesus have overcome the power of sin. According to Gustav Aulen's classic study of the atonement, *Christus Victor* (1970), there are three main types of atonement theory: Christus Victor, satisfaction and moral influence. The earliest of these and the one w hich is most characteristic of the teaching of the early Church is Christus Victor, which he refers to as 'the classic type'. This type emphasises Christ's victory over the power of sin, death and the Devil; hence, the designation Christus Victor. It begins from the conviction of God's enmity towards humans because of sin. According to St Irenaeus in the second century CE, through Christ's incarnation, human obedience, death and resurrection and the coming of the Holy Spirit, God has destroyed the power of the Devil and freed Christians from condemnation (Aulen, 1970, pp. 16–35). God has rescued human beings from the domination of the Devil so that they can then find their freedom in serving him.

In the early Church the general belief was that Christ had overcome the Devil in a cosmic battle between good and evil, in which the cross at first appeared like a defeat for God and a victory for the Devil, but then at the resurrection was revealed to be the destruction of the Devil's power and Christ's victory (Weaver, 2001, pp. 14–15). One influential way of explaining how this happened was to say that Jesus' death was a ransom paid to the Devil to free sinners from his power, or even that it was a trick played on the Devil (Aulen, 1970, pp. 47–55). But however it was explained, the essential point of the Christus Victor theory is that 'It is the sin itself that is overcome by Christ, and annihilated; it is from the power of sin itself that man is set free' (Aulen, 1970, p. 148).

Satisfaction theory was first elaborated by St Anselm, Archbishop of Canterbury (1033–1109) (Anselm, 1909), and is the theory which has been dominant in the Western Church since the Middle Ages. It is found in both the sacrificial understanding of Jesus' death in Roman Catholicism and the idea of penal substitution in Evangelicalism. Its central idea is that Jesus died vicariously on our behalf. Anselm put forward a theory which to modern ears sounds very strange but which was deeply rooted in the feudalism of his day. He suggested that God's 'honour' had been affronted by human sin and that although he loved humanity he could not overlook this fact. Hence, in his love he found a way to satisfy his honour by sending Jesus to die in place of the human race and thereby atone for the affront he had received. In later versions of this theory put forward by Luther and Calvin at the Reformation, Jesus did not die to satisfy God's honour but his justice; his death pays the penalty for sin which humans have incurred and, therefore, God forgives them if they believe in Christ (George, 1988, pp. 62–73, 213–16; Westerholm, 2004, pp. 32–3, 48–9).

The moral influence theory was developed by Peter Abelard, a contemporary of Anselm, in response to and in disagreement with him. Because it is primarily concerned with the way in which Jesus' death changes human beings, Aulen describes it as 'the subjective type'. In the moral influence theory the emphasis is not on any change that happens in God, but on the alteration in human consciousness as a result of witnessing the death of Jesus. People discover that the God whom they had thought was judgemental and unloving is in fact loving towards them, so much so that he sent his only Son to die to show them how much he loved them: 'Thus, for Abelard, Jesus dies as a demonstration of God's love' (Weaver, 2001, p. 18). Consequently, Abelard attached no particular

importance to Jesus' death beyond its power to move humans to love
and he rejected any idea that God required satisfaction for human sin
(Aulen, 1970, pp. 95–7): 'He emphasises especially that Christ is the great
Teacher and Example, who arouses responsive love in men; this love is
the basis on which reconciliation and forgiveness rest. Here he quotes
Luke vii. 47: "Much is forgiven to them that love much"' (Aulen, 1970, p.
96). In the moral influence theory, humans are rescued from themselves,
from their fear of God or obduracy in resisting God; in effect, from their
own autonomy over and against God's authority. They are, implicitly, at
the same time rescued from the power of sin over them, although this is
not personified as the Devil nor is it defeated in battle by God.

Although all these theories indicate that God has found a way to forgive human sin through the death of Jesus, it is noteworthy that all three
start from the assumption of God's alienation from humanity because of
sin and the inevitability of his punishment of human sinners without the
intervention of Christ. They all, therefore, promote an implicitly abusive
understanding of the nature of God's relationship with the human race
and, although in their different ways they account for a change in God's
stance from condemnation to forgiveness, none of them suggests that
any alteration has taken place in the character of God as a result of the
atonement; he remains both loving and just. In other words, he continues to be a controlling and abusive lover.

Christus Victor is based on the recognition of a fundamental duality
in God's attitude to humanity similar to that found in the Hebrew Bible.
As Aulen describes it:

> God is at once the all-ruler, and engaged in conflict with the
> powers of evil. These powers are evil powers, and at the same time
> executants of God's judgment on sin. God is at the same time the
> Reconciler and the Reconciled. His is the Love and His the Wrath.
> The Love prevails over the Wrath, and yet Love's condemnation of
> sin is absolute. The Love is infinite and unfathomable, acting *con-
> tra rationem et legem*, justifying men without any satisfaction of
> the Divine justice or any consideration of human merit; yet at the
> same time God's claim on men is sharpened to the uttermost.
>
> (Aulen, 1970, p. 155)

From this perspective, Christ's death has defeated the power of evil over
the human race. However, without it God would have continued as the
enemy of humanity because of sin.

In satisfaction theories Jesus' death may be described as either a
propitiation or an expiation for sin or simply as a sacrifice but, whatever
term is used, the essential point of satisfaction theories of the atonement

is that Jesus has died instead of us; without his self-offering all humanity would have been damned and those who do not believe in him will be damned in any case. Human beings are rescued from the wrath and condemnation of God, but the totalitarian nature of God's rule is not changed thereby. In essence, these theories substitute Jesus for human 'sinners' as the victim of God's violence. God's abusiveness and tendency to use violence is not 'healed', rather it is diverted onto Jesus who suffers its full extent.

Translated into human terms, which is what the use of the metaphors of father and son inevitably invites, this transaction does not appear credible, let alone just. The idea that a father would ever feel it necessary to punish a son with the death penalty is difficult enough to accept, although there are examples of this happening in human history, such as the son of a king who rebels against him. That a father would think it an acceptable and just punishment to kill his son in someone else's place is simply obscene. This portrait of God makes no sense unless God is regarded as completely pathological and so full of rage, not justice, that he has to unleash it on someone. If so, this God is a prime example of someone suffering from the psychology of an abuser who hits out at his partner when he is himself emotionally disturbed or, better, of a man who has a row with his partner and then goes and beats up his child in order to get rid of his inner tension.

In addition, the view of justice implicit in this theory is unjust. The punishment for the offence, whether it is to God's honour or his law, is completely unrelated to the sin. It takes place outside the relationship of which it is a part, in other words, it has nothing whatever to do with the person whose sin it is supposed to atone for. God sends his son to be born as a man in order for him to be killed, so that he does not have to kill the rest of humanity. His son accepts this mission, dies and, consequently, God forgives those people who accept this sacrifice on their behalf, but not anybody else. As such, this approach is in continuity with the collective idea of punishment practised in ancient Israel whereby any member of a family or tribe might be punished for the crime of another, and a man's sins could be visited on his descendants. It treats punishment as something which need have no necessary connection with either the person who offends or the actual consequences of the offence. Justice is not concerned with righting the wrong but with punishing the offence (Brown & Parker, 1989, p. 7). The punishment merely has to take place; the one who commits the offence does not have to experience the punishment; all that is necessary is that someone suffers and dies! It is incomprehensible how such a transaction can be considered just, let alone loving. As Julie M. Hopkins says: 'It is morally abhorrent to claim that God the Father demanded the self-sacrifice of his only Son to balance the scales of justice ... A god who punished through pain, despair and violent death is not a god of love but a sadist and a despot' (Hopkins, 1995, p. 50; cited by Weaver, 2001, p. 134; cf. Brown & Parker, 1989, p. 8).

Although, the moral influence theory does not share the obviously abusive potential of the other two theories, it is still based on the assumption that God will punish sinners if they are not freed from their sin. It is much more positive about human beings than the other two theories, attributing to them the ability to be moved to repentance by Jesus' suffering and death. Even so, as Joanne Carlson Brown and Rebecca Parker point out: 'The moral influence theory is founded on the belief that an innocent, suffering victim and only an innocent, suffering victim for whose suffering we are in some way responsible has the power to confront us with our guilt and move us to a new decision' (Brown & Parker, 1989, p. 12). This is actually a pretty grim view of the human capacity to change or gain insight and one which still requires a victim to die. It also contains within it the assumption that an individual's suffering may be redemptive for others, an idea which has the potential to encourage destructive forms of self-sacrifice and sado-masochism amongst the devout.

However it is understood, the depiction in each of these atonement theories of God as a father who willingly sends his son to die for the human race looks all too like an abusive relationship. Admittedly the terms 'father' and 'son' are metaphors and cannot be applied literally to the internal relations of the Holy Trinity. Nevertheless, their use immediately associates the Trinity with human familial relationships and inevitably, as a consequence, with the possibility of them being abusive. The description of Jesus' death as intended by God the Father makes the link definite.

THE SACRIFICE OF ISAAC

The abusiveness of God towards his son is replicated by the Church towards those who follow his son: they are also expected 'to carry their crosses' and to imitate Christ. Crucifixion becomes the model of sanctity promoted for Christians to imitate, carrying with it the dangerous implication that God desires his children to suffer and that only by suffering are his followers able to please him. The uncomplaining obedience of Christ is also put forward as a model for emulation. Both unconditional obedience and the unresisting acceptance of suffering are found in one of the most disturbing stories in the Bible, the sacrifice of Isaac (Gen. 22:1–18), which has often been taken by Christian commentators as a precursor of the sacrifice of Jesus. This story illustrates the dangers of this spirituality of imitation when the relationship between God the Father and God the Son is translated into the dynamics of a human relationship.

Here is an instance of a father who breaks the bonds of paternal love and determines to sacrifice his own child in obedience to God, and of a child who meekly accepts this abuse from his father. The radical psychoanalyst Alice Miller has made a study of the depiction of the sacrifice of Isaac in Christian art. Beginning from two paintings by Rembrandt, she notices that all such pictures portray Abraham looking away from Isaac at heaven and, furthermore, that in Rembrandt's versions Abraham has covered Isaac's face with his hand so that he cannot see (Miller, 1990, pp. 135–45). She asks how Isaac, an adult, could let his father sacrifice him without any resistance or questioning, and answers:

> How can a person lying on a sacrificial altar with hands bound, about to be slaughtered, ask questions when his father's hand keeps him from seeing or speaking and hinders his breathing? Such a person has been dehumanised by being made a sacrifice; he no longer has a right to ask questions and will scarcely even be able to articulate them to himself, for there is no room in him for anything besides fear. (Miller, 1990, p. 139)

To be sacrificed is to be put in the ultimate position of abuse. Miller compares modern young men who are taught to go off to fight in wars by the state to Isaac – a comparison also made by Wilfred Owen in his poem, 'The Parable of the Old Man and the Young': 'Then Abram bound the youth with belt and straps,/ And builded parapets and trenches there,/ And stretchèd forth the knife to slay his son' (Owen, 1985, p. 151). Miller adds the further observation that:

> Neither does the father ask any questions. He submits to the divine command as a matter of course, the same way his son submits to him. He must – and wants to – prove that his obedience is stronger than what he calls his love for his child, and as he prepares to carry out the deed his questions vanish. He doesn't ask God for mercy or look for a way out, and if the angel didn't intervene at the last moment, Abraham would become the murderer of his son simply because God's voice demanded it of him. In the pictures I examined, there is no pain in Abraham's face, no hesitation, no searching, no questioning, no sign that he is conscious of the tragic nature of the situation. All the artists, even Rembrandt, portray him as God's obedient instrument, whose sole concern is to function properly. (Miller, 1990, pp. 140–41)

This state of mind is a deeply disturbing example of the psychological and ethical perversion that can be engendered by a Christian believer's surrender of self to God. Such Christian depictions of the sacrifice of Isaac should be read as an expression of the abusive potential within Christianity, rather than as anything to do with Israelite religion or Judaism. They function as typological images portraying certain attitudes typical of Christian spirituality when it is based on a sacrificial reading of Christ's death and combined with the conviction that his followers are called to imitate both his unquestioning obedience and his total self-surrender to the will of his Father that he die.

A person who adopts this form of spirituality, under the influence of the psychology of abuse that is inextricably intertwined with it, can be persuaded not only to endure the worst forms of abuse, even murder, passively and uncomplainingly, but also to commit the most evil actions, overriding even the most sacred obligations towards his own family, 'in the name of God'. This is all the more the case when a believer has developed an unhealthy form of emotional dependency upon God, one which replicates that of some abused women upon their abusers. As Elie Godsi explains:

> Once the victim comes to feel helpless, worthless and yet at the same time responsible for the abuse, a distorted identification with the perpetrator, and an emotional dependency on them, sometimes takes place. The victim's identity can become defined by their association with their abuser and they can remain compliant and passive in relation to them in situations that are unrelated to the abuse. This is the ultimate form of powerlessness, whereby the victim's entire sense of their own existence becomes dependent on the relationship with their abuser. This sometimes leads to an experience of being totally under the abuser's control and at the mercy of almost their every wish and command; it is as if the victim becomes spellbound. (Godsi, 2004, p. 88)

Insofar as Christians are emotionally dependent upon their relationship with God in this way, especially if they have been subjected to abuse in their human relationships, there is a danger that the experience of being totally committed to him may result in such passive powerlessness in response to what they take to be the will of their divine lover. This makes them particularly vulnerable to being abused or exploited by their God's official representatives in the Christian community. There is, therefore, a direct line running from the abusive dynamics implicit within Christian teaching about the crucifixion of Jesus and contemporary scandals about sexual and other abuse within the Church.

Chapter 8

THE CROSS AND THE CYCLE OF ABUSE

The foregoing analysis may seem excessively gloomy. If the Christian religion promotes an oppressive spirituality of blind obedience and suffering, why have so many people believed in it as 'good news'? Christianity promises new life. Sufficient people must have experienced it as providing just that for it to have survived and prospered for almost 20 centuries. Wherein then lies its positive potential? The answer to this question is both straightforward and highly complex. Jesus taught a simple message of the forgiveness of sins for those who repent and follow him. Numerous individuals have indeed been released from the burden of guilt by accepting that forgiveness and have found belonging and purpose through following him and joining the Church. In addition, believers have taken Jesus' death on the cross at face value as a demonstration of the great love of God without being aware of or concerned by the negative implications that I described in the last chapter. Furthermore, Christianity does contain a remarkable and potentially liberating challenge to the psychology and dynamics of abuse, but it is set in the context of the crucifixion of Jesus and, thus, is highly paradoxical and ambiguous and open to interpretations which may be used to support oppressive and abusive practices.

In this chapter we will investigate the potential of the story of Jesus' life and, especially, his death to contribute to both abusive and counter-abusive forms of religious belief. It will be helpful to examine ambiguities in the Gospels and the other New Testament documents in order to understand how such contrasting interpretations of the significance of Jesus have been derived from the same source. At this point I shall be presenting neither my own method of handling these ambiguities nor seeking to discern 'the authentic message of Jesus' from the ways in which his followers have interpreted it, but will simply concentrate on indicating how the cross has been assimilated to the cycle of abuse, despite many potentially transformative and liberating elements in Jesus' teaching and practice.

THE KENOSIS-GLORIFICATION PARADIGM

The nearest there is in the New Testament to a definitive summary of the spiritual significance of Jesus' life, including his birth, death and resurrection, is found in St Paul's Letter to the Philippians:

Your attitude should be the same as that of Christ Jesus:

Who, being in very nature God,
did not consider equality with God
something to be grasped,
but made himself nothing,
taking the nature of a servant,
being made in human likeness.
And being found in appearance as a man,
he humbled himself
and became obedient to death –
even death on a cross!
Therefore God exalted him to the highest place
and gave him the name that is above every name,
that at the name of Jesus every knee should bow,
in heaven and on earth and under the earth,
and every tongue confess that Jesus Christ is Lord,
to the glory of God the Father.

(Phil. 2:5–11)

This is the passage on which Brueggemann based his division of the Psalms into psalms of orientation, disorientation and new orientation. According to St Paul, Jesus willingly gave up his glory in heaven, taking the status of a servant, voluntarily accepting humiliation, and being obedient to death on the cross. This movement is the exact opposite of the attempt to make other people an extension of oneself in order to fulfil one's own needs and desires that results in abusive and controlling behaviour. However, the cross is not the end of the story; Jesus dies but then he rises again and is exalted to reign in heaven 'in the highest place' and to receive the obeisance of all people, 'that at the name of Jesus every knee should bow'. Although this passage does not mention it, Jesus' exaltation is often also linked to his role as the future judge of all, sometimes accompanied by the apostles (Matt. 19:28; Luke 22:30).

The significance of this passage in relation to the cycle of abuse is profoundly ambivalent, an ambivalence which is located at the heart of the central Christian conception of what Jesus Christ did and how his followers are expected to respond. On the one hand, his renunciation of dominance, known in theology as his self-emptying (in Greek, *kenosis*), and his refusal to adopt violent means to defend himself against his accusers, appear to be counter-abusive. There are many statements in the New Testament which are opposed to human grandiosity and power-seeking. The fundamental Christian insight from this perspective is that violence is not overcome by violence but by refusing to turn the violence back upon the oppressor. This strategy introduces a radically new possibility into the cycle of abuse; in response to oppression, instead of being an unwilling victim or moving from being a victim to a victimiser, it puts forward a third option for an abused person to follow: non-violent acceptance of victimisation as a means of overcoming violence and evil. This response is enjoined on all those who follow Jesus: 'Your attitude should be the same as that of Christ Jesus.' On the other hand, Christ's self-denial and acceptance of suffering and death is a highly ambivalent model for Christians to follow. As we noted in the last chapter, over the centuries it has given rise both to forms of spirituality which have been self-destructive and to attitudes towards others which have been highly abusive.

Moreover, Christ's kenosis is only the first movement in a process which culminates in a reversal of victimhood in the form of his resurrection, exaltation and coming in judgement. In the New Testament there are numerous references to the future return of Jesus to judge the world in which he is depicted as an old-fashioned absolute monarch or else a warrior with the power to inflict punishments, including torture and death, on those who resist him (e.g. Mark 14:62; Rev. 19:11–21). This portrayal puts in question the degree to which Jesus' teaching and example actually contradict the pattern of dominance and subordination or overcome the cycle of abuse; and there are worrying indications that Jesus' radicalism was associated with a reversal of victimhood, at least in the minds of some of his followers. This is a possibility celebrated in the Magnificat, in which Mary says:

> He has performed mighty deeds with his arm;
>   he has scattered those who are proud in their inmost
>   thoughts.
> He has brought down rulers from their thrones
>   but has lifted up the humble.
> He has filled the hungry with good things
>   but has sent the rich away empty.
>
>   (Luke 2:51–53)

It appears that at any rate some of the early Christians expected Jesus to engage in a traditional reversal of victimhood, whereby the original victim replaces his victimisers and then rules over them. Tragically, whatever Jesus may have intended, his followers have over the centuries often used his exaltation to rulership in heaven and future return to rule on earth as a justification for their own dominance over others in the present ordering of the world.

It is not clear whether the meaning of Jesus' movement from glory through self-emptying and death to glory for his adherents is that self-denial and non-violence are means by which to end the cycles of violence and abuse amongst humans or, conversely, that they are an alternative route to enjoying ultimate domination. This ambiguity arises in part, I suggest, because of the confusion between Jesus the human being, who accepts martyrdom and provides a model for the behaviour of his human followers, and Jesus the second person of the Trinity, who leaves his place at the right hand of God and returns to it again and then participates in the dominance of God over his creation. The doctrine of the incarnation, which holds that Jesus was both God and human, having two natures which were united in one person without separation and without confusion, means that the Jesus who is in a position of voluntary subordination and the Jesus who is the dominant ruler of the world are the same; and that both are both God and human. The consequence is that the attributes of the deity and of a human tend to become muddled and capable of being attributed to both Jesus' divine and human natures. This means that his exaltation can easily be interpreted as a compensation for his kenosis and compromise the latter, so that it looks like neither a true surrender of divine dominance nor an authentically selfless act of human obedience to God. The result is that the humble self-emptying of the second person of the Trinity becomes not a true surrendering of dominance, but a merely temporary entering into the realm of change and mortality in submission to the will of the Father which is subsequently reversed through an exaltation to cosmic rule. Likewise, after his resurrection, Jesus the man is regarded as participating in the rule of God over creation, and his exaltation as a human being comes implicitly to contradict the humility of his voluntary acceptance of suffering and death.

Moreover, even though the kingdom of God disrupts the old order of dominance and subordination in human relationships, it does not bring about a similar change in the relations between humans and the deity. God remains the one who has the right to expect and to extract obedience from his human creatures. The sayings of Jesus that challenge attempts at domination confront the *human* tendency to seek power and control *over other human beings*. However, they in no way acknowledge or critique the potential *abusiveness of God* implicit within this view of the deity. Jesus failed to recognise the double oppression – that is, by both

God and humans – which we identified as a core element of Israelite experience; and the New Testament authors follow his example. Indeed, the specifically Christian Scriptures actually contain significantly less questioning of the justice of God than the specifically Hebrew ones.

The problem is that, even apart from the violence of the cross for which, since he sent his Son to die, he is ultimately responsible, God's wrath and its accompanying violence is as present in the New Testament as it was in the Old, even though for the most part the violence is delayed until the second coming of Christ. Apocalyptic passages are especially full of visions of divine violence which are psychotic in their intensity and venom, particularly in the book of Revelation, whose visions surpass even the worst excesses of the Old Testament; for example, the description of 'the seven bowls of God's wrath' in chapter 16, of which the following is a sample: 'The second angel poured out his bowl on the sea, and it turned into blood like that of a dead man, and every living thing in the sea died' (Rev. 16:3).

The ambiguity about whether Jesus is truly advocating a transformation in human relationships that would dispense with the cycle of abuse or is promoting a different means towards dominance is further encouraged by numerous paradoxes and apparent contradictions in the teaching attributed to him in the Gospels as well as in that of the New Testament in general. In order to make sense of these disparities, we will examine these different aspects of his message in relation to the pattern of kenosis followed by exaltation found in Philippians. This progression may be divided into three phases: firstly, voluntary renunciation of privilege and adoption of the lowest place in relation to others; secondly, struggle with evil leading to apparent defeat, including a refusal to use violence to fight the enemy; thirdly, victory over evil and exaltation to a position of dominance over not just former enemies but the whole of creation.

This enquiry will take into account not only attitudes found in the New Testament but also the ways in which they have been developed both in the early Church and by contemporary interpreters. Unfortunately, because of limitations of space this survey can only be a very selective sampling of the available evidence. However, since my intention is only to show that these perspectives exist in either the biblical documents themselves or commentaries upon them, rather than attempting an exegesis and assessment of what each passage 'really means' (if such a thing is possible), this brief treatment will, I hope, suffice. We will be focusing on the relation of Christian interpretations of Jesus to the cycle of abuse, and on how they encourage or counteract the psychology of abuse amongst believers. The connection is unclear because many elements of the teaching attributed to Jesus and of his practice can be taken either way. Please note that I shall not be concerned with questions of either historicity or authenticity. In other words, for the purpose of this investigation what matters is not whether or not Jesus actually spoke the words attributed to him, but that the early Christians treated them as if he had and, therefore, regarded them as an authoritative guide to his teaching.

FIRST PHASE: VOLUNTARY RENUNCIATION OF DOMINANCE

Undoubtedly, Jesus preached a radical gospel which challenged the religious and secular authorities and reversed the normal social hierarchy. After the disciples had been arguing about 'who was the greatest,' he said, 'If anyone wants to be first, he must be the very last, and the servant of all' (Mark 9:35), a saying backed up by his action of washing the disciples' feet at the Last Supper, accompanied by these words: 'You call me "Teacher" and "Lord," and rightly so, for that is what I am. Now that I, your Lord and Teacher, have washed your feet, you also should wash one another's feet. I have set you an example that you should do as I have done' (John 13:13–15). In addition, in the beatitudes he proclaimed the blessedness of the meek, the poor, and so on (Matt. 5:1–12; Luke 6:20–23). He also commanded the rich young man to sell everything (Mark 10:17–22; Matt. 19:16–22; Luke 28:18–23) and said: 'How hard it is for the rich to enter the kingdom of God' (Mark 10:23–26; Matt. 19:23–24; Luke 28:24–25). These passages are extraordinarily subversive of normal social order, and there are many others that are equally so.

However, there is a dark side to Jesus' encouragement of the renunciation of dominance. It is not entirely voluntary; there is a threat behind it:

> If anyone would come after me, he must deny himself and take up his cross and follow me. For whoever wants to save his life will lose it, but whoever loses his life for me and for the gospel will save it. What good is it for a man to gain the whole world, yet forfeit his soul? Or what can a man give in exchange for his soul? If anyone is ashamed of me and my words in this adulterous and sinful generation, the Son of Man will be ashamed of him when he comes in his Father's glory with the holy angels. (Mark 8:34–38)

Jesus' message is given in the context of the coming of the kingdom of God, which is an event which includes judgement and the potential for eternal condemnation. All people are at risk of being on the receiving end of divine violence if they do not conform to Jesus' injunctions.

Even so, the positive side of Jesus' expectation of the kingdom is that he proclaimed the fulfilment of Old Testament prophecies about the coming of the Day of the Lord, which includes the ending of injustice: 'The Spirit of the Lord is on me, because he has anointed me to preach good news to the poor. He has sent me to proclaim freedom for the prisoners and recovery of sight for the blind, to release the oppressed, to proclaim the year of the Lord's favour' (Luke 4:18–19). He also treated women in a manner which contradicted the patriarchal norms of his times, including making them the primary witnesses to his resurrection (Mark 16:1–8; Matt. 28:1–10; Luke 24:1–10; John 20:10–18). Many feminist scholars claim that Jesus advocated the replacement of traditional patri- archal norms with a radically new society in which all people would be equal (e.g. Fiorenza, 1983), and liberation theologians argue that his primary concern was to resist political oppression and liberate the poor (e.g. Gutierrez, 1974; Miranda, 1982).

Jesus did indeed tell his followers not to live as those who find their satisfaction in this world, but to put God first and renounce the attempt to dominate others or accumulate wealth: 'You cannot serve God and money' (Matt. 6:24; Luke 16:13; cf. 1 Tim. 6:6–10). However, historically commentators have been divided about his intentions. Whether or not Jesus was concerned to bring about a change in the political and eco- nomic structures of the present world has been debated for centuries by biblical scholars and theologians. Some have concluded that the king- dom of God is an eschatological or heavenly reality and that Christians are not expected to follow Jesus' 'impractical' commandments or to seek for radical social change this side of the Apocalypse. Others have seen his message of the coming of the kingdom as extremely radical political- ly, requiring his followers to be committed to fundamental, even revolu- tionary, political transformation; and have concluded that it was the chief reason why he was executed. It continues to be a matter of dispute between Christians whether they should take Jesus' teaching as an endorsement of direct action to change economic and political struc- tures in the light of the entry of the kingdom of God into this world, or whether they should be indifferent to the affairs of this life, apart from the duty to care for the poor and sick, because the present order is passing away.

Whatever Jesus may have intended, the first Christians do appear to have imitated him in his renunciation of worldly power and wealth, holding their goods in common (Acts 2:44–45). However, this practice does not seem to have been sustained for long, and the more revolu- tionary aspects of Jesus' message appear to have been toned down quite quickly. The New Testament authors continued to emphasise the necessity of caring for the poor, for example: 'If anyone has material possessions and sees his brother in need but has no pity on him, how can the love of God be in him?' (1 John 3:17; cf. Jas. 2:14–26), but this was in the context of an overall acceptance of the social structures of the world in which they lived. Moreover, *Jesus' message of voluntary subordination was interpreted by some Christians as an injunction to submit to the contemporary patriarchal and hierarchical ordering of society.* Wives were to obey their husbands, children their parents, and slaves their masters, though husbands, fathers and masters were exhorted to treat their subordinates kindly (Eph. 5:22—6:9; 1 Pet. 2:18—3:7). Christians were expected to be submissive even when their superior was harsh or if he was also a Christian (1 Pet. 2:18; 1 Tim. 6:1–2); and the same attitude was to be directed towards those in positions of secular authority: 'Everyone must submit himself to the governing authorities, for there is no authority except that which God has established' (Rom. 13:1; cf. 1 Pet. 2:13–17). Such texts have provided a justification for subsequent generations to argue that the present structure of society is divinely ordered and that, therefore, Christians are commanded by Christ to obey their secular rulers, however unjust they may be.

SECOND PHASE: NON-VIOLENT ACCEPTANCE OF MARTRYDOM

The conviction that, in Jesus, God became human, suffered and died and that, therefore, he shares in the human predicament and in human suffering, has been a source of considerable comfort to many Christians who have faced suffering, including not only martyrdom but also abuse, oppression, slavery, poverty and sickness. As Jon Sobrino says:

> On the positive side the cross presents a basic affirmation about God. It says that on the cross God himself is crucified. The Father suffers the death of his Son and takes upon himself all the sorrow and pain of history. This ultimate solidarity with humanity reveals God as a God of love in a real and credible way rather than in an idealistic way. From the ultimate depths of history's negative side, this God of love thereby opens up the possibility of hope and a future.
>
> (Sobrino, 1978, p. 371; quoted by Brown & Parker, 1989, p. 23)

Furthermore, Jesus' death makes possible a theological understanding of suffering as salvific. This idea is not unique to the New Testament. It was already present in the Hebrew Bible in the figure of the suffering servant found in Deutero-Isaiah, whose description of the servant was taken by the early Christians as a prophecy of Christ's death:

> He was despised and rejected of men,
>   a man of sorrows, and familiar with suffering.
> Like one from whom men hide their faces
>   he was despised, and we esteemed him not.
> Surely he took up our infirmities
>   and carried our sorrows,
> yet we considered him stricken by God,
>   smitten by him, and afflicted.
> But he was pierced for our transgressions,
>   he was crushed for our iniquities;
> the punishment that brought us peace was upon him,
>   and by his wounds we are healed.
> We all, like sheep, have gone astray,
>   each of us has turned to his own way;
> and the Lord has laid on him
>   the iniquity of us all.
>
>   (Isa. 53:3–6)

Commentators are unclear who the servant was – it may be that Israel is meant – but for our purposes it does not matter. What is important is that this passage was hugely influential on the Christian interpretation of Jesus' death. The Gospels state unequivocally that Jesus had to die: 'He then began to teach them that the Son of Man must suffer many things and be rejected by the elders, chief priests and teachers of the law, and that he must be killed and after three days rise again' (Mark 8:31); and his death was understood to be necessary in order to fulfil the Scriptures (Luke 24:44). In short, it was the will of God which Jesus freely undertook, as he said in Gethsemane: 'Abba, Father, everything is possible for you. Take this cup from me. Yet not what I will, but what you will' (Mark 14:36).

The idea that suffering can be redemptive for others and can also be a means of coming close to Christ by imitating his suffering, 'being crucified with Christ' (Gal. 2:20), as Paul puts it, has opened the way for the development of various spiritualities of self-sacrifice. On the one hand, these may encourage believers to acts of self-denial and courage in the face of injustice and oppression which are heroic. On the other hand, they may result in masochistic forms of religious practice or the use of Christian teaching to abuse or exploit others, as we observed in the last chapter.

A good example of the first possibility is the book of Revelation, the heart of whose message, according to Richard Bauckham, is: 'that the church redeemed from all nations is called to suffering witness which, by virtue of its participation in Jesus' sacrificial witness, can bring the nations to repentance of idolatry and conversion to the true God' (Bauckham, 2001, p. 1296). Suffering may also be a powerful force in the struggle for justice in this life, as Martin Luther King, Jr. asserted:

> The non-violent say that suffering becomes a powerful social force when you willingly accept that violence on yourself, so that self-suffering stands at the center of the non-violent movement and the individuals involved are able to suffer in a creative manner, feeling that unearned suffering is redemptive, and that suffering may serve to transform the social situation.
>
> (Quoted in Washington, 1986, p. 47; quoted in Brown & Parker, 1989, p. 20)

Brown and Parker comment on this passage: 'The problem with this theology is that it asks people to suffer for the sake of helping evildoers to see the evil of their ways. It puts concern for the evildoer ahead of concern for the victim of evil. It makes victims the servants of the evil-doers' salvation' (Brown & Parker, 1989, p. 20). This is the kind of argument that has been used to encourage abused women to stay with their partners or slaves to obey their masters in the hope of converting them.

However, it is also true in the contemporary world that the witness of the martyrs may be experienced by persecuted Christians as bringing salvation. Thus, Jon Sobrino, writing from the context of the Church in El Salvador, argues that martyrdom has 'salvific power' (Sobrino, 2003, p. 103) and identifies 'the crucified peoples' in South America with the suffering servant, saying that they bring salvation because they offer values that are not offered elsewhere; have evangelising potential; offer hope and great love; are ready to forgive their oppressors; have generated solidarity; and offer faith (Sobrino, 2003, pp. 155–63). This perspective is particularly potent because it is associated with the belief that 'Jesus' death is the result of his option for the poor and the oppressed' (Ela, 1988, p. 108; quoted by Tesfai, 1994, p. 7). In other words, the martyrs who die because they seek to follow in Jesus' struggle against injustice witness to the power of his death to overcome evil.

Even so, God's solidarity with suffering humans is profoundly paradoxical when it is recalled that on the cross it is God who is abandoned by God. One theologian who has grappled with this excruciating paradox is Jürgen Moltmann. In *The Crucified God* he presents a theology of the cross that begins with Jesus' abandonment. He says:

> Jesus died crying out to God, 'My God, why hast thou forsaken

me?' All Christian theology and all Christian life is basically an answer to the question which Jesus asked as he died … Either Jesus who was abandoned by God is the end of all theology or he is the beginning of a specifically Christian, and therefore critical and liberating, theology and life. (Moltmann, 1974, p. 4).

Moltmann speaks about the abandonment as 'something which takes place within God himself', as 'God against God', and he links Jesus' cry to 'the cry of the wretched for God and for freedom out of the depths of the sufferings of this age' (Moltmann, 1974, pp. 152–3). In Jesus, God shares in solidarity with the wretched of the earth, but he does so as the victim of his Father in heaven. His situation is reminiscent of that of Job who appealed to God his vindicator against God his oppressor. For Moltmann, there is hope in the fact that human suffering is also God's suffering:

Only if all disaster, forsakenness by God, absolute death, the in-finite curse of damnation and sinking into nothingness is in God himself, is community with this God eternal salvation, infinite joy, indestructible election and divine life … There is no suffering which in this history of God [i.e. the Son being forsaken by the Father] is not God's suffering; no death which has not been God's death in the history on Golgotha. Therefore there is no life, no fortune and no joy which have not been integrated by his history into eternal life, the eternal joy of God. (Moltmann, 1974, p. 246)

Brown and Parker object to Moltmann's theology of 'the suffering God' on the grounds that he suggests that Jesus 'incited violence against him-self' by confronting the guardians of the religious tradition and is, thus, 'blaming the victim' for his death. They point out that believing that 'suf-fering gives life' numbs 'your resources for confronting perpetrators of violence and abuse', and that such a conviction may encourage Christians to think that they need to suffer in order to be like God and to be good. They conclude: 'This theology is offensive because it sug-gests that acceptance of pain is tantamount to love and is the foundation of social action' (Brown & Parker, 1989, pp. 18–19). Nevertheless, there has to be some means of showing how God is involved positively in human suffering if theology is to be able to speak constructively to those in pain. This is an issue to which we will have to return.

How Jesus' acceptance of death on the cross is interpreted has obvi-ous political implications. Commentators from an establishment point of view are much more likely to emphasise those elements of Jesus' teaching which promote non-violence and the acceptance of current social structures and the authority of the present rulers of the world.

Those with a radical political agenda emphasise the more subversive and activist aspects. Jesus adopted a policy of non-violence which he encouraged his disciples also to follow. He said that his kingdom was not of this world (John 18:36). He refused to allow a crowd to make him king by force (John 6:15). He also refused to lead an armed rebellion against the Roman occupation and rebuked the disciple who cut off the ear of the high priest's servant (Matt. 26:50–56; Luke 22:49–53). He entered Jerusalem on a humble colt rather than a warrior's horse (Mark 11:1–11; Matt. 12:1–9; Luke 19:28–38), and he told his followers:

> You have heard that it was said, 'Eye for eye, and tooth for tooth.' But I tell you, Do not resist an evil person. If someone strikes you on the right cheek, turn to him the other also. And if someone wants to sue you to take your tunic, let him have your cloak as well. If someone forces you to go one mile, go with him two miles. Give to the one who asks you, and do not turn away from the one who wants to borrow from you. You have heard that it was said, 'Love your neighbour and hate your enemy.' But I tell you: Love your enemies and pray for those who persecute you, that you may be sons of your Father in heaven. He causes the sun to shine on the evil and the good, and sends rain on the righteous and the unrighteous. (Matt. 5:38–45)

Such teachings of Jesus, combined with his acceptance of death on the cross and refusal to fight to defend himself from arrest, have inspired numerous Christians to refuse to engage in violence. As Michael Hardin says: 'Jesus does not repay humanity with violence, which it dealt him. By not participating in violence, Jesus breaks the mechanism of violence and opens the way for a new obedience. Vengeance is not part of the high priestly work of Christ' (Hardin, 2000, p. 111; quoted by Weaver, 2001, p. 63). The early Christians followed Jesus' example of non-violence. Even though they were subjected to periods of persecution both by Jewish leaders, including Saul, and by the Roman Empire during which many were martyred, they accepted martyrdom without violent resistance.

Jesus' non-violence is one of his most radical actions, containing the potential for a dissolution of the cycle of violence, especially when taken in conjunction with his loving attitude towards enemies. However, Jesus' policy of non-violence is not necessarily as acquiescent as it at first appears. The liberation theologian José Miranda argues that our impression of Jesus' teaching has been biased by pro-establishment translations. For instance, he points out that 'My kingdom is not of this world' should be translated *'from* this world' (John 18:36). In other words, it comes from outside this world, from God, but it is very much present in this world and requires changes in the current organisation of society (Miranda, 1982, pp. 65–7, italics in original). Similarly, Wink argues that the apparent passivity of 'giving the cloak', 'turning the other cheek' or 'going the extra mile' is not that at all but an assertive form of non-violent resistance. Each of these actions would embarrass or humiliate the oppressors in ways that modern people do not appreciate because of our ignorance of the culture of Jesus' time (Wink, 1992, pp. 175–84). Furthermore, some of Jesus' sayings and actions do encourage violence. Miranda argues that the command to 'love your enemies' does not preclude the use of violence to deprive the rich of their privileges. He says that establishment theologians

> deliberately forget Luke 22:36, 'Whoever has no sword, let him sell his tunic and buy one.' They also purposely forget Matthew 10:34: 'I came not to bring peace, but the sword.' They pass over the fact that Matthew 23 is a page full of *verbal violence* unique in all literature of all time. And most of all they pass over the fact that according to John 2:14–22, Matthew 21:12–13, Mark 11:15–17, and Luke 19:45–46, *Jesus used physical violence* to drive the traders from the temple. (Miranda, 1982, p. 76, italics in original)

THIRD PHASE: EXALTATION TO A POSITION OF DOMINANCE

How far the first Christians actually intended to bring about economic or political change is debatable. Whatever may have been the practice of the first generations, those who came after appear to have been increasingly assimilated to the norms of their social context, whilst being sustained by the belief that Christ on the cross had defeated evil. They looked to Christ's second coming to make his victory over iniquity manifest through overthrowing the power of the Roman Empire. In other words, they resorted to the eschatological defence to sustain them in their imperilled and marginal social position. Their hope of the second coming of Christ to judge the world and of a life with him in heaven helped them to resist persecution (e.g. Rev. 7).

However, this does not mean that they adopted a forgiving or loving attitude towards their enemies. At least in the book of Revelation, that aspect of Jesus' teaching was entirely overlooked, being replaced by a strong desire for vengeance on their oppressors. The seer John says:

> When he opened the fifth seal, I saw under the altar the souls of those who had been slain because of the word of God and the testimony they had maintained. They called out in a loud voice, 'How long, Sovereign Lord, holy and true, until you judge the

inhabitants of the earth and avenge our blood?' (Rev. 6:9–10)

The Christians for whom this book was written may have left vengeance to God, but they still most definitely wanted vengeance, and this vengeance was directed against the Roman Empire, which is represented in Revelation by the beast from the sea (Rev. 13:1–9) (Bauckham, 2001, p. 1297).

Historically, the hostility of the Empire was indeed overcome, but not by violence nor by the coming of the Lord Jesus on clouds of glory on the apocalyptic Day of the Lord. Instead, the Emperor Constantine converted to Christianity and made observance of the Christian religion legal (313 CE), and in the 390s the Emperor Theodosius I banned pagan religion. As a consequence, the Church became one of the most important arms of the imperial administration. This development was a dramatic reversal of victimhood which paralleled the reversal from persecution to heavenly rule experienced by Christ, and which brought about equally dramatic changes in the Church's conception of the religious significance both of the present aeon and of the imperial government.

After Constantine's conversion, the royal imagery used about Christ in the New Testament was increasingly applied to the Emperor as the divinely appointed ruler whose role was to ensure that society was ordered according to God's laws. Thus, by the middle of the fourth century the Roman Ambrosiaster stated that 'the King [emperor] bears the image of God, just as the bishop bears the image of Christ', and the orator Themistus asserted that 'the emperor is an emanation of that divine nature; he is providence nearer the earth; he looks toward God from all directions, aiming at imitation of Him in every way' (quoted by Freeman, 2003, p. 258). In effect, an identification was made between the Emperor and the rule of God which completely contradicted Jesus' teaching about the transformation of human relationships of dominance and subordination in the kingdom of God. This resulted in an equally profound change in the ethical orientation of the Church. As J. Denny Weaver explains, prior to Constantine:

> Being Christian meant to live the life modelled by Jesus, the head or lord of the church. On the other hand, the emperor symbolized the empire. Once Christianity became the religion of the empire and of the social order, and the continuation of Christianity was linked to the success of the empire, preservation of the empire or the institution of the social order became the decisive criterion for ethical behavior, and the emperor or ruler became the norm against which the rightness of a behavior such as killing or truth-telling was judged. (Weaver, 2001, pp. 84–5)

In other words, the Church adapted its teaching to the ethics of the establishment and became one of the most important social structures that supported and enforced imperial rule. Consequently, the socially radical aspects of the teaching of Jesus were marginalised, along with the expectation of an eschatological disruption of the present world. In their place, emphasis was put on individual salvation from personal sin, albeit within the community of the Church, and an expectation of reward or punishment for the individual in the hereafter. This focus on the individual was ultimately encapsulated in satisfaction theories of the atonement, which all stress the role of Christ's death in bringing forgiveness for individual sin and completely ignore the structural or systemic aspects of sin, such as the corruption or injustice of governments (Weaver, 2001, p. 89).

In the centuries since Constantine, the hierarchical difference between God and humanity has often been used by Christian rulers and theologians to defend hierarchical differentiation amongst humans. Secular and ecclesiastical rulers and others in positions of leadership have frequently identified themselves with 'the Lord's anointed' or the apostles or have asserted divine sponsorship in some form and, thereby, claimed authority over other people in the name of God. Indeed, this strategy has been adopted to justify some of the most despotic regimes in history. After all, if a person is chosen by God and rules by divine right, nobody else has the right to resist his decisions. Moreover, Jesus' teaching about subordination has been applied to the relationship between a ruler and his subjects, who have been encouraged to obey their ruler because, as St Paul said, 'He is God's servant, an agent of wrath to bring punishment on the wrongdoer' (Rom. 13:4b). Thus, Jesus' radical and subversive proclamation of the kingdom of God has been co-opted as an ideological justification for the power and privilege of the dominant kingdoms and classes of this world, a process which has been replicated in our time in the war on terror.

Chapter 9

IMPERIAL THEOLOGY, OPPRESSION AND SCAPEGOATING

IMPERIAL THEOLOGY AND INTERNALISED OPPRESSION

The kenosis–exaltation paradigm has been used in a completely illegitimate way to reinforce the authority of Christian rulers. Alongside the identification of a ruler with Christ or, more modestly, with the authority of Christ, the teaching that the devout should imitate Christ has been used extensively by Christians in positions of power to encourage those subordinate to them to accept their subordination passively as a form of virtue pleasing to God. Thus, the kenosis part of the kenosis–exaltation paradigm has been split off from the exaltation part and, whereas the ruler has been identified with the exalted Christ, the ruled have been identified with the passive and suffering Christ. In this way the voluntary submission of Jesus to his Father has been used to encourage Christians to accept political and social subordination and injustice in the name of Christ, and their suffering at the hands of oppressive governments and social structures has been interpreted as an imitation of Christ pleasing to his Father.

This teaching is one of the chief means by which the psychology of the abused has been replicated in believing Christians, especially those who have been in subordinate social positions, as Brown and Parker explain in relation to the lives of women:

> Christianity has been a primary – in many women's lives *the* primary – force in shaping our acceptance of abuse. The central image of Christ on the cross as the savior of the world communicates the message that suffering is redemptive. If the best person who ever lived gave his life for others, then, to be of value we should likewise sacrifice ourselves. Any sense that we have a right to care for our own needs is in conflict with being a faithful

follower of Jesus. Our sufferings for others will save the world. This message is complicated further by the theology that says Christ suffered in obedience to his Father's will. Divine child abuse is paraded as salvific and the child who suffers 'without even raising a voice' is lauded as the hope of the world. Those whose lives have been deeply shaped by the Christian tradition feel that self-sacrifice and obedience are not only virtues but the definition of a faithful identity. The promise of resurrection persuades us to endure pain, humiliation, and violation of our sacred rights to self-determination, wholeness, and freedom … Our internalization of this theology traps us in an almost unbearable cycle of abuse. Our continuing presence in the church is a sign of the depth of our oppression. (Brown & Parker, 1989, pp. 2–3)

Numerous examples could be given of how the splitting of the image of Christ into the Lord in glory and the suffering redeemer has been used to promote the acceptance of abuse and oppression by Christians, but because of limited space I will only give two, drawn from widely disparate geographic regions and theological standpoints. The first example comes from Latin America where Roman Catholicism predominates. Walter Altmann describes how during the history of colonisation two images of Christ predominated over others: 'a dead Jesus and Jesus as a celestial monarch'. On the one hand:

Like the king on earth, Jesus is the monarch in the sky. In fact, the paintings and sculptures of Jesus in heaven at that time represent him as an Iberian king: seated on a throne, luxuriously dressed, and ornamented with a golden crown. It is clear: the power and glory of this Jesus are not instruments of change nor agents of limitation for the terrestrial powers, but are quality attributes that Jesus saves for himself. The power that is actually exercised remains in the hands of the terrestrial kings.

(Altmann, 1994, p. 81)

On the other hand, Altmann points out that the image of the dead Jesus 'is defenceless and impotent', and says that this image and the people's devotion to it have 'an alienating role: the people identify themselves with the suffering of Christ and his spilled blood, but they are not mobilized to transform their situation of suffering.' He concludes: 'When, on the one side, the power of Christ is transferred to heaven in the image of the effective terrestrial power of the king and, on the other side, a defeated Jesus is left for identification with and devotion of the people, systems of domination are obviously being supported' (Altmann, 1994, pp. 81–2).

The second example comes from South Africa and draws on the Calvinist theology of the Afrikaners. At the beginning of the nineteenth century a certain Reverend M. C. Vos, who was working in South Africa, recorded a conversation with the owner of some Black slaves in which he was trying to persuade the slave owner to allow him to evangelise his slaves. He pointed out the dangers of slaves rebelling and continued:

> But if we could have the opportunity to teach them that there is such a thing as divine providence, that nothing happens without the will of God, that this God is a God of order and that just as they have to serve earthly masters, so their masters must serve God. Just as they are punished by their masters when they are disobedient, so their masters are punished by God if they disobey him. If we also make clear to them that the things which seem unbearable to us are the will of God for our good; and that indeed, if they had stayed in their free country they would never have heard about the saving grace of our Lord and on dying would have been lost for ever. Now fortunately they were brought to a Christian country where they have the opportunity to learn to know our Lord and Savior Jesus Christ, who is able to give them eternal happiness. Once they understand this, they will change. Instead of entertaining rebellious thoughts, they will say: If this is the case, I will be content with what I am and I will do my best to serve my master obediently and with joy. (Quoted by Boesak, 1978, pp. 104–5)

This is a blatant example of the deliberate and manipulative use of Christian teaching in the service of social domination. It shows clearly how the identification of Jesus' submission to God with that of subordinate human beings to their social 'superiors' can provide a theological justification for dominance and even slavery that may be used as a form of ideological control. All too often in Christian history the story of the crucifixion has been misused in this way to encourage many different kinds of people to submit to Christian White patriarchal rule. As Julie M. Hopkins says:

> Not only women, but Black slaves in the West Indies and antibellum America, Indians in Latin America, Africans, peoples from the Indian Subcontinent and Asiatics were 'kept in place' by a form of Christianity which engendered passivity and an ethic of self-sacrifice. (Hopkins, 1995, p. 52; quoted by Weaver, 2001, p. 135)

THE MORAL DEFENCE AND ORIGINAL SIN

The passivity and obedience of believers has also been encouraged by the doctrine of original sin. A prominent feature of the psychological inheritance that Christians received from the Jewish religion was the moral defence, the denigration of self in order to preserve the idea that God is good. As we have observed, Paul was convinced that all humans were in subjection to sin: 'all have sinned and fall short of the glory of God' (Rom. 3:23), a conviction which he supported by referring to several passages in the Old Testament that speak about the sinfulness of the human race (Rom. 3:10–18). He also used the story of Adam and Eve (Gen. 2:4—3:24) to bolster his claim that the whole human race is corrupted by sin: 'sin entered the world through one man, and death through sin, and in this way death came to all men, because all sinned' (Rom. 5:12). This is a clear expression of the moral defence. Paul's negative view of the descendants of Adam was later incorporated into Christian doctrine. The Christian religion is based on the conviction that the relationship between God and those made in his image has broken down and, furthermore, that human beings are *entirely at fault* for this breakdown and are *completely unable to help themselves* out of the bondage of sin. This is a very negative view of the human predicament, one which compares with the sense of helplessness and the poor self-image of many an abused woman or an oppressed people.

Thus the Christian story begins, like the Hebrew one, in a situation of slavery, even if the enslavement is not to a human oppressor, and the purpose of Christ's birth is to enter the human context in order to rescue God's people. Just how that slavery is conceived determines the nature of the liberation that Christians believe Jesus has achieved. The most influential theory in the Western Christian tradition about that slavery was developed by St Augustine of Hippo in the early fifth century and is known as 'original sin'. Augustine created a view of human nature that attributes all blame for the suffering in the world to humanity on the basis of the sin of Adam and Eve. According to him, all people have inherited the guilt of Adam's sin in eating the fruit of the tree of the knowledge of good and evil. He even credited infants with guilt, despite the fact that they have no ability to act with moral responsibility. In this way God, *who is the one who imposed and implemented the punishment* of our first parents, was exonerated from any blame for the disordered state of our 'fallen' world (Kelly, 1977, pp. 361–6).

In Augustine's view, Adam and Eve were born with free will and the ability to obey God. However, they chose to sin and thus lost not only their innocence but also their ability not to sin. They bequeathed to their descendants both the guilt of the first sin and, despite their continuing possession of free will, 'a cruel necessity of sinning' which could only be overcome by the grace of God. As J. N. D. Kelly explains: 'By this he means, not that our wills are in the grip of any physical or metaphysical determinism, but rather that, our choice remaining free, we spontaneously, as a matter of psychological fact, opt for perverse courses' (Kelly, 1977, pp. 365–6). In short, human beings are incapable by their own efforts of obeying God and are utterly dependent upon God's grace for their salvation (Westerholm, 2004, pp. 9–10).

This view of human nature is equivalent to some of the most negative self-images internalised by abused women from the criticisms directed at them by their abusers. Humans are incapable of doing good by their own efforts. They are born guilty and are, despite the doctrine that the creation was made good, effectively worthless and wicked, being justly punished simply for existing! Such an attitude when directed towards oneself is a form of internalised oppression. It completely undermines any sense that individuals have either the right or the capacity to act autonomously and, thus, renders Job's protest pointless before it has even been uttered.

The view of creation as *fallen* has unfortunate echoes of the myth of redemptive violence, which has made it possible for Christians to interpret it from the perspective of this myth. The story of the Fall states that God's originally good creation has been corrupted. The rot has got into the nature of things and, as a result, human nature now possesses a tendency to produce chaos and evil if it is not carefully controlled. Consequently, without domination humans will abandon themselves to sin. Implicit in the doctrine of original sin is a requirement for those who are responsible for the ordering of society to impose constraints on these disruptive animals for the common good.

A belief in the Fall and original sin supports Christian spiritualities of control according to which human nature has to be subdued and (often literally) beaten into submission to the decrees of God. This can be seen in attitudes towards children and their education. Alice Miller describes how negative views of children have given rise to cruel and abusive forms of child-rearing which she calls 'poisonous pedagogy' (Miller, 1987). The doctrine of original sin has obviously contributed to such practices, for example:

> The young child which lieth in the cradle is both wayward and full of affections; and though his body be but small, yet hath he a reat [wrong-doing] heart, and is altogether inclined to evil ... If this sparkle be suffered to increase, it will rage over and burn down the whole house. For we are changed and become good not by birth

but by education ... Therefore parents must be wary and circum-
spect ... they must correct and sharply reprove their children for
saying or doing ill.

(Robert Cleaver and John Dod, *A Godly Form of Household
Government*, 1621; quoted by Miller, 1987, unnumbered)

Thus, ironically, the doctrine of original sin has contributed to patterns
of childcare and education that have been intrinsically abusive and
which have, therefore, damaged children psychologically in just those
ways which are most likely to replicate the cycle of abuse, especially
when the cross has been used as a justification for imposing severe
punishments upon children. *Divine child abuse has generated human
child abuse.*

The Augustinian tradition has encouraged not just child abuse but
political oppression. Its very pessimistic view of human nature has been
easily co-opted into a justification for authoritarian forms of Christian
government. Such corrupt, self-seeking, naturally criminal and aggressive individuals as fallen human beings are hardly capable of ruling
themselves, any more than 'the young child which lieth in the cradle'.
Instead, they need to be kept in order by a strong, if beneficent, government. As Felicity de Zulueta comments about Augustine's views:
'Clearly, those in power favoured a belief system that emphasised man's
inability to govern himself because of his inherent depravity; such a
doctrine could be used as an instrument of social control ... if men are
made to feel inherently guilty, they are easier to control' (de Zulueta,
1993, pp. 14–15).

PREDESTINATION AND THE TYRANNY OF GOD

Predestination is another doctrine developed by Augustine which has
been used by believers to abuse or oppress other human beings. For
Augustine, predestination was a logical consequence of original sin: if
the human ability not to sin has been destroyed by the Fall, then the only
way in which humans can be rescued from their propensity to sin is by
the gracious intervention of God. Since not all people respond to God's
grace and even the ability to respond to God's grace is a gift of God, it
follows that the reason that some do and some do not lies in the will of
God. Hence, the ultimate fate of each individual is determined by the
predestining decision of God. A belief in predestination finds considerable support in the Old Testament emphasis upon the choice by God
of the Hebrews as his chosen people. As we have seen, this choice
depended entirely on God's 'grace' and had nothing to do with the
Hebrews' virtue or worldly importance. It appears quite arbitrary.

The doctrine of predestination is in continuity with another Old

Testament theme, one which we have not yet examined – namely, that of 'the hardening of hearts'. The most prominent victim of the hardening of hearts was the Pharaoh who refused to let the Hebrews leave Egypt. When God commissioned Moses to go to tell Pharaoh to set his people free, he promised to 'harden Pharaoh's heart' so that 'he will not listen to you', in order that God could judge Egypt and demonstrate his power to the Egyptians (Exod. 7:1–5). This is only one of numerous references to the hardening of Pharaoh's heart (Exod. 4:21; 7:3, 13; 9:12, 34; 10:1, 20, 27; 11:10; 14:4, 8), a fate that the Egyptians also suffered (Exod. 14:17). Whenever Pharaoh was inclined to do as Moses requested, God ensured that he reneged by hardening his heart. In like manner, he made sure that the Israelites would have to fight the Canaanites for possession of the Promised Land:

> Except for the Hivites living in Gibeon, not one city made a treaty of peace with the Israelites, who took them all in battle. For it was the Lord himself who hardened their hearts to wage war against Israel, so that he might destroy them totally, exterminating them without mercy, as the Lord had commanded Moses.
>
> (Josh. 11:19–20)

Other victims who had their hearts hardened include Sihon, king of the Amorites (Deut. 2:30), and Absolam, son of David (2 Sam. 17:14). In addition, the Israelites as a people had their hearts hardened by God (Isa. 6:10; 63:17), something which, according to all four of the Gospels, continued into the time of Jesus in order *to prevent them from believing in him* (Mark 4:11–12; Matt. 13:11–15; Luke 8:10; John 12:39–40; cf. Acts 28:26–27)!

St Paul took up the idea of the hardening of hearts in order to account for the failure of the majority of the Jews to respond to the preaching of Jesus and, after his death, that of the apostles. He was aware that many of the early Christians struggled to reconcile God's apparent arbitrariness with a belief in God's justice. Even so, he defended God's justice, speaking about 'God's purpose in election' (Rom. 9:11) and referring explicitly to Pharaoh:

> What then shall we say? Is God unjust? Not at all! For he says to Moses, 'I will have mercy on whom I have mercy, and I will have compassion on whom I have compassion.' It does not, therefore, depend on man's desire or effort, but on God's mercy. For the Scripture says to Pharaoh: 'I raised you up for this very purpose, that I might display my power in you and that my name might be proclaimed in all the earth.' Therefore God has mercy on whom he wants and he hardens whom he wants to harden. One of you will

say to me: 'Then why does God still blame us? For who resists his will?' But who are you, O man, to talk back to God? 'Shall what is formed say to him who formed it, "Why did you make me like this?"' (Romans 9:14–20)

Ironically, Paul's 'defence' of God is actually an assertion that he has the right to be arbitrary because he is God, and that humans do not have the right to fair treatment because they are his creation! Nor do they have the right to challenge God's judgements or protest about his treatment of them. Paul's attitude is even more repressive than that of the Hebrew Bible, which at least gives canonical status to Job and the complaining psalms. Significantly, his 'justification' of God's arbitrariness, along with his teaching about the sin of Adam, was the seed-bed within which Augustine's views about predestination grew.

From the perspective of this book, predestination puts all people in the ultimate situation of abuse with regard to God. Human beings have a total inability either to resist or to escape from their abuser, who will ultimately assign everyone either to bliss in heaven or to eternal torture in hell solely according to his whim. There could be no more extreme theological expression of the psychology of the abused than this belief. It completely outlaws any protest against the injustice of God and, thereby, encourages passivity and depression in the face of the apparent arbitrariness of God. What is the point of standing up against divine oppression, if there is nothing you can do to change your fate since God has decided your eternal destination before you were born?

Belief in predestination may lead to a sense of fatalism or despair but, conversely, it may equally function as a source of pride. If a person is able to imagine himself to be amongst those who have been chosen to go to heaven, he may become arrogant and use this conviction as the basis for lording it over others whom he does not believe are saved. Not surprisingly, the idea of predestination has been used to support the oppression of one group of humans by another. In this case, the oppressors have identified themselves with the elect of God, those chosen or predestined to bliss, and they have used their spiritually privileged position to justify their domination over another group who are benighted in unbelief, whether as heathens or heretics. Very often this ideological use of a belief in predestination has been combined with the chosen people defence to produce a very effective rationalisation of racial superiority and colonialism.

CHRISTIAN CHOSEN PEOPLE THEOLOGY
As a minority under Roman rule Christians were persecuted and, like the ancient Hebrews, they used the chosen people defence to

compensate for their endangered condition and marginal social status. They came to regard themselves as the New Israel. All the Gospels show 'the Jews' rejecting Jesus. Paul argues that the promises of God to Israel have now been inherited by those who believe in Christ (Rom. 9—11; cf. Acts 28:28), an assertion repeated in the imagery of the book of Revelation, which concludes with a vision of the New Jerusalem descending from heaven to a new earth (Rev. 21:1–4).

The early Church supported its claim to be the New Israel by the use of a form of biblical interpretation known as 'typology'. In this method historical events recorded in the Old Testament are taken as 'types' or blueprints of present events which indicate the significance of those events and how the faithful should behave now. The identification of the Church with Israel is itself an example of typological interpretation. The advantage of typology for believers is that, once particular contemporary events are deemed to be equivalent to events in the history of Israel, conclusions can be drawn about what to expect and how to respond to them on the basis of the Israelite precedent (Longley, 2002, pp. 104–5). Thus, for example, the book of Revelation compares the Roman Empire to Babylon, and looks forward to the destruction of that oppressor of Christians just as, according to the Old Testament, the original Babylonian Empire was overcome by the power of God (Rev. 18). Such typological comparisons continue to be a feature of contemporary religious and political rhetoric. For example:

> When President Ronald Reagan addressed the British House of Commons in 1982, those with a sharp ear for biblical typology would have caught his reference to an 'Evil Empire' – the part of the world ruled by the Soviets – as a parallel to the corrupt and cruel Neo-Babylonian Empire which had taken the Jews into captivity in 587 BC. (Longley, 2002, p. 110)

Typological interpretation has been used by many Christian groups to identify themselves with God's chosen people and to claim the privileges of Israel for themselves, very often asserting that they had been given their own promised land or a special role by God. In these claims the chosen people defence tends to merge with belief in predestination to produce the conviction in specific Christian nations that they, rather than Christians as a whole, are the new chosen people who are predestined by God to fulfil a special imperial and civilising destiny over other nations or races. For example, such a self-description was held by Germany, Britain, Russia and France during the periods of their imperial success (Lieven, 2004, pp. 33–6).

Often the idea of chosenness has been explicitly linked to ethnic or racial differences, a link also found in the Bible. For instance, in Ireland a belief in their chosenness was widespread amongst Ulster Protestants who used it to justify their dominance over and dispossession of Irish Catholics during the plantations. Drawing on the tradition of the Covenanters of the sixteenth and seventeenth centuries, they had 'a sense of being a special group that has been set apart by God and given the land of Ulster as a form of promised land' (McGlinchey, 1996, p. 40), a conviction which inspired their resistance to Home Rule in the late nineteenth and early twentieth centuries.

The doctrines of chosenness and predestination have also supported the idea of the superiority of White races over those of other colours, a belief which has often been used as a rationalisation for colonialism. For example:

> British imperialism was underpinned by the belief that the British people were a 'new' Israel chosen to fulfill a divine mission and, more importantly, that their election was determined by their racial and cultural superiority over those they were destined to rule. (Maimela, 1994, p. 43; cf. Longley, 2002)

Likewise, in South Africa, the Afrikaners had 'a theological sense of being a chosen people with a mission, namely to create a new "white" nation in dark Africa as a beacon of Christian civilization,' an outlook which ultimately gave birth to Apartheid (Maimela, 1994, p. 44; cf. Longley, 2002, p. 198).

MIMETIC RIVALRY AND SCAPEGOATING

When different countries or religious sects each believe that they are God's chosen people, a conflict inevitably arises between them, especially if they are also involved in a competition for land or material resources. In human history, the combination of incompatible religious claims with ethnic or national rivalries has been one of the most significant causes of inter-communal violence and war. A highly influential explanation both of such rivalry and of scapegoating has been provided by René Girard, a literary critic who has written extensively about the link between religion, social order and violence. According to Girard, interpersonal conflict is fuelled by what he calls 'mimetic violence'. *Mimesis* means imitation. In Girard's theory, human desire has a mimetic quality – in other words, we come to desire something because someone else desires it. *We learn what to desire by copying others.* He distinguishes between biologically conditioned needs or appetites, such as those for food, warmth and physical comfort, and desire, which is acquired through social interaction and conditioned by cultural norms and expectations.

The mimetic process is unproblematic while there is enough of whatever is desired to go round, but when there is scarcity, mimetic desire leads to rivalry as separate individuals compete for the same resource and, thus, to conflict which, if unchecked, escalates into violence. Girard believes that humans lack the instinctual responses which act as breaking mechanisms on fighting animals. Thus, the imitative and escalating violence that happens when two or more rivals compete for possession of the same desired object will continue unchecked unless some non-instinctual restraint intervenes or one party overpowers the other (Girard, 1987, pp. 13–19; cf. Kirwan, 2004, pp. 14–37).

He argues that the sacred exists as the means whereby inter-communal violence is turned into co-operation. This happens when the conflict within a group becomes so bad that there is what Girard calls a 'mimetic crisis' – in other words, the group is threatening to dissolve into a fight of 'all against all'. At this point, those who are competing with each other find somebody else to blame for causing the disruption. They unite in murdering this person, who is chosen arbitrarily to be a scape-goat. Thus the conflict of 'all against all' becomes that of 'all against one', and the unity of the group is restored through combining in antagonism towards the scapegoat. For this process to work, the victim must be in some sense an outsider in relation to the group so that there is no one in the community who might exact revenge for his murder. Originally such murders are spontaneous events, but later on they become formalised and re-enacted as ritual sacrifice (Girard, 1987, p. 24; cf. Kirwan, 2004, pp. 38–62).

By blaming the victim the members of the community deny any responsibility for the problems in their group and establish their own 'innocence'. The community then prohibits the conflictual behaviour associated with the victim with the intention of preventing the violence arising again. The victim is also in some sense divinised or regarded as sacred, and God or the gods are invoked as guarantors within the community of the prohibitions that have been brought into existence. Subsequently, such prohibitions give rise to communal myths and laws, and to a social order and culture based upon them. The original murder is forgotten, indeed the myths associated with the sacrificial cult disguise the fact that there was at the beginning an historical murder. Violence between individuals is contained because its use is now reserved to the divinity, who is believed to use it to enforce these prohibitions, and to the divinity's representatives (Girard, 1987, p. 41). On the basis of cross-cultural anthropological study, Girard believes that the murder of scapegoated victims is the founding event of all religions and cultures:

the scapegoat mechanism is the secret hidden at the heart of the sacred (Girard, 1988). I do not accept the whole of Girard's theory by any means. In my opinion, it has serious deficiencies, in particular, the idea that scapegoating is the *sole cause* of religion and culture seems to me to be a presumptuous and completely unjustifiable denial of the multiple influences upon human religious and cultural development, and of the alternative theories of the origin of religion suggested by disciplines as disparate as psychology, sociology, anthropology, history, economics, semiotics and neurophysiology, not to mention philosophy, theology and religious studies.

Nevertheless, Girard's identification of the role that mimesis plays in the generation of desire is a most valuable contribution to our understanding of human conflict, if not a complete explanation. Mimetic rivalry is not limited to material goods; it may also centre on the possession of abstract or metaphysical attributes. In the religious context it appears to be an important element in the rivalry between different 'chosen peoples'. Since there can only be one chosen people, the assertion by any particular group of its chosenness is also a claim to religious, if not political, superiority and inevitably creates a competitive response in other groups. Such rivalry has occurred on a number of occasions in the history of the Judaeo-Christian tradition. An early example is when the exiles who returned to Jerusalem excluded the people of the land, who subsequently set up their own Samaritan religion. This process was repeated when the early Christians were rejected by the Jewish synagogue and then claimed that they were the New Israel. A much later example, and one of great significance for American identity, occurred at the Reformation when the Reformers asserted that they had taken over as God's chosen people from the Roman Catholic Church. Naturally, the Reformers or Protestants, who were divided into many distinct sects, competed with each other to establish which of them was truly God's people. The competition amongst themselves and with Roman Catholicism gave birth to a series of wars of religion and much religious persecution over the next 200 years.

Many of the early European settlers of North America were Protestants who had left their original countries behind because of persecution or marginalisation, and had set out for the New World in order to live the kind of Christian life that they believed God required of them. These colonists frequently regarded themselves and their particular co-religionists as the genuine chosen people in contradistinction to the 'corrupt' and 'unfaithful' Christian churches that they had left behind and whom they had replaced. The idea that one chosen people has been replaced by another is known as 'supersessionism'. An important aspect of this conception is that the previous chosen people has been rejected by God because of its sin (Longley, 2002, pp. 65–100). As Clifford Longley explains, after the Reformation a 'distinct Protestant supersessionism' developed 'focused on the emerging English nation-state':

> The Jews had been unfaithful to their covenant, and been superseded by the early Church. But the Catholics had also proved unfaithful to their covenant, probably at about the time the papacy emerged, post-Constantine, as a new Roman Imperium ... And so it was presumed that the Catholics too were repudiated by God. They stood, in relation to Protestants, as Jews had stood in relation to Catholics. In fact it is not difficult to see a further sequence: the English in turn proved unfaithful to their covenant, and so God made a new covenant with America. Black American Christians would eventually take it a stage further still – white America had failed, and so the covenant had passed on again.
>
> (Longley, 2002, pp. 88–9)

For those who believe in supersessionism, God's decision to choose a new people, in Christian terminology, 'the elect', is a source of self-esteem and reassurance, but God's changeability also introduces an element of insecurity: if he has rejected his previously chosen people, the fear is that he could also reject the new one if its members do not live up to his requirements. The consequence of this way of thinking is that the new chosen people become very concerned with maintaining their purity so that God will not punish them in the same way that he punished Israel. The consequence is scapegoating, as was the case in post-exilic Israel. It becomes necessary for the chosen ones to defend themselves from any suggestion of sin or failure, the latter of which implies a loss of God's favour. The necessity to maintain a sense of their own purity, at least in their own eyes, encourages those who regard themselves as the elect to see all sin and failure in other people, beginning with the group whom they have replaced as the chosen people. Hence, the extreme hostility towards Roman Catholics evinced by Protestant sects. The other major object of aggression is any other group also claiming to be God's chosen people. Thus, supersessionism is a breeding ground for intolerance.

Not surprisingly, 'the displaced group, no longer "chosen", is presumed by the successor group to be intent on conspiring to undermine it' (Longley, 2002, p. 108). For example, Longley points out that:

> Once Catholics regarded themselves as successors to the Jews as

God's Chosen People, the Jews fell foul of the principle that 'he that is not with me is against me' (Matthew 12:30). They were deemed enemies of the 'Chosen People', whether they saw themselves that way or not. They were presumed to act in that way. Logically, to be the enemy of God's work was to be in league with the devil. (Longley, 2002, p. 107)

The rejection of a superseded group's right to maintain its own beliefs is easily generalised to include all oppositional sects, an intolerance which St Augustine sought to justify through the doctrine that 'error has no right'. As the Irish theologian Joseph Liechty explains:

> This doctrine was developed by St Augustine in the fourth or fifth century to justify the use of state coercion to suppress his heretical opponents: because they are radically in error, they have no right to express or hold their beliefs. Ever since, the doctrine has been put to similar use as the principle behind every use of coercion, especially state coercion, for religious purposes. Error has no right is the doctrine behind penal laws, inquisitions, forced conversions, and similar ugly stains on Christian history. (Liechty, 1995, p. 1)

It should be noted that there is a functional equivalence between the idea that error has no right and the dynamic in domestic abuse when an abusive partner disallows the rights of the other to be heard because he determines the truth and she is 'stupid'. Liechty points out that when the belief that error has no right is combined with the belief that there is only one true Church – or, we may add, one chosen people – the result is likely to be sectarianism:

> if you believe that error has no right, then the chances are your truth claim will be made disastrously, because if your church is the one true church *and* error has no right, then it is your duty to see that error is suppressed by whatever means necessary. Therefore tolerance is no virtue – tolerance is a deadly vice. In terms of our definition of sectarianism, note that this combination of doctrines operates by demonising enemies and justifies their domination.
>
> (Liechty, 1995, p. 2, italics in original)

These doctrines reinforce the grounds for domination already contained in a sect's conviction of predestination and chosenness. Thus, for instance, in Ireland Protestants used this combination of beliefs as the grounds for the political oppression of those whom they had superseded. Catholics, whom Protestants believed were condemned by God to the eternal exclusion of hell, were subjected to persecution and consigned to a subordinate social and economic position in this life.

Such scapegoating creates unity amongst the 'elect'. As Girard suggests, a common enemy is very useful for binding a faction together. Deviant members of the community may also be picked out for censure or punishment, including exclusion or execution. In this way, the sect may 'cleanse' itself of impurity and seek to retain God's favour, in the same way as the ancient Israelites sought to do so when they executed their 'sinful' members. Scapegoating may also promote group conformity and cohesion. To this extent, Girard appears to be correct: internal conflict is overcome by finding a scapegoat onto whom the community can project its conflicts and deviance. However, contrary to Girard, in intra-communal conflict there is often a need to keep the scapegoat alive in order to maintain the projection of the negative and thereby to ensure internal group solidarity. This process is better explained by Erich Neumann's theory of scapegoating, which I described in Chapter 5, than by Girard's theory. However, this is not the place to debate the relative merits of theories of scapegoating.

It seems to me that Girard's theory of mimetic rivalry is extremely relevant to the war on terror in which there is clearly a competition between three distinct entities, each of which claims in one way or another to be the chosen people. Firstly, there is the United States of America which since the days of the earliest settlers has regarded itself as the chosen people sent out to a new Promised Land by the providence of God. Secondly, there is the State of Israel which is a nation explicitly founded as the homeland of the Jews, who are the original chosen people. Thirdly, there is the Muslim *umma* or international community which in Muslim theology is regarded as the people chosen by God to receive his final revelation, one that has superseded that given to the Jews and the Christians just as the *umma* has superseded them as the people whom God favours. From this perspective the war on terror is a war of religion. Certainly, it can only be properly understood when the religious dimensions of the conflict are recognised.

Since it is a war between competing chosen peoples, the war on terror is also marked by numerous instances of scapegoating. Both President Bush and Osama bin Laden believe that the other is the epitome of evil with no right to hold his beliefs. However, this scapegoating does not resolve the conflict nor does it give birth to a religion in the way Girard's theory suggests. Instead, it arises from mutually incompatible religious convictions and results in violence. There is no check on this mimetic rivalry. In addition, the practice of scapegoating is combined with a sense of innocence and victimisation on the behalf of all the parties involved. Furthermore, all three 'chosen peoples' draw heavily on the theological ideas which we have explored in this book and which I have argued are associated with the cycle of abuse. There is, therefore, a direct connection between the cycle of abuse, the theology produced by that cycle and the war on terror which we will now examine in detail.

Chapter 10

THE MYTH OF AMERICA

AMERICA AS A RELIGION

The idea that the war on terror is a war of religion is supported by the observation that the United States of America promotes itself as a religious or mythic entity. In a manner that is distinct from almost all other peoples, large numbers of Americans adopt a religious attitude towards their country, one that is very heavily influenced by Judaeo-Christian imagery and theology. Thus, in many respects *the American nation functions as a form of religion*; it is the object of the kind of devotion that is normally reserved for a god. This may seem an extreme claim, but I am by no means the first person to make such a suggestion. Herbert Croly, the first editor of the *New Republic*, wrote in 1909:

> The faith of Americans in the country is religious, if not in intensity, at any rate in its almost absolute and universal authority. It pervades the air we breathe. As children, we hear it asserted or implied in the conversation of our elders. Every new stage of our educational training provides some additional testimony on its behalf. Newspapers and novelists, orators and playwrights, even if they are little else, are at least preachers of the Truth. The skeptic is not controverted; he is overlooked. It constitutes the kind of faith which is the implication, rather than the object, of thought, and consciously or unconsciously, it enters largely into our personal lives as a formative influence. (Quoted by Lieven, 2004, p. 22)

The theological roots of this 'religious faith' in America are to be found in several identifications that Americans have conventionally made between their country and images central to Christianity. In this chapter we will examine the most important ones:

- America as the chosen people or New Israel;
- America as the New Eden or paradise;
- America as the messiah or saviour of the world;
- America as the kingdom of God or heavenly Jerusalem.

In addition, the self-image of the United States is heavily influenced by the myth of redemptive violence and, although most Americans have never heard of Marduk, there is an implicit identification of America with Marduk (see Chapter 4).

These five identifications act as foundational metaphors which when combined generate a highly exalted view of the role of the United States in the world and in the intentions of God. The resulting 'theology' does not quite amount to a religion; America does not claim to be God, but God is frequently summoned to bless America and is expected to do so. Even so, Americans often portray their country in language reminiscent of Jesus Christ and often implicitly, if unconsciously or unintentionally, identify it with Christ. Thus, they attribute to the American nation a divine messianic character and regard it in a similar manner to the Byzantine Emperor when he was depicted as the earthly representative of the exalted Christ. Perhaps, rather than saying that America is a religion, the best description of the religious nature of Americans' devotion to their nation is to say that it is a form of Christian heresy which implicitly identifies America with Christ. The Church's teachings about Christ have been transferred wholesale to the United States, with the result that Americans wrap it in messianic imagery and imagine it to be a latter-day saviour of the world. Insofar as the nation is treated with a reverence that amounts to worship, this heresy is also a form of idolatry.

This is the case despite the fact that the Constitution makes a separation between Church and State. Indeed, paradoxically, this separation makes it possible for the United States to function as a religious entity (Longley, 2002, p. 69). After the Revolution, since no place was provided for an official or established form of religion, a religious vacuum was created at the heart of the American nation. An exalted conception of America itself seems to have stepped into the void, and to have provided the unifying ideology around which the diverse collection of revolutionary colonists and later immigrants coalesced. This development was anticipated by the attitudes of many of the early settlers who regarded the destiny of their colonies as divinely inspired. This conviction was foundational of the Constitution of the newly independent nation. Because it is believed to enshrine this God-given destiny, Americans have an extraordinarily exalted view of their Constitution, one which is much closer to how members of religions treat their sacred texts than how most other nationalities regard their own constitutions (Sardar & Wyn Davies, 2004, p. 65). The Constitution is regarded as 'pure and perfect' and is 'the basis of what writer and journalist Daniel Lazare calls American "civic religion"', to which he says 'liberals and conservatives' are 'united in their devotion' (Lazare, 1996, p. 3; quoted in Sardar & Wyn

Davies, 2002, pp. 165–6). The flag also commands a loyalty and adulation that to an outsider often appears to be verging on the idolatrous.

AMERICA AS THE CHOSEN PEOPLE OR NEW ISRAEL

The origins of the religious view of the United States are to be found in the beliefs of the first settlers in New England, who were Puritans who regarded the establishment of the early colonies as a response to a call by God to be a new chosen people. They brought with them the idea of predestination which was prominent in the theologies of the Reformers Luther and Calvin, especially the latter (Westerholm, 2004, pp. 39–41, 54–5). Although both of them said that no one was able to know whether or not he was amongst the elect, their followers conveniently ignored this teaching and took the fact that they themselves believed in Christ, and that their worldly endeavours were successful, as a sign of God's favour indicating their chosen status. When their conviction of predestination to heaven was combined with the chosen people defence applied to their own religious sect, or to the American people as a whole, the result was a view of their new continent as a new Promised Land and of themselves as the new chosen people. For instance:

> In 1640, one New England assembly passed an eminently straight-forward series of resolutions:
> 1. The Earth is the Lord's and the fullness thereof. Voted
> 2. The Lord may give the earth or any part of it to his chosen people. Voted
> 3. We are his chosen people. Voted
> (Quoted in Sardar & Wyn Davies, 2002, p. 156)

And, in a sermon in 1799 the Reverend Abiel Abbot said:

> It has often been remarked that the people of the United States come nearer to a parallel with ancient Israel, than any other nation upon the globe. Hence *Our American Israel* is a term frequently used; and common consent allows it apt and proper.
> (Quoted by Lieven, 2004, p. 188, italics in original)

Since the settlers were the new 'chosen people' and the North American continent was the new Promised Land, the settlement was not a mere colonial occupation, but an act of divine providence through which the Almighty would create a New Israel. As John Rolfe said in 1617 about the Virginia colony: 'What need we fear but to go up at once as a peculiar people, marked and chosen by the finger of God to possess it' (Sardar & Wyn Davies, 2002, p. 151). This is a religious vision *par excellence*, and one which has been expressed over the intervening period in some very high-flown language with some equally inflated religious allusions (Armstrong, 2001, pp. 83–5). For example, in the nineteenth century, novelist Herman Melville (1819–91) wrote:

> We Americans are the peculiar chosen people – the Israel of our time; we bear the ark of the liberties of the world. God has pre-destined, mankind expects, great things from our race; and great things we feel in our souls. The rest of the nations must soon be in our rear. We are pioneers of the world; the advance guard, sent on through the wilderness of untried things, to break a path into the New World that is ours. (Lieven, 2004, p. 33)

However, the dark underside of the settlers' typological identification of themselves with Israel meant that the existing inhabitants of the land were regarded as Canaanites whom they were justified in displacing or annihilating. *The Exodus–Conquest paradigm lies at the core of American identity and inspired the conquest of the Native American tribes who occupied the land the settlers coveted.* Thus, as Anatol Lieven says:

> from the very first days of the American colonies, the settlers' belief that they were a people chosen by God was accompanied by an Old Testament belief that God was a 'God of Warre.' The image of the ancient Israelites and their battles with their neighbours was used to justify wars against latter-day 'Amalekites,' whether Indian or French, and God was held to fight for [English-speaking] America in those wars. (Lieven, 2004, p. 127)

For instance, in 1689 Cotton Mather used the references to the Amalekites in Exodus 17:13–16 and 1 Samuel 15:3 to justify wiping out Native Americans whom he regarded as 'deserving of vengeance and total destruction' because they had attacked the settlers (Niditch, 1995, pp. 3–4). Similar Old Testament imagery was used in battles against the French, including by the British before the War of Independence. Thus, 'a sermon preached by Samuel Woodward after the conquest of Montreal by the British General Wolfe in 1760 presents the victory in terms of Israel's triumph at the sea in Exodus 14–15' (McDonald, 2004, pp. 30–31). Subsequently, Britain was also included in the list of enemies whom God helped to vanquish; for example, at the time of the Revolution, George Washington was compared to Moses and the British to Egypt (Longley, 2002, p. 113).

AMERICA AS THE NEW EDEN OR PARADISE
The fear of losing God's favour and hence of losing their status as the new chosen people was prominent amongst the New England Puritan

settlers who, consequently, emphasised the need for purity to avoid the ever-present danger of provoking God's wrath (Longley, 2002, pp. 156–7). However, confusingly, they also held a conviction of America's innocence. 'The earliest settlers wrote they had found a new Eden, the land of Canaan, an earthly Paradise' (Sardar & Wyn Davies, 2002, p. 152). In other words, they thought that they had escaped the corruption of Europe and they determined to set up a society in the New World free from the problems of the old one. This intention was associated with the myth of America as a vast uninhabited wilderness waiting for the first civilising influence of humanity, a myth that ignored the existence and culture of the Native Americans.

Paradoxically, the resulting national theology diverged significantly from the theological traditions that the Protestant colonists brought with them, whilst coexisting with those official religious teachings. According to this view, the land of America was uncorrupted, but everywhere outside this New Eden was fallen, sinful and a potential source of pollution of the pristine territory that the colonists inhabited. In effect, even if not explicitly, the settlers restricted the doctrine of original sin to the world outside their colonial boundaries, while the territory inside them remained a realm of 'original sinlessness'. The frontier between American 'civilisation' and the 'savage' realm of the untamed Native American tribes came to be seen as the boundary between good and evil. This is a classic piece of scapegoat thinking which was easily linked to the Exodus–Conquest paradigm. We have seen that the Native Americans were regarded as Canaanites. Consequently, they represented sinfulness, and their threat to the goodness of the American people provided a further justification for their dispossession.

This dualistic mode of thinking has had a very significant influence upon the way Americans conceive of themselves and their relationship to the rest of the world. As Lieven notes:

> This belief in American innocence, of 'original sinlessness,' is both very old and very powerful. It plays a tremendously important role in strengthening American nationalism and in diminishing the nation's willingness to listen to other countries, viewed in turn as originally sinful. This belief in national sinlessness, like all such beliefs, contributes greatly to America's crowning sin of Pride – the first deadly sin and, in medieval Catholic theology, the one from which all other sins originally stem.
>
> This is in origin a New England Puritan, or 'Yankee,' myth stemming from the idea of the settlers as God's elect, born again in the New World and purged of the stews and sins of England and Europe. (Lieven, 2004, p. 53)

The belief in America's sinlessness is certainly shared by President Bush, who famously asked after the 9/11 attacks, 'Why do they hate us, when we are so good?' (quoted by Chomsky, 2003, p. 83). Apart from being a stunning piece of self-deception, the really important thing to recognise about this statement is that it was made in complete sincerity and is, according to many commentators, representative of an attitude which is widespread in the United States; one which is combined with an equally genuine puzzlement that other nations do not understand that America is exceptionally committed to freedom and democracy and so is exceptionally good (Sardar & Wyn Davies, 2002, pp. 198–9; Lieven, 2004, p. 49). As President Bush put it, 'I'm amazed that there's such mis-understanding of what our country is about that people would hate us. I'm – like most Americans, I just can't believe it because I know how good we are' (Lieven, 2004, p. 52). This failure to see themselves as others see them leads many Americans to misunderstand the antagonism directed towards them; instead of recognising it as a response to the *actions of the United States* that have harmed other peoples, the enmity of their opponents is interpreted as a hostility towards *American values* (LeVine, 2005). Hence, Bush has said that those who hate America do so because they hate the freedom Americans enjoy (Lieven, 2004, p. 74). At this point, it needs to be stressed that not all Americans think like this – there is, after all, a strong movement of opposition to President Bush and the policies of his administration. Many are able to acknowledge and campaign against the 'sins' of their country, and many at the time sought to make 9/11 an occasion for national self-reflection. However, unfortu-nately, the dominant voices in politics and the media crowded them out and presented any criticism of American policies as equivalent to treach-ery or to being a fellow traveller with the al-Qaeda terrorists.

The myth of American sinlessness contributes to its reluctance to listen to other nations. Since America is an innocent country founded and protected by God, who has given it a special mission in the world to spread knowledge of the true way to live, there is nothing that Americans can learn from other peoples; rather, others should listen to America and thereby become enlightened. As Professor John Gray says:

> Today, the idea that America embodies all that is good in the world is an article of faith in the 'new strategic doctrine' presented to the US Congress in September 2002, in which President Bush declared that there is 'a single sustainable model for national success': American democracy and free enterprise. This Wilsonian faith in universal democracy owes something to the European Enlight-enment, but it is at bottom an indigenously American creed, rooted in the belief that the United States has been chosen by God

to bring freedom and virtue into a benighted world.

(Gray, 2004, p. 125)

This attitude is associated not only with a disdain for those who disagree with America or, more narrowly, its government, but with the adoption of policies based implicitly on the doctrine that error has no right. Since America is the standard-bearer of Truth, those who disagree with America are in error. Because they are wrong and are resisting the onward march of Truth, they have no right to hold onto their own beliefs nor to hold America to account for its actions nor to oppose America's God-given 'right' to impose its own convictions upon them. The combination of the assumption of America's innocence with the dogma that error has no right appears to lie behind many actions of the United States' government that would otherwise be incomprehensible in a body that claims to believe in freedom and democracy, and to promote them worldwide; for example, the internment of 'enemy combatants' at Guantánamo Bay without trial and in contravention of the Geneva Conventions (Barber, 2004, p. 18).

This outlook reflects what is often referred to as 'American exceptionalism'. This is the conviction that the United States is not like other nations and does not have to behave like them or observe the same laws or conventions as others do, that it is a law unto itself. In part this idea is based on 'the presumption of American virtue' (Barber, 2004, p. 69), but it also draws heavily on the idea that the American nation is the latter-day chosen people. This exceptionalism is well illustrated by Phyllis Schlafly, one of the leaders of the Christian right, who in 1998 said that:

> Global treaties and conferences are a direct threat to every American citizen ... The Senate should reject all UN treaties out of hand. Every single one would reduce our rights, freedom and sovereignty. That goes for treaties on the child, women, an international court, the sea, trade, biodiversity, global warming, and heritage sites ...
>
> Our Declaration of Independence and Constitution are the fountainhead of the freedom and prosperity Americans enjoy. We Americans have a constitutional republic so unique, so precious, so successful that it would be total folly to put our necks in a yoke with any other nation. St Paul warns us (II Corinthians 6.14): 'Be ye not unequally yoked together with unbelievers, for what fellowship hath righteousness with unrighteousness? And what communion hath light with darkness?' The principles of life, liberty and property must not be joined with the principles of

genocide, totalitarianism, socialism and religious persecution. We cannot trust agreements or treaties with infidels.

(Quoted by Lieven, 2004, p. 16)

Schlafly's words are a good example of reverence for the Constitution, which here is treated on an equal footing with the New Testament, as well as of the beliefs that error has no right and that America is virtuous. Another influential American belief about good and evil is 'Manichaeism' (Barber, 2004, p. 57). According to Manichaeism, the cosmos is divided between good and evil principles which are engaged in an eternal combat with each other. As we have seen, America tends to view the world as divided into good and evil, to identify itself with the good and to present itself as the standard-bearer of good in the battle against evil. America's exceptionalism and conviction of its own virtue when combined with this Manichaean view of the world result in a justification for the United States to dominate the world. As Benjamin Barber explains:

> Exceptionalism, then, offers special rationalizations both for the isola-tionism that has tried to separate America from the world's tumult and for the interventionism that has pushed America out into its very heart. An idealist American foreign policy goes abroad in the name of the virtues of home and remakes the world in its own image not because it wants to dominate the world but because (it believes) it can only be safe in a world that is like America. Isolationism – an older, more conser-vative tradition – is no less wedded to the idea of American virtue, hop-ing, however, that a doctrine of independence secured by geography and arms (two oceans in the nineteenth century, an antiballistic shield in the twenty-first) will afford virtue the protection it requires. It may seem odd that a policy of reclusive separation from the world and a policy of aggressive intervention in the world are born of a single idea. Yet making the world safe for democracy has translated all too easily into making America safe from the world and making America hege-monic in the world. In both cases, America prefers not to get 'entan-gled' or to know the world too well.
>
> (Barber, 2004, pp. 78–9)

Alongside the belief in America's original sinlessness and a Manichaean outlook on the world, Americans often have an attitude towards human freedom which is Pelagian, even though this is inconsistent with Manichaeism. Pelagius was the contemporary of St Augustine against whose ideas Augustine developed the doctrine of original sin. Pelagius taught that human beings were capable of obeying the commands of

God through their own efforts. He rejected Augustine's teaching that the sin of Adam had resulted in the corruption of the human ability to obey God. In other words, he said that the human will was still free and able to choose to do good. It did not require any special intervention of divine grace to make it possible for humans to succeed in their battle against temptation (Kelly, 1977, pp. 357–61). This point of view was condemned by the Church as heretical. The American version of this heresy is the conviction that the world is perfectible and, furthermore, that the United States has been chosen by God to perfect it in the image of America, the innocent and the good. John Gray denies that America is Manichaean because it does not believe in an eternal conflict between good and evil but, rather, that the battle against evil can be won:

> For all its unremitting piety, American culture is far removed from the traditional Christian doctrine that human life is marked indelibly by sin. Rather, American culture is animated by what has always been seen as a heresy – Pelagius' doctrine that human nature is not inherently flawed but instead essentially good … When George W. Bush uses the language of evil to describe the international system, he is doing more than transpose theological categories into the always morally ambivalent realm of diplomacy and war, where they plainly do not belong. He is endorsing the heretical belief that evil can be banished from the world by an act of human will. Bush is inordinately fond of talking up the threat posed to the world by evil forces; but he evinces not the slightest doubt that, given the right kind of moral resoluteness, they can be wholly destroyed. Far from being grounded in the Christian insight that humans have an ingrained predilection for evil, he is driven by a militant version of the Pelagian faith that human will can eradicate the evils we find in the world. In contrast, Europeans see the choices that have to be made in international relations as being unavoidably among evils. Long experience has taught them that in dangerous conflicts the best intentions can have the most horrific results. No doubt they continue to hope for a better world, but they are always conscious of the danger of too much enthusiasm. Even where Europeans seem entirely secular in outlook, history has made most of them instinctive Augustinians.
>
> (Gray, 2004, pp. 126–7)

President Bush's speech at the service at the National Cathedral after 9/11 confirms Gray's assessment. Perversely, Bush declared war on terrorism during an address given from the pulpit of a cathedral dedicated to the worship of 'the prince of peace'. He said to the nation: 'Our responsibility to history is already clear: to answer these attacks and rid the world of evil' (quoted by Wallis, 2005, p. 143). Note that he did not say 'this evil' but 'evil' unqualified. In the war on terror, American Pelagianism, its belief that the world is perfectible, is especially dangerous for the peace of the world, because it encourages American leaders to think that they can win such a war and destroy evil, which is utterly absurd, and, consequently, that they do not need to engage in self-reflection nor to attend to the reasons why the United States is hated by so many people throughout the world (Sardar & Wyn Davies, 2002; cf. LeVine, 2005), nor to consider changing their own behaviour. The dangerous combination of a Manichaean belief that the world is divided between the forces of good and evil with the Pelagian belief that good can actually defeat evil appears to be the core conviction that underlies the administration's prosecution of the 'war on terror'.

AMERICA AS THE MESSIAH OR SAVIOUR OF THE WORLD

The belief that America is the chosen people is very often associated with the conviction that it has a special God-given destiny to develop and spread its own divinely inspired social order, the 'perfect' embodiment of freedom and democracy, to all humanity. America is, thus, a saviour or messiah called to redeem the other peoples of the world from their imperfect or malfunctioning forms of government. Indeed, through doing so, the American people will demonstrate the superiority of their civilisation. As Robert Kagan explains:

> For those early generations of Americans ... The proof of the transcendent importance of the American experiment would be found not only in the continual perfection of American institutions at home but also in the spread of American influence in the world. Americans have always been internationalists, therefore, but their internationalism has always been a by-product of their nationalism. When Americans sought legitimacy for their actions abroad, they sought it not from supernational institutions but from their own principles. That is why it is was always so easy for so many Americans to believe, as so many still believe, today, that by advancing their own interests they advance the interests of humanity. As Benjamin Franklin put it, America's 'cause is the cause of all mankind.' (Kagan, 2003, pp. 87–8)

Hence, Ziauddin Sardar and Merryl Wyn Davies conclude that 'America is a messianic dream of global dimensions; its mission is to be the human future' (Sardar & Wyn Davies, 2004, p. 105; cf. Gray, 2003, p. 99), a view supported by the following words of President Woodrow Wilson, who held that in World War I, America 'had the infinite privilege of fulfilling her destiny and saving the world' (Lieven, 2004, pp. 32–3).

President George W. Bush belongs very much to this tradition. On the first anniversary of the September 11 attacks he said the following whilst speaking on Ellis Island, for many years the point of debarkation for immigrants in New York:

> Be confident. Our country is strong. And our cause is even larger than our country. Ours is the cause of human dignity; freedom guided by conscience and guarded by peace. *This ideal of America is the hope of all mankind.* That hope drew millions to this harbor. That hope still lights our way. And the light shines in the darkness. And the darkness will not overcome it.
>
> (Cited by Dark, 2005, p. 14, italics added)

The reference is to John 1:15, which says: 'The light shines in the darkness and the darkness has not understood [or overcome] it.' The light in this case is the incarnate Word of God, according to Christian theology the second person of the Trinity who became man as Jesus Christ. President Bush was, therefore, equating the United States of America with God the Son, the Saviour of the world; even though in Christian theology Christ is 'the hope of all mankind' and not America.

There is no possibility that this identification of America with Christ was accidental. President Bush's well-tuned publicity machine no doubt produced the speech with the deliberate intention of evoking the biblical echoes. In addition, Bush is a born-again Christian who is steeped in the Bible and must have known what these allusions meant. Furthermore, he has made a similar comparison on other occasions, notably in a State of the Union address, during which he said: 'there's power, wonder-working power, in the goodness and idealism and faith of the American people' (Dark, 2005, p. 15). This is a reference to a hymn which proclaims 'the wonder-working power' of 'the blood of the Lamb who was slain' – in other words, of Christ, who is, according to Christian theology, 'the Lamb of God who takes away the sin of the world'. Once again President Bush was suggesting that America is Christ and that its role is to save the world. This is not just a conflation of America with Christ; this is blasphemy!

President Bush is, as far as one can tell, a genuinely devout and convinced Christian who would not deliberately utter blasphemy. Hence, it is likely that the conflation in his speeches of Christian teaching about Christ with the idea of the United States as a messianic figure is a result of the combination of bad theology with a good rhetorical image, rather than a deliberate intention to commit blasphemy. Nevertheless, it is shocking that such words could be uttered by a President of the United States without the Christian leaders of that country rising up with one accord to correct his error. That only a very few Christian leaders challenged his language (Wallis, 2005, p. 149; Dark, 2005, p. 15), shows the extent to which the distorted theology of the myth of America has taken over the religious imagination of this most church-going of nations.

AMERICA AS THE KINGDOM OF GOD OR HEAVENLY JERUSALEM

Very closely connected with the conception that America is going to save the world is the view that it is going to usher in the kingdom of God, or that it is already a manifestation of the kingdom of God which is destined to spread out until it covers the whole world. This vision was one of the inspirations of the Revolution:

> Timothy Dwight (1752–1817), president of Yale University, spoke enthusiastically of the revolution ushering in 'Immanuel's Land,' and of America becoming 'the principal seat of that new, that peculiar Kingdom which shall be given to the saints of the Most High.' In 1775, the Connecticut preacher Ebenezer Baldwin insisted that the calamities of the war could only hasten God's plans for the New World. Jesus would establish his glorious Kingdom in America: liberty, religion, and learning had been driven out of Europe and had moved westward, across the Atlantic. The present crisis was preparing the way for the Last Days of the present corrupt order. (Armstrong, 2001, p. 83)

The idea that America is the kingdom of God is also expressed by comparing it to the heavenly Jerusalem. This comparison was made as early as 1630 by John Winthrop, who became Governor of Massachusetts colony. As he sailed to America, he wrote: 'We must consider that we shall be a City upon a Hill, the eyes of all people shall be upon us' (Sardar & Wyn Davies, 2002, p. 151). The 'city upon a hill' is a typological reference to Matthew 5:14: 'You are the light of the world. A city on a hill cannot be hidden.' In using this biblical reference, Winthrop was implicitly saying that America is the heavenly Jerusalem, an implication subsequently adopted by President Ronald Reagan. In a speech Reagan explicitly mentioned Winthrop and went on to refer to America as a 'shining city on a hill', thereby conflating the two elements in this biblical verse, the city and the light. Clifford Longley explains the highly compressed typological references in this metaphor:

Jesus' words referred to in Matthew are themselves typological, for his hearers would have understood instantly that he was alluding to Mount Zion, the hill on which the city of Jerusalem was founded by King David a thousand years before. In Jewish literature Zion is synonymous with the Jewish homeland, longed for by exiles from a distance. In Christian literature it becomes spiritualised into the capital city of the Kingdom of Heaven, in other words no place actually on earth (except, in the eyes of a John Winthrop or a Ronald Reagan, when it is identified with America).

(Longley, 2002, p. 110)

The consequence of regarding the United States as the kingdom of God is, as Hans Morgenthau once said, that: 'History has a discernible direction and destination. Uniquely among all the nations of the world, the United States comprehends and manifests history's purpose' (quoted by Chomsky, 2005, p. 187). In 1845 this purpose had already been described by John L. Sullivan as America's 'manifest destiny' when he asserted that Americans had:

the right of our manifest destiny to overspread and to possess the whole of the continent which providence has given us for the development of the great experiment of liberty and federalitive [sic] development of self government entrusted to us. It is the right such as that of the tree to the space of air and the earth suitable for the full expansion of its principle and destiny of growth.

(Sardar & Wyn Davies, 2002, p. 178)

This vision is alarmingly reminiscent of the latter-day Nazi expansionist notion of lebensraum ('room to live'), and shows how the chosen people ideology of the early settlers developed into a general assumption of American superiority over other nations, along with the right of the United States to dominate not only North America but also the southern continent. This idea was enshrined in the Monroe Doctrine, named after President Monroe who in 1823 asserted: 'that the American continents … are henceforth not to be considered as subjects for future colonization by any European powers' (quoted by Brogan, 1999, p. 255). This doctrine was subsequently developed into an expectation that the United States would dominate South America without interference from the imperial powers of Europe.

In the last century, the American sense of entitlement to control its own hemisphere grew into a belief that it had the right to intervene anywhere in the globe where it considered its 'interests' to be at risk. Certainly, the last half of the twentieth century was marked by American interventions in the affairs of other nations to a remarkable degree.

These have included actual military action (ranging in extent from the Vietnam War down to the invasion of Grenada) as well as financial or military support for 'friendly' governments, often of an oppressive nature completely at odds with the United States' much-vaunted role of promoting democracy (e.g. Saddam Hussein's Iraq and Saudi Arabia). They have also frequently taken a covert form, including the training and financing of revolutionaries or terrorists (e.g. the Islamic rebels in Afghanistan from which al-Qaeda originated, and the Contras in Nicaragua). William Blum lists almost 70 United States interventions in other nations since 1945, many lasting several years (Blum, 2005; cf. Sardar & Wyn Davies, 2002, pp. 92–101).

This history may be regarded negatively as the unwarranted interference of the United States in the internal affairs of independent countries in pursuit of its own political and economic interests, or it may be given a wholly different interpretation and seen as the costly and disinterested sacrifice made by the American people as they fulfilled their messianic role. Naturally, President Bush adopts the latter alternative. In remarks made to Coast Guard graduates in 2003, he said:

> Because America loves peace, America will always work and sacrifice for the expansion of freedom. The advance of freedom is more than an interest we pursue. It is a calling we follow ... As a people driven to civil rights, we are driven to define the human rights of others. We are the nation that liberated continents and concentration camps. We are the nation of the Marshall Plan, the Berlin Airlift and the Peace Corps. We are the nation that ended the oppression of Afghan women, and we are the nation that closed the torture chambers of Iraq ... America seeks to expand, not the borders of our country, but the realm of liberty.
> (Quoted by Barber, 2004, pp. 59–60)

Even so, since 9/11 the Bush administration has taken the assumption of America's right to rule to its logical conclusion and outlined a programme for world dominance:

> In the vision set out in its National Security Strategy of 2002 ... embodying the so-called Bush Doctrine, American sovereignty was to remain absolute and unqualified. The sovereignty of other countries, however, was to be heavily qualified by America, and no other country was to be allowed a sphere of influence, even in its own neighbourhood. In this conception, 'balance of power' – a phrase used repeatedly in the NSS – was a form of Orwellian doublespeak. The clear intention actually was to be so strong that other countries had no choice but to rally to the side of the United

States, concentrating all real power and freedom in the hands of
America. (Lieven, 2004, p. 13)

This policy statement was linked to a declaration that the United States
has the right to take pre-emptive action to ensure its security not just
against imminent attack, but against anybody who presents a potential
threat (Micklethwait & Wooldridge, 2004, p. 213). From the administration's perspective, the world is so dangerous that America can only be
defended by attacking its enemies before they have gathered sufficient
power to be able to harm America; and America has no option but to act
in this manner because there is no other course by which its innocence
and superior way of life may be defended from those who envy it so
much that they are intent on destroying it.

Even though it does not use explicitly religious language or make
reference to the Judaeo-Christian tradition, the assertion in the Bush
doctrine that the United States has the right to world hegemony is a
direct development out of the belief that the United States is God's
instrument for the salvation of humanity, whether America is seen as the
chosen people, the saviour of the world or the kingdom of God.
However, the religious roots of this vision are seriously compromised by
the fact that the ideal being promoted by the United States is not
Christianity but neo-liberal capitalism which has nothing to do with the
Bible. Indeed, in many respects this economic creed, which promotes
unregulated trade and market forces and is not concerned with equality
or social justice or the environment, is contrary to biblical teaching,
especially the condemnations of usury (e.g. Lev. 25:37) and of traders
who seek to become rich at the expense of the poor in the Hebrew
Scriptures (e.g. Amos 2:6–7). The Jewish and Christian idea of the
eschatological Day of the Lord ushering in the kingdom of God has been
transformed by neo-conservative theorists into the idea of a this-worldly
secular kingdom of God initiated and ruled over by the United States of
America, which functions as the messiah for the new order, and into
whose sphere of control all nations will ultimately be drawn as into the
kingdom of God.

This is the implicit conviction which lies behind Francis Fukuyama's
book, *The End of History and the Last Man* (1992), which, soon after the
fall of the Soviet Union, asserted that history had now reached its conclusion in the democratic capitalism promoted by the United States. This
view, as the title clearly suggests, is a secularised expression of the
Judaeo-Christian expectation of a final consummation of history in the
kingdom of God. In Fukuyama's case, the end of history may not be
ushered in by the apocalypse, but his theory is nevertheless based on an
eschatological perspective. John Gray argues that the belief in human

progress advanced by Western science, including economics, is inherited from the Christian belief that history is moving in a linear direction
towards a final consummation. For Gray, 'The global free market is the
offspring of the marriage of Positivist economics with the American
sense of universal mission' (Gray, 2003, p. 48), and both Marxism and
neo-liberal economics are examples of a post-Christian faith in human
development – they both 'aim to save mankind' (Gray, 2003, p. 104). If
Gray is correct, we may conclude that the United States is now in thrall
to a political ideology which is the perverse offspring of the conjunction
of two Christian heresies, the myth of America and neo-liberal economics, both of which assert that they provide the universally applicable
model of society which the whole world should follow. The consequence
of these beliefs is the American drive for universal hegemony. As Sardar
and Wyn Davies point out:

> Fukuyama, and other proponents of American empire, give the
> rest of the world three stark choices: disappear, without a trace and
> complete with your culture and values, from history and the
> future; be subdued by American military technology and become
> a colony of the benevolent empire; or embrace American
> consumerism in its totality and be reduced to a cipher.
> (Sardar & Wyn Davies, 2004, p. 218)

They conclude: 'imperialism is a logical product of the very idea that
American culture is universal' (Sardar & Wyn Davies, 2004, p. 223).

AMERICA AS MARDUK

Worryingly, the American messiah does not come to inaugurate the
kingdom of God on clouds of glory; rather, he seeks to do so by the force
of his military, political and economic dominance over the globe. This is
where the myth of redemptive violence is particularly influential upon
the myth of America. We have observed that the myth of redemptive
violence, the idea that evil can only be overcome by force, is implicit
within both the Exodus–Conquest paradigm and its eschatological
equivalent, the Day of the Lord. Both these themes have been incorporated by the myth of America, which is consequently a form of the
myth of redemptive violence. To this extent, Walter Wink is correct
when he claims that the myth of redemptive violence is 'the real religion of America' (Wink, 1992, p. 13). Members of the present administration repeatedly claim that they are fighting for freedom, democracy
and Christian values. However, even a cursory look at the rhetoric they
use shows clearly that the war on terror is based on the myth of
redemptive violence rather than the teaching of Jesus, especially when it

is recalled that in the Gospels he rejects the path of violence.

Terrorists represent Tiamat, the chaos which threatens to destroy the order of American society and American dominance of the world. America is clearly Marduk, the god who will give security to other nations provided they accept his leadership unquestioningly (see Chapter 4). The war is advanced through violence, which the American government claims is able to defeat terrorism or, at least, to make America and the world as a whole a safer place. It seems clear that the American government believes in the myth of redemptive violence, and is also convinced that the violence used by the United States against terrorism and in defence of democratic capitalism is justified by its special relationship to God and its divinely sanctioned role in the world. These 'justifications' are very neatly combined with America's sense of sinlessness, its Manichaean belief in the eternal battle of good and evil, and its conception of the frontier as the boundary between good and evil to produce an image of America as a modern warrior god or Marduk who maintains order over evil and chaos in the world through force of arms. An astonishing statement by President George W. Bush perhaps proves the point: 'the war in Iraq is really about peace' (quoted by Godsi, 2004, p. 234).

The vision of America as a bulwark against chaos is much older than the Bush administration. In 1898 Senator Albert J. Beveridge made a speech which neatly combined the idea of America as Marduk with that of America as the chosen people, along with an unquestioned sense of racial superiority:

> God has ... made us the master organizers of the world to estab-
> lish system where chaos reigns. He has given us the spirit of
> progress to overwhelm the forces of reaction throughout the earth.
> He has made us adept in government that we may administer
> government among savage and senile peoples. Were it not for such
> a force as this, the world would relapse into barbarism and night.
> And of all our race He has marked the American people as His
> chosen nation to finally lead in the regeneration of the world. This
> is the divine mission of America, and it holds for us all the profit,
> all the glory, all the happiness possible to man.
>
> (Quoted by Nelson-Pallmeyer, 2005b, p. 9)

However, contrary not only to this panegyric, but also to the American myth and the illusion of American sinlessness, the United States is a country founded on some of the worst crimes against humanity – genocide of Native Americans and enslavement of Africans – and it has suffered an extremely destructive civil war and continues to be riven by internal conflicts and extremes of inequality. The serpent is well established in 'Paradise' and has already persuaded numerous of its residents to eat of the tree of the knowledge of good and evil. Since both the negative side of its history and the current divisions in the nation exist, the American people and its government can only maintain a belief in their nation's virtue and identification with God's chosen people by scapegoating or ridiculing those who question or oppose American policies. Of course, not all Americans live in such denial, but those who do can only maintain their illusions through denial and scapegoating.

The history of the United States has been marked by the selection of a long series of scapegoats onto whom its inhabitants have projected the responsibility for the existence of evil, in general, and specific deficiencies in the American commonwealth, in particular. Thus, as we have already noted, the original settlers scapegoated the Native Americans, Roman Catholics and the French, and the revolutionaries scapegoated the British. Scapegoats have included both internal and external enemies. Amongst internal enemies, the Blacks have been prime candidates for the White majority, especially, though by no means exclusively, in the South. The mutual scapegoating of the North and South led to the Civil War, which, rationally, should have destroyed the idea of American innocence forever. The North and the South have continued to act as scapegoats for each other, as do liberals and conservatives at the present time.

For most of the latter part of the twentieth century the Soviet Union was the chief external scapegoat, President Reagan's 'Evil Empire'. The existence of this enemy, which was in competition with the United States for world dominance, proved a very useful means of promoting the internal cohesion of the USA. However, after the collapse of the USSR, America lost its primary scapegoat and was at risk of having to face and acknowledge its own negative behaviour. Contrary to Girard, if scapegoating is to work as a means of overcoming internal conflict, it is necessary either to have a quick succession of scapegoats or to keep the scapegoat alive in order to maintain the projection of evil. *America needs a perpetual scapegoat if it is to avoid both dealing with its internal divisions and recognising the evil, oppressive and unjust actions of which it has been and is still often guilty.* Hence, the USA replaced the USSR first with the 'axis of evil' or 'rogue states' and then, more generally, with terrorists or Islamists, recently relabelled as 'Islamo-fascists'.

The 9/11 attack provided the leaders of America with a very convenient new scapegoat, and the prosecution of the war on terror, which is now being referred to as 'the long war' by members of the current administration, provides a continuing justification for the adoption of interventionist policies abroad, the building up of America's already excessive military might and the restriction of liberty and civil rights in the 'homeland', ironically in the name of protecting the freedom which America is supposed to embody. The American reaction to 9/11 is, we may conclude, a multi-faceted defence of its own exalted view of itself based on the myth of America, which, in essence, identifies the United States with the promise of divine redemption in the Jewish and Christian religions. In the light of this analysis, the war on terror is most definitely a war of religion, even if the 'religion' being 'defended' by the war is a secularised Christian heresy whose adherents do not consciously acknowledge that the God they worship is not the God of Israel or the Holy Trinity of the Christian faith, but *America itself*.

Chapter 11

VICTIMS AND VIOLENCE IN THE WAR ON TERROR

AMERICANS AS VICTIMS

Having established that the United States functions in many respects like a religion and that the war on terror is in essence a war of religion, I want now to locate this 'war' in the cycle of abuse and show how it grows out of and reinforces the psychology of the victim. I will begin with the American people. Since the Exodus–Conquest paradigm and the Day of the Lord are both forms of the reversal of victimhood, and both of these themes have been incorporated by the myth of America, we would expect the psychology of those who believe in this myth to participate in the psychology of the victim. This may seem a surprising thing to say in view of the United States' massive military and political superiority in the contemporary world. However, the origins of many of those who emigrated to America over the last four centuries suggest otherwise.

Many of the early immigrants to the colonies were Puritans who had left Northern European Protestant countries. Some had done so because they were being persecuted or faced the threat of persecution from state authorities who regarded their beliefs as too extreme or subversive. Others had simply rejected the values and religious practices of the societies from which they originated and were seeking to establish a pure religious community in the New World. This is why they were so prone to see America as a new Promised Land and themselves as a new chosen people. As we have seen, this complex of beliefs is a product of the cycle of abuse and it appears reasonable to assume that experiences of persecution or marginalisation in their countries of birth had initiated these immigrants into the cycle of abuse before they left or, at least, primed them to behave in oppressive ways to the 'uncivilised' and 'heathen' peoples who already inhabited North America. Not surprisingly, they proceeded to behave abusively towards the Native Americans, whom, following the example of the ancient Israelites, they regarded as barely human and without human rights.

Thus, *the cycle of abuse, in the form of a past experience of victimisation*

*followed by divinely guided salvation resulting in a reversal of victimhood,
became central to American identity*; all the more so since many later
immigrants were also the victims of persecution, oppression, poverty or
starvation in their countries of birth. A sense of victimisation was also
experienced by the Confederate States which suffered humiliation and
bitterness as a result of their defeat in the Civil War. Of course, Native
Americans and Black slaves were also victims but, ironically, victims of
the myth of America and of the immigrants who believed in it. The
importance of these experiences of victimisation for American identity
is emphasised by Lieven, who draws particular attention to those of Irish
immigrants:

> One other factor should be kept in mind, because it fits into wider
> American patterns of defeat and the embittered nationalism which
> they help produce: the Irish sense of historical defeat, oppression
> and dispossession by England. For if the Confederate South's
> historical experience of defeat is unique among America's geo-
> graphical sections: Irish, Poles and other American immigrants all
> brought with them ethnic memories of defeat much worse than
> those of the south. Even southern Italians had been conquered,
> despised and exploited by northern Italians, while Jews and
> Armenians had suffered infinitely more horrendously. Indeed, in
> many cases it was precisely the attacks and oppression they had
> suffered which brought the immigrants to America's shores.
> All these groups have had a tendency to compensate for past
> humiliations and sufferings by glorifying national power – and, of
> course, in many cases (the Irish included), by seeking to harness
> that power to the achievements of their own national aims. Many
> have sought to overcome their exclusion from the centers of
> national power, wealth and prestige by becoming '200 percent'
> American nationalists. (Lieven, 2004, p. 135)

The exaltation of the American nation and its divinely appointed destiny
in the American myth looks like an over-compensation for the prior victimisation and humiliation of a large proportion of both the original and
the subsequent immigrants, as well as for the defeat of the South. These
victims all found in the myth of America (and 'the American dream' of
individual success) a route to the reversal of victimhood and, even when
individually they did not succeed materially, they could gain a sense of
importance and value through identifying with the nation chosen by
God.

9/11 AND THE MYTH OF AMERICA

We have seen that the Hebrew Bible contains three attitudes to the relationship between God and the current social order: God as the one who supports and legitimates the social hierarchy; God as the one who fights on behalf of the oppressed and underprivileged against unjust rulers and enemies; and, God as the one who himself judges, persecutes or abandons his faithful followers. Chosen people theology is associated positively with the first two and negatively with the last. In the case of the ancient Hebrews, God began as the God of the slaves in Egypt and then became the God of the conquerors and rulers of Canaan. This progression from being victims to being oppressors is typical of religious or ethnic groups who identify themselves with God's chosen people and who subsequently gain political power, and is an expression of the reversal of victimhood which takes place in the cycle of abuse.

Before the 9/11 attacks the American nation was in a position similar to that of the Hebrew kingdoms before the fall of Israel to the Assyrians and Judah to the Babylonians: the majority of its citizens or their ancestors had experienced a reversal of victimhood and, as a result, had gained a position of prosperity and apparent security in the 'Promised Land'. They had come to take this state of affairs for granted, indeed, to see it as an entitlement because of their virtue and commitment to freedom and democracy. One reason why the 9/11 attacks were so shocking, I suggest, is that they destroyed the American people's illusion of invulnerability secured both by divine favour and protection and by their vast military arsenal, and raised the question, at least at a subliminal level, of whether God's favour still rested with them. In chosen people theology prosperity and success are signs of God's approval, whereas adversity and defeat are signs of God's disfavour or judgement. al-Qaeda's success put the religious nature of the American project in doubt because it raised the possibility that God had abandoned his favour and protection, or that the myth of America is false, or even that God's favour lay elsewhere – with Muslims! Even for secular Americans, the attack shattered their sense of security and put a question mark against their conviction of their country's destiny and innocence. In other words, it challenged their 'faith in America', which is, I contend, an implicitly religious attitude even when it is not acknowledged as such.

Some commentators suggested that the Islamist aggression against the American people was a response to their own aggressive actions in the Muslim world. If this were true, it would undermine the whole myth of America and its central role in compensating for its citizens' past

victimisation or current economic or social marginalisation. Thus, the
9/11 attacks presented the American people with a choice: either to
examine themselves to see if they were in any way at fault, or to reassert
their conviction of chosenness and innocence against the doubt that the
attacks inevitably raised. Despite the existence of large numbers of
Americans who were ready to undertake this self-examination, unfortunately, the government and, it appears, the majority of the people
chose to do the latter. Hence, the question, 'Why do they hate us?' was
answered by concentrating on the faults of the attackers. This approach
was accompanied by a collective resistance to self-examination and an
hostility to anyone who dared to suggest that there might be some
justification for the attackers' motives, even if not their methods. Instead
of listening to the complaints of Osama bin Laden and his followers,
they were belittled by many pundits as fanatical and evil terrorists who
were acting out of an irrational hatred that could not be justified. In
this way, America could be portrayed as the innocent victim of
unprovoked aggression, and its status as the injured party could be co-
opted as a justification for retaliation. Stanley Hauerwas describes
President Bush as needing to do something to return the situation to
normal:

> So he said, 'We are at war.' Magic words necessary to reclaim the
> everyday. War is such a normalizing discourse. Americans know
> war. This is our Pearl Harbor. Life can return to normal. We are
> frightened, and ironically war makes us feel safe. The way to go in
> the face of September 11, 2001, is to find someone to kill.
> Americans are, moreover, good at killing. We often fail to acknowl-
> edge how accomplished we are in the art of killing. Indeed we, the
> American people, have become masters of killing. We now con-
> duct war in such a manner that only the enemy has to die. You can
> tell that our expertise in war-making embarrasses some in our mil-
> itary, but what can they do? They are but following orders.
>
> So the silence created by destruction was soon shattered by the
> need for revenge – a revenge all the more unforgiving because we
> cannot forgive those who flew the planes for making us acknowl-
> edge our vulnerability. The flag that flew in mourning was soon
> transformed into a pride-filled thing; the bloodstained flag of
> victims transformed into the flag of the indomitable American
> spirit. We will prevail no matter how many people we must kill to
> rid ourselves of the knowledge that Americans died as victims.
> Americans do not get to die as victims. They have to be heroes. So
> the stock trader who happened to work on the seventy-second
> floor becomes as heroic as the police and firefighters who were

doing their job. No one who died on September 11, 2001, gets to die a meaningless death. That is why their deaths must be avenged.

(Hauerwas, 2004, pp. 202–3)

The myth of redemptive violence was highly useful in this project. The al-Qaeda terrorists were represented in terms that are clearly reminiscent of the chaos monster, Tiamat: they were threatening civilisation and needed to be destroyed by force of arms. However, the attacks also put in question the United States' belief in the effectiveness of violence to protect the nation. The superpower armed with more weapons than the combined arsenals of the next ten or more nations discovered that its weaponry did not protect it from attack. The destruction of the Twin Towers exposed a profound sense of vulnerability in the American people which had been disguised by the apparent impregnability of their territory. From a psychological perspective, their weapons stockpile looks like a massive over-compensation for a fundamental sense of insecurity in the world and an unacknowledged fear that they may not be so special as they claim. This insecurity was brought to consciousness by the 9/11 attacks, and the administration immediately sought to push it back into the unconscious by producing a military response to the terrorist assault.

Hence, President Bush declared a 'war on terror' and attempted to destroy the threat posed by the newly revived chaos monster, Islamic terrorism, through force of arms: in particular, by invading Afghanistan and, subsequently, Iraq, even though the latter had no known connection with al-Qaeda and no involvement with 9/11. These invasions and the Bush doctrine, especially the assertion of a right to military pre-emption, look like the attempts of members of the present administration to reassure themselves of their own superiority and that their reliance on God and violence (or, unconsciously, on the God of Violence) will continue to protect them. In terms of the psychology of abuse, the Bush doctrine is equivalent to the threat of violence of an abusive man who is using it to protect his own unacknowledged vulnerability, internal conflicts, threatened manhood and sense of inferiority.

This is all the more dangerous in the context of the black-and-white thinking of President Bush himself, and his own psychological history. By his own admission, George Bush is an alcoholic who has ceased to drink. However, he has managed to do so not through joining Alcoholics Anonymous or following a 12-step programme, but through religious conversion to born-again Christianity. Whilst in no way wishing to challenge the genuineness of either his conversion or his sobriety, the troubling aspect of this means of escaping from the clutches of a drink problem is that it involves no growth in self-awareness. Even though one who uses religious conviction to fight drink acknowledges his fault in drinking, he calls on the power of God to defeat the power of drink and avoids an examination of the psychological motivations that lead him to drink – a stage that is normally necessary for successful long-term recovery. Without such deep-seated emotional change, these underlying problems can only be kept in control by the strength of an overwhelming religious conviction. This procedure necessitates considerable use of repression and eventuates in the unavoidable accompaniment of repression – namely, scapegoating.

Of course, one can only speculate about the internal psychological dynamics of George Bush but, on the basis of the evidence of his oft-proclaimed division of the world into good and evil, and his identification of America with goodness, it seems a reasonable conclusion to suggest that he is using his position as President of the United States of America as one means of fighting his own inner demons, through attacking them in projection in the external world, especially in the form of al-Qaeda and other 'terrorists'. If this speculation is correct, he will have no motivation whatsoever to seek to understand the actions of, nor to enter into negotiation with, his enemies. To do so would undermine his carefully erected psychological defences and mean that he would have to face those aspects of himself that he has pushed out of his consciousness. This psychological hobbling of the leader of the so-called 'free world' is alarmingly hazardous for the peace of humankind.

ZIONISM AND THE PALESTINIANS AS VICTIMS

The importance of chosen people theology and of the psychology of the victim in the myth of America helps to explain the commitment of American governments to the State of Israel. Israel's strategic importance has a great deal to do with it as well. However, only the religious and ideological motivations of this policy make America's extraordinary partiality for Israel explicable. There is a very great similarity between the national mythologies of Israel and the United States which arises from the fact that they both originate in chosen people theology and the Exodus–Conquest paradigm. Indeed, the original inspiration for Zionism and the justification for the foundation of a Jewish homeland in Palestine lies in this paradigm. Without it, no one would have thought it appropriate for millions of Jews to migrate to the Holy Land.

Historically, Zionism represents a major shift in Jewish consciousness. Since the Jewish revolt against Roman rule in 66 CE, which resulted in the destruction of the temple in Jerusalem in 70 CE, the Jewish people had been unable to take part in the administration of a territory of their own. They had been dispersed across the globe and subject to social marginalisation, prejudice and sporadic persecution. In addition, for centuries they had functioned as scapegoats for Christians in Europe and, in the nineteenth century, were often the victims of pogroms in Poland and Russia. Then some of the Jews of Eastern Europe decided to change the ancient policy of non-violent passivity in the face of these attacks and Zionism was born. Its essence is the idea that the Jews will never be safe until they possess their own independent state in which to defend themselves. The obvious candidate for this honour was Israel, the land which, according to the Bible, God had given to the Jews.

Zionism did not find immediate widespread support within the Orthodox Jewish community. Many traditional rabbis condemned it as a heresy because they believed that the promise made by God, that the Jews would return to Israel, could only be fulfilled by the intervention of God in his own good time. To seek to bring it about by human agency was, therefore, an impious attempt to pre-empt the will of God (Armstrong, 2001, pp. 149–50; Rose, 2005, pp. 31–2). Even so, sufficient Jews, whether secular or religious, were convinced by the arguments for a Jewish state to begin migrating to Israel, and the Zionist movement was formally established at its first congress in Basel in 1897.

Until the nineteenth century, Jews were a very small minority in Palestine living at peace with their Muslim and Christian neighbours under the rule of the Muslim Ottoman Empire. At the beginning of the nineteenth century the Jewish population of Palestine was only about 25,000. By 1914 it had grown to 60,000 or 10 per cent of the total popu-lation, and by 1936 it had swelled to 400,000 or 30 per cent of the population (McTernan, 2003, pp. 108–10). The Zionists regarded Pales-tine as 'a land without people for a people without land'. However, this perception was false and its use as a slogan was a piece of disingenuous propaganda. Palestine was already highly populated and suffering from a shortage of good land (Rose, 2005, p. 89).

It should be noted that Zionism was a movement of Ashkenazi or European Jews who had been subjected to persecution in Europe for centuries. It was not supported by Sephardic Jews who lived in Muslim lands and who were well integrated with the local populations and had not suffered such persecution. Indeed, Sephardic Jews were in many cases subjected to discrimination and exploitation by the Ashkenazi in Israel (Giladi, 1990). Furthermore, from very early in the Zionist move-ment some at least of the immigrants behaved in a way that shows clear evidence of a reversal of victimhood, including denigration and exploitation of the Arabs, a tendency that appears to have continued to the present day. In 1891 the Russian Jewish writer Ahad Ha'am wrote about the behaviour of immigrants:

> Really, we could have learnt from our past and present history that we should not arouse the anger of the natives of the country through atrocious deeds. We must also be wary in our dealings with the foreign people among whose ranks we have started to renew our life. We must forge relations with them based on love, honour, correctness and justice. But what are our brethren doing in the Land of Israel? The complete opposite. They were slaves in exile and suddenly they have found themselves living a life of absolute freedom, the barbarous freedom that could only exist in the Ottoman Empire. This sudden change gave birth in them to the tendency to tyranny which is what happens usually with the slave who becomes king. They deal with the Arabs with an unjustified excess of harshness and hatred. They beat them and despise them for no reason whatsoever, and are, moreover, proud of it.
>
> (Quoted by Giladi, 1990, p. 40)

Apart from the behaviour of Ashkenazi Zionist immigrants, the deliberate incursion of Jews into Palestinian territory with the intention of establishing a majority Jewish state was inevitably experienced by the existing inhabitants as an act of aggression which they resented and resisted. Consequently, there was often tension between the Arab residents and the Jewish immigrants, leading to occasional incidents of inter-communal violence for which both sides blamed the other (La Guardia, 2001/2003; Lochery, 2004). The British government made matters worse by making incompatible promises to each side of self-government, including the Balfour declaration of 1917 supporting the establishment of a home for the Jewish people in Palestine (McTernan, 2003, p. 109–10).

Then came the Holocaust. It is impossible to overstate the psychic trauma inflicted on the Jewish people by the systematic attempt of the Nazis to exterminate them. Six million Jews died. European Jewry was either annihilated or dispersed. The unspeakable suffering of the Jews reinforced the argument of Zionists for a Jewish nation, and the guilt and compassion of the Christian nations of Europe and America, who had either colluded with anti-Semitism or failed to prevent the Holocaust, assured their agreement. Thus, a Jewish state came into being in Israel in 1948.

From the Palestinian and broader Arab perspective the foundation of Israel was completely unacceptable. As far as they were concerned, Israel had no right to exist. They were the victims of a deliberate intrusion into their ancestral lands and they saw no reason why they should accept a Jewish state. Furthermore, they had been betrayed by the British who had promised them a majority Arab state. Their outlook may be understood by a comparison with a proposal by Theodor Herzl at the Second Zionist Conference in Basel (1898) for the Jewish homeland to be located not in Palestine but in Uganda (Armstrong, 2001, p. 151). This idea appears completely preposterous. The Jews had no connection with Uganda and no possible justification for going there, apart from the fact that they needed to go somewhere if they were to found an independent nation. For the Jews to have dispossessed native Ugandans would, from our contemporary perspective, seem completely indefensible. In the late nineteenth century it was possible for this suggestion to be put forward because imperialist attitudes were common. The proposal to set up a Jewish state in Palestine was made at a time when the European nations took an arrogant attitude towards the rest of the world and thought that they had the right to dispose of the lands of 'lesser' peoples. It rests on the implicit assumption that the rights of the Arab inhabitants of Palestine are of no account. The comparison with Uganda indicates how much Zionism owes to nineteenth-century imperial attitudes.

The only significant difference between the settlement of Jews in Israel and in Uganda, and the only possible rationalisation for the former, is the chosen people theology of the Hebrew Scriptures. In 1898 the delegates to the Second Zionist Conference resoundingly rejected the Ugandan proposal. Although, ironically, many of the early Zionists were atheists, the power of their identification as Jews with Israel was stronger than their religion, which provided the only possible justification for the establishment of a homeland in Israel rather than anywhere else. Why then should the Arabs of Palestine have been expected to accept 'the right of Israel to exist'? As Anatol Lieven says:

> It cannot be emphasized too strongly that if the Palestinian Arabs in the 1930s and 1940s had agreed that a large part of Palestine – where they were still a large majority and had until recently been an overwhelming one – should be given up to form the state of Israel, they would have been acting in a way which, as far as I am aware, would have had no precedent in all of human history ...
>
> In other words, however one might condemn the Palestinians and Arabs for their long delay in coming to terms with the reality of Israel, to blame them for initially resisting that reality is to engage in moral and historical idiocy. While condemning the Arabs as demons, it suggests they should have acted as saints.
>
> (Lieven, 2004, p. 194)

Even the first Prime Minister of Israel, David Ben-Gurion, recognised very clearly why the Arabs refused to accept the existence of Israel. He is reported to have said in private:

> Why should the Arabs make peace? If I were an Arab leader I would never make terms with Israel. That is natural: we have taken their country. Sure, God promised it to us, but what does that matter to them? Our God is not theirs. We came from Israel, it's true, but two thousand years ago, and what is that to them? There has been anti-Semitism, the Nazis, Hitler, Auschwitz, but was that their fault? They only see one thing: we have come here and stolen their country. Why should they accept that?
>
> (Quoted by Lieven, 2004, p. 196)

In effect, the Palestinians were being asked to pay the price for both the Holocaust and the persecution of European Jews by Christians over many centuries, and the Europeans were being let off scot-free. It would have been much more just for a Jewish homeland to have been established in, say, a province of Germany or in Poland or Russia than in Palestine. It is not surprising, therefore, that when Israel became independent in 1948, the surrounding Arab nations invaded with the intention of destroying the new-born Jewish nation. What was surprising was that they lost the war and, as a consequence, 750,000 Arabs were displaced from the territory of Israel. Subsequently, the Arabs suffered a further major defeat in 1967 in the Six Day War, through which Israel gained control of the Golan Heights, the West Bank, Gaza and the Sinai peninsula, thenceforth known collectively as the Occupied Territories. Although Sinai was later returned to Egypt under the terms of a peace treaty, the other territories remain under Israeli control.

Any discussion of the rights and wrongs of the situation in Israel–Palestine is bound to be controversial (e.g. compare Ateek, 1989, with Lochery, 2004), but it is undeniable that Palestinians have suffered considerably under the Israeli occupation. Their movements have been highly controlled and their access to work and financial and material resources has been severely limited. They have been subjected to military raids on civilian areas to assassinate 'terrorists' or as collective punishment, and to the bulldozing of houses. In particular, many have been dispossessed of their land and sources of water by the establishment of Israeli settlements and the building of the 'defensive' wall separating Israel from Palestinian areas, the land for which has been confiscated *without compensation*. The vast majority of these actions are in breach of the Geneva Conventions or United Nations' resolutions.

From the Palestinians' perspective, they are clearly the victims, as Dr

Abdul Aziz Rantisi, one of the founders of the Hamas movement, told Mark Juergensmeyer:

> 'It is important for you to understand,' he said, 'that we are the victims in this struggle, not the cause of it.' ... 'You think we are the aggressors,' Rantisi said. 'That is the number one misunderstanding. We are not: we are the victims.'
>
> (Juergensmeyer, 2003, p. 75)

Their sense of injustice and frustration has been so severe that the Palestinian people have now taken part in two *intifadas* or uprisings, the last of which is still ongoing. Some amongst them, including the Palestinian Liberation Front, Hamas, Hizbullah (a Lebanon-based group) and Palestine Islamic Jihad, have at various times during the occupation gone so far as to organise armed resistance in the form of terrorist attacks and the last three of these organisations have been instrumental in suicide bombings (McTernan, 2003, pp. 118–20). Furthermore, in the summer of 2006 Hizbullah actually fought a war with Israel, which failed to drive it from its base in southern Lebanon.

JEWS AND ISRAELIS AS VICTIMS

From the Israelis' perspective, the situation looks very different; they are not the aggressors but the victims. The rabbi and Jungian analyst David Freeman, in commenting on the oppressive practices of the State of Israel, attributes the behaviour of Israel to the identification of the Jews with their historical victimhood. He relates how in 1988, early in the first *intifada*, Israeli soldiers were filmed maltreating a Palestinian boy, who had been throwing stones at them, and asks: 'What was going on in the minds of the soldiers as they performed these brutal actions?' He answers:

> Deep down inside themselves, probably without being at all aware of it, these soldiers were screaming in terror at that boy, 'Why are you persecuting us?' In some hidden place within themselves they were experiencing the boy as being the victimiser and themselves as the victims. (Freeman, 1991, p. 2)

Freeman points out how the repressed rage of the victim

> will even permit him to victimise others in the very manner in which it was once done to him. At this very deep level inside himself, the victim and the victimiser are one. There is no distinction except in their individual subjective perception of themselves. The murderous anger of the victim, the chthonic [underground, i.e. deep-seated] rage inside him provides so powerful an unconscious

defence mechanism that he is virtually omnipotent.

(Freeman, 1991, p. 3)

I was present at Freeman's original talk, which inspired in me a long process of gestation out of which this book has ultimately been born. Although he has no direct responsibility for its contents, I want to acknowledge my debt to him. In terms of the cycle of abuse, his description is an acute observation of the process through which the victim's rage gives rise to a reversal of victimhood.

In speaking about this reversal in relation to the State of Israel, Freeman broke a taboo on criticising Israel. Since then this taboo has, if anything, become stronger; it is certainly very widespread in the United States and, to a lesser extent, in Britain. Anyone who raises any questions about Israeli actions is likely to be assaulted with accusations of anti-Semitism, if he is a Gentile, or of being a self-hating Jew, if he is Jewish. However, if I am to locate the Israeli–Palestinian conflict within the cycle of abuse which the Jews have suffered and, hence, to be in a position to place it within the wider cycle of abuse which has given rise to the war on terror, it is necessary for me, even though I am a Christian priest, to risk commenting on the influence of the psychology of the victim on the behaviour of Israel.

The birth of Zionism was a momentous event in the history of Jewish victimisation. From the perspective of the cycle of abuse, it represents the moment when an abused woman decides that she will no longer tolerate being beaten up by her partner and begins to look for a means of escape to a place of safety, or attempts to fight back. Similarly, in the case of violent child abuse, it is quite common for an abused boy, when he has grown big enough, to retaliate physically against his father. The first organised use of violence in Jewish self-defence began with the establishment of units for this purpose in response to the Russian pogroms of 1904 and 1905 (Rose, 2005, p. 122). Subsequently, violence was used by Zionists both in self-defence by Jews who had settled in Palestine and offensively by Jewish terrorist groups, such as Irgun and the Stern Gang.

The Holocaust made the status of the Jewish people as archetypal victims unassailable. It also raised considerable theological problems for them. How could God have abandoned his people to the extermination camps? How could they maintain their faith in the face of their sense of betrayal by rage at God? The conquests of Israel and Judah and the Exile in Babylon were an extreme trauma for the sixth-century BCE Israelites which resulted in a radical transformation of their faith, including positioning the moral defence at the heart of their relationship to God. But what could the Jews have possibly done that would justify the Holocaust as a just punishment? How does anyone ever recover from the kind of nihilistic experience here described by Elie Wiesel?

> Never shall I forget that night, the first night in the camp, which has turned my life into one long night, seven times cursed and seven times sealed. Never shall I forget the little faces of the children, whose bodies I saw turned into wreaths of smoke beneath a silent blue sky.
> Never shall I forget those flames which consumed my faith forever.
> Never shall I forget that nocturnal silence which deprived me, for all eternity, of the desire to live. Never shall I forget those moments which murdered my God and my soul and turned my dreams to dust. Never shall I forget these things, even if I am condemned to live as long as God Himself. Never.
>
> (Wiesel, 1960, p. 32; quoted by Blumenthal, 1993, p. 249)

It was inevitable that such experiences should have produced some very dark responses indeed, including Wiesel's own play *The Trial of God*:

> The play, which is a modern re-reading of the Book of Job, is set in the midst of the Chmielnitsky (Cossack) massacres of the Jews in 1348–1349. God is put on trial by an innkeeper named Berish, three wandering Jews, and a defending attorney called Sam, abbreviated from Samael, one of the names of Satan.

Berish insists on holding God responsible:

> If He insists upon going on with His methods, let Him – but I won't say Amen. Let him crush me, I won't say Kaddish. Let him kill me, let Him kill us all, I shall shout and shout that it's His fault ... To you, judges, I'll shout, 'Tell Him what He should not have done; tell Him to stop the bloodshed now ...' I live as a Jew, and it is as a Jew that I die – and it is as a Jew that, with my last breath, I shall shout my protest to God! And because the end is near, I shall shout louder! Because the end is near, I'll tell him he is more guilty than ever!
>
> (Wiesel, 1979, pp. 133, 156; quoted and introduced by Blumenthal, 1993, p. 250)

Coming so soon after the Holocaust, the establishment of the State of Israel seemed to many religious Jews like a response from the God who had so inexplicably abandoned them to their hideous fate. According to Jacqueline Rose, it carried a religious significance even for secular Jews: 'With the birth of Israel, nationalism became the new messianism – the aura of the sacred, with all its glory and tribulations passed to the state' (Rose, 2005, p. 8). Even though she acknowledges that not all its citizens believe in its divine mandate, she argues that 'messianism colors Zionism, including secular Zionism, at every turn' (Rose, 2006, p. 28). In other words, the State of Israel has come to have a 'religious' significance for Israelis, indeed for Jews worldwide, whether they are religious or secular, practising or not; one which is closely bound up with the restoration of Jewish identity and confidence after the trauma of the Holocaust.

The founding of Israel came as balm upon the Jews' collective shame for being the victims of the Nazis – all the more so after the victory of 1967 restored the borders of Israel almost to those laid down in the Bible, with the exception of land to the east of the River Jordan. Shame is not an aspect of the Holocaust which is normally mentioned; yet it is an emotion often experienced by victims of abuse or oppression. It is a sign of their sense of worthlessness because of their inability to help themselves. After such a massacre as the Holocaust it would be natural for its survivors to feel shame, alongside rage and grief or the numbness of trauma. Significantly, some of those Jews who had emigrated to Israel before the Second World War, and who had not been victims of the German persecution, reacted with shame towards those who had survived it and who afterwards came to settle in Israel (Rose, 2005, p. xiv). The explanation for this response, it seems to me, is that the Holocaust cut at the roots of their attempts through Zionism to escape from weakness and victimisation. Their co-religionists' failure to save themselves, followed by their arrival in the Holy Land, pushed the Zionists back into a fellowship with victims that they thought they had escaped.

Shame is a symptom of narcissistic injury and is one of the major motivations of abusive behaviour in individuals. A man may compensate for a sense of shame by 'proving his worth' through dominating someone else, be it a woman or other men. A group may do the same and dominate another group. It is, therefore, essential to take account of the role of shame in both the attitudes of Jews worldwide to Israel and the behaviour of Israelis towards the Palestinians. To those Jews for whom the existence and success of Israel function either as a compensation for a profound collective sense of shame or as a reassurance of God's existence and faithfulness, any suggestion that the nation is less than perfect, let alone itself guilty of injustice or even crimes against humanity, will be rejected out of hand because it is too threatening to their psychological defence mechanisms. This observation is supported by the following comment of David Blumenthal, although he refers to guilt rather than shame. The two often exist side by side. However, it seems to be easier to acknowledge guilt than shame, and so one should always be on the look-out for the presence of shame when people are speaking about guilt. In the context, shame seems a more appropriate word than guilt:

> The most unspoken of the horrors of contemporary Jewish existence is the possibility of the destruction of the State of Israel. This event would evoke unbearable guilt in contemporary Jewry and would provoke an unparalleled loss of faith in God among Jews. For this reason, defense of the State of Israel, not defense of Jewish religion, is the litmus test of loyalty for Jews everywhere. (Blumenthal, 1993, p. 242, note 11)

In this psychological and spiritual context, how is it possible for contemporary Israelis to be self-critical? This is where the blindness of the Exodus–Conquest paradigm to the humanity and rights of the original inhabitants of the Promised Land is so very unhelpful. It seems that in Israel today the original pattern of invasion and conquest is being lived out again, but in an admittedly much milder form. This time there has been no original invasion by the Jews, but instead organised immigration followed by territorial expansion as the result of conquest in wars initiated by external invaders; and there has been no systematic genocide, but instead systematic harassment and oppression of an occupied people and expropriation of their resources, especially water and land for Jewish settlements.

Sometimes the Israeli government is compared to the Apartheid regime in South Africa. This is too extreme a comparison, although there are similarities – in particular, the exclusivist nature of the Israeli State, which gives all Jews 'the right of return' to Israel whilst denying resident non-Jews and Palestinians civil rights equivalent to those enjoyed by Jews. For example, a recent law has denied Palestinians who marry Israelis the right to reside in Israel, although that right is enjoyed by any other nationalities marrying Israelis who are entitled to Israeli citizenship (Rose, 2005, p. 51). Such policies look remarkably like racism, although whether or not that term is regarded as appropriate will depend on whether Jewish and Israeli identities are regarded as based on religion, ethnicity, race or nationality. Sometimes, Israel is defended against the charge of racism on the grounds that Jews of different skin colours are allowed to settle there, but the racism built into the foundations of the State of Israel is that of discriminating between Jews and non-Jews, and privileging Jews over non-Jews *simply because they are Jews*. This is an inescapable concomitant of the idea of a Jewish homeland. Jewish Israelis may make excuses for why they think that that discrimination is necessary, but it is still discrimination on the grounds of race, religion or ethnicity of the kind that is outlawed by anti-discrimination laws in the United States and most other Western countries.

Perhaps a more helpful comparison than with South Africa under Apartheid is that with the plantations undertaken by Ulster Protestants in the seventeenth century, during which Irish Catholics had their land confiscated and given to Protestants to farm. Israeli settlements seem to me to be a modern equivalent. Certainly, the similarity is recognised by the Protestant and Catholic communities of Belfast. For a number of years I was a frequent visitor to Belfast, and observed that amongst the Irish and Republican paramilitary flags on the Catholic Falls Road were numerous Palestinian ones, and on the Protestant Shankill Road Israeli flags flew alongside those of Britain, Ulster and Protestant para-militaries. This is not surprising because what Israel and Ulster and, indeed, Apartheid South Africa and the United States of America have in common is chosen people theology, according to which the previous inhabitants of the land that the 'chosen people' has occupied are 'Canaanites' whom it is legitimate for them to dominate or, indeed, exterminate. As we have seen, this theology is a product of the cycle of abuse and acts as a compensation for victimhood and the shame that accompanies it and, consequently, often results in a reversal of victim-hood. The modern history of Israel demonstrates how pernicious it can be.

Even so, the remarkable thing is that a large number of Israelis are self-critical and do not support the mistreatment of Palestinians, including a number of 'refusenik' soldiers who have refused to serve in the Occupied Territories (Rose, 2005). It is important to remember that Israel is actually a very diverse society and that major differences and tensions exist between different groups of Israelis, including between religious and secular and Ashkenazi and Sephardic Jews (Giladi, 1990; Rosenthal, 2005). Nevertheless, when they are on the receiving end of suicide attacks, it is understandably difficult for Jewish Israelis to see the Palestinians as human beings to whom they are joined by common bonds of compassion and morality, and to whose legitimate grievances they should attend. If David Freeman is right that Israelis are likely to interpret Palestinian resistance as yet one more example of the hostility of a subhuman oppressor and to retreat into the psychology of the victim, even if the 'oppressor' is only a boy throwing stones, how much more is this the case if he is a suicide bomber who creates carnage in their cities and wishes, like the Arab nations who have attacked them in the past, to drive them into the sea?

MUSLIMS AS VICTIMS

The grievances of the Palestinians are one of the major inspirations for the campaign of terror launched by al-Qaeda. However, in the view of Osama bin Laden and his associates, it is not just Palestinians, but the worldwide Muslim community, or *umma*, which is the victim of American and Israeli aggression. On 23 February 1998, bin Laden and other leaders of Jihad groups in Egypt, Pakistan and Bangladesh issued a *Declaration of the World Islamic Front for Jihad against the Jews and Crusaders*, laying down the reasons why all Muslims should engage in *jihad*, religious war, against America, Israel and their allies. These included the presence of American troops on Arabian soil, the 1990 invasion and subsequent blockade of Iraq, the occupation of Jerusalem by the State of Israel and its 'killing of Muslims in it', and America's general subjugation of the Arab states of the Middle East (Lewis, 2004, pp. xxii–xxv). In addition, in a statement issued soon after the 9/11 attacks, bin Laden listed numerous places in which 'the brutal enemy' was 'continuing the war he has started against Islam and Muslims many decades ago', including Palestine, Iraq, Bosnia–Herzegovina, Kashmir, Chechnya, Afghanistan, the Central Asian republics, East Timor, Somalia, and the Philippines; and added: 'We say that all the Muslims that the international Crusader–Zionist machine is annihilating have not committed any crime other than to say God is our Allah' (quoted by Scheuer, 2005, pp. 129–30).

For bin Laden, America is the aggressor against the Islamic community in numerous conflicts and, from a Muslim point of view, all the examples he gives are more than plausible. There is a widespread perception in the Muslim world that America is not concerned with the interests of Muslim people or freedom or democracy, but with its own interests regardless of the negative effects of its policies on the inhabitants of the countries it dominates. This is a perception that is not limited to terrorist organisations or religious fundamentalists or the poor and uneducated; it is found amongst sophisticated and Westernised Muslims as well, and is by no means only a recent phenomenon. According to Noam Chomsky:

> Forty-four years ago President Eisenhower and his staff discussed what he called the 'campaign of hatred against us' in the Arab world, 'not by the governments but by the people.' The basic reason, the NSC [National Security Council] advised, is the recognition that the US supports corrupt and brutal governments and is 'opposing political and economic progress,' in order 'to protect its interests in Near East oil.' The *Wall Street Journal* and

others found much the same when they investigated attitudes of
wealthy westernized Muslims after 9/11, feelings now exacerbated
by US policies with regard to Israel–Palestine and Iraq.

(Chomsky, 2005, p. 195)

In his statements bin Laden refers again and again to Crusaders and
Zionists. Although to Western ears these terms may sound like extreme
rhetoric and the latter reeks of anti-Semitism, they should be taken very
seriously. For most Europeans the Crusades belong to a distant history
which seems to have nothing to do with us today, but for Muslims they
are very much part of a living communal memory which holds in mind
centuries of conflict with the Christian world. From this perspective,
Israel appears typologically to be a re-establishment of the Crusader
kingdom of Jerusalem of the early Middle Ages. In 1095 Pope Urban II
launched the First Crusade with the avowed intention of wresting the
sacred places in the Holy Land from Muslim control. For a while the
Crusaders succeeded in setting up a Christian kingdom in Palestine. The
behaviour of the Crusaders was brutal in the extreme and they left a
lasting impression of Christian aggression and barbarity in the Muslim
mind, for whom they represent the archetypal Christian invader. For
Muslim terrorists, whom Mary Habeck refers to as 'Jihadists', the
Crusades were a deliberate attempt to destroy Islam which is being
repeated by their contemporary successors America, Israel and their
allies (Habeck, 2006, pp. 88–92, 165).

The success of the Crusaders produced a problem for Muslim theology. This was because Islam had inherited much from the chosen
people theology of Judaism and Christianity. Although the religion of
Islam began amongst the Arabs and they have a proprietorial attitude
towards it (Manji, 2005, pp. 151–76), the Qur'an does not designate any
particular race as a chosen people. Instead, like the Church in the
Christian religion, the *umma* or Muslim nation itself functions as a kind
of chosen people. Believers as a whole are regarded as having a special
relationship with Allah which is different from that of unbelievers.
Those who practise Islam, which entails submission to Allah's will, can
be assured of Allah's favour and, ultimately, a place in Paradise. Also like
Christianity, Islam contains a theory of supersession. Jews and
Christians were both previously entrusted with his revelation by Allah
but they proved unfaithful and corrupted that revelation. However,
now Allah has revealed his final, complete, infallible and uncorrupted
revelation to Muhammad which is gathered in the Qur'an. This is the
one truth and it applies to all peoples; none can contradict it or improve
upon it (Habeck, 2006, pp. 47–8). Islam is a universal religion to which
all peoples may belong, and its aim or, better, divine destiny is to become

the religion of the whole of humanity.

As in Jewish and Christian chosen people theology, Allah's favour is indicated by worldly success. Within a century of 622 CE, the official date of the foundation of Islam as a religion, the armies of Islam had created a vast empire. In the subsequent centuries the religion and culture of Islam grew to be the most powerful and most advanced in the world, with the exception only of China (Lewis, 2002, p. 6). Naturally, Muslims were aware of their political and cultural superiority and attributed it to the superiority of their religion. Hence, the establishment of a Crusader kingdom had very significant theological implications because it put in question the favour and protection of Allah. However, in the early thirteenth century these hated infidels were evicted and Palestine returned to Muslim control. Muslim dominance survived for some centuries after the Crusades. Nevertheless, in 1798 Napoleon landed in Egypt and began two centuries of European domination over North Africa and the Middle East which reached its apotheosis 120 years later: 'Every single Muslim majority country in the world, with the exception of parts of the Arabian Peninsula, was conquered by Europe by the end of World War I' (LeVine, p. 45).

It is undeniable that the last 200 years have been a time of defeat and humiliation for Muslims worldwide which has left a scar on their communal psyche. As Mark LeVine asks: 'What must it feel like to be a Muslim? To know that there is practically no part of the *ummah*, or Muslim nation, that hasn't been ruled by others, and today still remains, to a greater or lesser degree, under the influence, or even occupation, of the West and its allies?' (LeVine, 2005, p. 45). The shame of their collective humiliation has been a major factor in the development of terrorist groups such as al-Qaeda. As Professor Bernard Lewis explains:

> The revolutionary wave of Islam has several components. One of them is a sense of humiliation: the feeling of a community of people accustomed to regard themselves as the sole custodians of God's truth, commanded by Him to bring it to the infidels, who suddenly find themselves dominated and exploited by those same infidels and, even when no longer dominated, still profoundly affected in ways that change their lives, moving them from the true Islamic to other paths. To humiliation was added frustration as the various remedies, most of them imported from the West, were tried and one after another failed. (Lewis, 2004, pp. 18–19)

He adds that they gained 'a new confidence and sense of power' as a result of the oil crisis in 1973. Even so, this has not removed the subordination of Islam to the political powers of the West nor stemmed its cultural invasion of the Muslim lands. Consequently, some Muslims have come to the point of deciding to fight back.

According to mainstream Muslim thinking, there is a religious obligation on every able-bodied Muslim male to defend the *umma* from attack. The term used to describe this is *jihad* or struggle. In traditional teaching there are two types of *jihad*, the lesser *jihad* which is the military struggle and the greater *jihad* which is the spiritual struggle involved in fulfilling the obligations of the Islamic religion as a whole (Nasr, 1990, pp. 29–33; Esposito, 2002, pp. 26–70; Habeck, 2006, pp. 20–21). The lesser *jihad*:

> is to engage in an external struggle (fighting) with others to bring the Truth (Islam) to mankind. Jihad was never supposed to be about the forcible conversion of others to Islam – although under some rulers it became that – but rather about opening the doors to countries so that the oppressed peoples within could hear the Truth and, once Muslims conquered the land, have the privilege of being ruled by the just laws of Islam. (Habeck, 2006, p. 20)

It needs to be stressed that the understanding of *jihad* is contested within contemporary Islam. Although the four mainstream schools of Islamic jurisprudence 'all assume that Muslims have a duty to spread the dominion of Islam, through military offensives, until it rules the world … the vast majority of Muslims today have renounced this concept of a continuous offensive against the unbelievers.' In addition, the Qur'an contains different emphases and also affirms that 'there is no compulsion in religion' (Habbeck, 2006, pp. 116–17).

Furthermore, the methods of fighting *jihad* and who may be attacked during it are also matters of dispute between Jihadists and others. The Qur'an forbids both suicide and the killing of non-combatant women, children and slaves. Traditional Muslim jurisprudence has supported the restriction on killing such non-combatants, but male members of oppositional groups have universally been considered to be legitimate targets, even if they are non-combatants, with the exception of monks, old men (only in some interpretations), the insane and the disabled. Obviously, suicide bombings involve both suicide and indiscriminate killing and thus flout these restrictions. Even so, Jihadists appeal to certain Quranic texts to argue for the legitimacy of suicide bombings (Habeck, 2006, pp. 124–8). They also define the deaths of suicide bombers as martyrdom and, since the Qur'an promises a place in Paradise to those who die as martyrs whilst engaged in *jihad*, thereby claim the reward of Paradise for those who make this self-sacrifice. Like many others, this Jihadist assertion is contested by more moderate

Muslims. Without describing their arguments in detail, it is clear that, like the Bible, the Qur'an is open to numerous different interpretations and that Muslims, like Christians, are capable of using their sacred scripture selectively to support their actions. Jihadist groups have used it to provide religious 'justification' for heinous acts of violence, even though most Muslims disagree with their rationales.

Suicide bombing was first introduced into the Israeli–Palestinian conflict in 1994 after the murder of 29 Muslim worshippers at the Mosque of the Patriarch in Hebron by a Jewish settler named Baruch Goldstein. It represents an extreme reaction to victimisation and humiliation, and gives the powerless a sense of power. As John Esposito explains in answer to the question, 'What drives young Muslims to become suicide bombers?':

> Growing up oppressed and under siege, facing a future with little hope, high unemployment, and endemic poverty can produce anger and desire for revenge against those responsible. Just as among inner city youth in the United States, some of those young people lose all hope. For others, religion holds the answer. For a small minority, suicide bombing seems a proud and powerful response.
>
> Completely out of their league militarily when compared to Israel, these militant Palestinians boast of their new and most effective weapon. As student posters at universities in the West Bank and Gaza declare: 'Israel has nuclear bombs, we have human bombs.' Suicide is forbidden in Islam, but militant Palestinians do not see this as suicide. It is self-sacrifice for the cause of Palestinian freedom. The simplicity of the act enables an otherwise impotent individual to step into a crowd unnoticed and then with a simple detonation to wreak horrendous carnage. The use of concepts like jihad and martyrdom to justify suicide bombing provides a powerful incentive: the prospect of being a glorified hero in this life and enjoying Paradise in the next. (Esposito, 2002, pp. 99–100)

Thus, suicide bombing is a product of the cycle of abuse. Paradoxically, the self-annihilation of the suicide bomber becomes a form of self-assertion that both resists the oppressor and guarantees a posthumous reversal of victimhood for the bomber in the prospect of glory in Paradise, from which the oppressor will be excluded.

However, the vast majority of Muslims are not and never will be suicide bombers, and a large number are not even anti-Western. It should be emphasised that the attitude of Muslims to the West, even in the traditional Muslim heartlands in the Middle East and North Africa, is by no means uniform. Many Muslims are attracted to the freedoms and the consumer culture of the West (LeVine, 2005; Manji, 2005). Indeed, that is one of the major reasons why the Jihadists feel the need to attack America and its allies – they have too much influence and are 'corrupting' the purity of Islam. They view mainstream Muslims as not 'truly Muslim' and thus believe it is legitimate to direct their violent *jihad* against such 'apostates' (Esposito, 2002, pp. 71–117). Thus, from their perspective, the majority of those who claim to be Muslims are legitimate targets in their *jihad* and, especially, Muslim governments who co-operate with the United States and its allies.

Bin Laden appealed to the tradition of *jihad* when he declared war on America; and, from an Islamic perspective, *if America is accurately categorised as an aggressor*, he is correct to do so. The appropriateness of his response depends on how American actions are categorised and, once again, this is a matter of great dispute between Jihadists and mainstream Muslims. Bin Laden has adopted the most extreme view of *jihad* in Islam, which also has many more pacific interpretations. For him, this war is a religious obligation which is not only about territory but also about the truth of the Muslim religion. In the last analysis, it is about the conflict between the absolute claims of Islam and a Western culture which he views not only as hostile to those claims, but also as actively involved in seeking to destroy the Muslim religion by undermining Muslim culture and dominating Muslim lands politically and economically (Habeck, 2006). The attitude of bin Laden and other Jihadists is well summed up in some words of Hasan al-Banna, the founder of the Muslim Brotherhood and one of the leading Islamist theorists of the twentieth century:

> Our task in general is to stand against the flood of modernist civilization overflowing from the swamp of materialistic and sinful desires. This flood has swept the Muslim nation away from the Prophet's leadership and Qur'anic guidance and deprived the world of its guiding light. Western secularism moved into a Muslim world already estranged from its Qur'anic roots, and delayed its advancement for centuries, and will continue to do so until we drive it from our lands. Moreover, we will not stop at this point, but will pursue this evil force to its own lands, invade its Western heartland, and struggle to overcome it until all the world shouts by the name of the Prophet and the teachings of Islam spread throughout the world. Only then will Muslims achieve their fundamental goal, and there will be no more 'persecution' and all religion will be exclusively for Allah.
>
> (al-Banna, 1978, p. 30; quoted by Habeck, 2006, pp. 31–2)

This point of view is an extreme one within the wide spectrum of Muslim opinion, and it is supported only by a very small minority of Muslims. Nevertheless, the sense of victimisation by the Western world of the Muslim community appears to be widespread, and accounts for the status of bin Laden as a popular hero for many Muslims. In terms of the cycle of abuse, he represents the moment when an abused person decides to resist victimisation and to fight back against the abuser. Whatever we may think of his methods or his religious justifications for them, his resistance to America and the West symbolises the first stage in a reversal of victimhood for much of the Muslim world. As such, it is a very worrying development, especially since Jihadist ideology does not countenance anything other than a complete victory over those whom they consider to be the enemies of Islam.

Chapter 12

CONFRONTING THE HUMAN ABUSERS

A COMPETITION IN VICTIMHOOD

The tendency to identify a particular people with the chosen or elect of God is endemic in the monotheistic religions of revelation – Judaism, Christianity and Islam. The chief issue dividing them is the identity of the people whom God has chosen. A similar process of identification is found in the claims to religious authority made on behalf of their sacred scriptures, the Hebrew Bible, the New Testament and the Qur'an. Their teachings are identified with the revealed truth of God. The combination of such 'absolute truth' with the self-identification of a group as the chosen people, especially when associated with some version of the belief that error has no right, has enabled Jews, Christians and Muslims to commit the most evil atrocities in the name of God with a clear conscience. From the genocide of the Canaanites in the Hebrew Bible, through the persecutions, Crusades, wars of religion and colonialism that have marred Christian history, and the imperialist expansion of the Muslim empires, to the occupation of the West Bank by Israeli forces and the destruction of the World Trade Center, the violent consequences of the identification of monotheistic religion with the ideological interests of 'the elect of God' are apparent.

Americans, Palestinians, Jews, Israelis and Muslims all have grounds for considering themselves to be victims and all, therefore, have grounds for believing that the violence they commit is justified as self-defence. The situation in Israel–Palestine and the war on terror in general is marked by a competition in victimhood. Such mimetic rivalry makes it very difficult for the different parties to listen to each other; they are too intent on getting their own perspective and their own sense of injustice heard. Most situations of conflict are complex and in the majority of them all parties believe that they are the ones who are the victims. As the Croatian theologian Miroslav Volf points out:

> If the plot is written around the schema of 'oppressed' ('victims')

and 'oppressors' ('perpetrators'), each party will find good reasons for claiming the higher moral ground of a victim; each will perceive itself as oppressed by the other and all will see themselves as engaged in the struggle for liberation. The categories of oppression and liberation provide combat gear, not a pin-striped suit or a dinner dress; they are good for fighting, but not for negotiating or celebrating – at least not until the oppressors have been conquered and the prisoners set free. (Volf, 1996, pp. 102–3)

When the belief in victimhood is reinforced and 'justified' by appeal to religious traditions, some of which are completely intransigent, there is little possibility of reconciliation. Regrettably, in the war on terror these justifications make continual use of the chosen people theology of the Judaeo-Christian tradition or its close counterpart in the Islamic religion. Hence, the war on terror represents a modern expression of the political effects of the combination of chosen people theology with the reversal of victimhood contained in the Exodus–Conquest paradigm. The religious justification for violence provided by this theology has become an urgent issue which needs to be addressed for the peace of the world; all the more so since the United States is currently led by a conservative evangelical Christian who believes himself called by God to engage in a war against 'evil' (Wallis, 2005, pp. 140–41).

AGAINST THE MYTH OF AMERICA

As I have shown, the belief that the United States of America is a new chosen people has dominated American self-perceptions from the time of the first colonists until today, and has inspired and justified the territorial expansion of the United States within North America and its ambition for hegemony over the contemporary world. The history of the United States demonstrates only too clearly how chosen people theology combined with the Exodus–Conquest paradigm gives birth to imperialist aggression (Kiernan, 2005). It also demonstrates that the theological traditions that have been incorporated into the myth of America are not of merely academic or religious interest but are influential and determinative of modern politics and the fate of the world. As Jim Wallis, founder of the progressive evangelical group the Sojourners, argues:

> The real theological problem in America today is no longer the religious Right, but the nationalist religion of the Bush administration, one that confuses the identity of the nation with the church, and God's purposes with the mission of American empire. America's foreign policy is more than pre-emptive, it is theologi-

cally presumptuous; not only unilateral, but dangerously messianic; not just arrogant; but rather bordering on the idolatrous and blasphemous. George Bush's personal faith has prompted a profound self-confidence in his 'mission' to fight the 'axis of evil,' his 'call' to be commander and chief in the war against terrorism, and his definition of America's 'responsibility' to 'defend the hopes of all mankind.' This is a dangerous mix of bad foreign policy and bad theology. (Wallis, 2005, p. 149)

Because the American administration holds a false identification of the American people with the chosen people of God, a false belief in America's goodness and innocence, a false belief in America's special destiny and exceptional rights with regard to other nations, a false theology of evil, and a false belief in the myth of redemptive violence, it is attempting to solve the problem of terrorism through violence. Such a solution can only result in ever more destructive cycles of violence. Evil cannot be destroyed by force. Force creates cycles of violence and even 'victories' sow the seeds of future conflicts, as can be seen in the connection between the humiliation of the Germans after the First World War and the rise of Hitler to power.

If the present dangers to national security and world peace are to be averted, instead of answering violence with violence, the reasons not only why al-Qaeda launched its attack on 11 September 2001, but also why so many of the American people are resistant to self-examination and to acknowledging their own misdeeds, need to be understood. Many commentators have written analyses pointing out the grievances of nations that America has exploited or invaded or otherwise offended, especially Muslim and Arab countries in the Middle East (e.g. Sardar & Wyn Davies, 2002 & 2004; LeVine, 2005). It is clear that the United States is very far from innocent. Indeed, it has been guilty from the beginning. As Jim Wallis wrote in an article arguing that racism is 'America's Original Sin': 'The United States of America was established as a white society, founded upon the genocide of another race and then the enslavement of yet another' (Wallis, 2005, p. 308). The current administration very often replaces a commitment to its much-professed ideals of freedom and democracy with a cynical *realpolitik* that is quite prepared to support undemocratic and oppressive regimes, to undertake dubious undercover operations, to break the Geneva Conventions and flout international law, and to impose neo-liberal economic policies on unwilling nations in pursuit of its own political, strategic and economic interests (Hamm, 2005). However, it is equally clear that the present administration is not prepared to admit its own double standards and hypocrisy, and that many Americans will not do so either.

I have suggested that the idea that the ancient Hebrews were the chosen people acted as a psychological defence which compensated for the humiliation entailed in their slavery or economic and political marginalisation. It also gave them the hope that their God would come to rescue them and, in the story of the Exodus and the Conquest of Canaan, their hopes were fulfilled through a dramatic reversal of victimhood. I think it reasonable to assume, unless otherwise proven, that when chosen people theology is adopted by a group, race or nation, it is operating as a defence against the narcissistic wounds or inadequacies of the ethnic group which applies that theology to itself *whether or not those claims are justified theologically.*

This is the case even when that people is successful or, like the United States, the most powerful nation in the world. We should remember that grandiosity is the other side of an unconscious sense of inferiority and shame in a narcissistic personality. It does not exist in a group or a person that is genuinely self-confident. Hence, whenever we observe it in an individual or a people, we would be wise to seek to identify the hidden shame which is fuelling the grandiosity. The grandiosity of the United States, and especially its current administration and those theorists who promote American empire, is an obvious candidate for such an investigation. The self-regarding notion of the nation contained in the myth of America, which dismisses the rights and opinions of other countries, is a symptom of group narcissism.

Curiously, although the myth of America is based on, and finds support in, the chosen people theology of the Judaeo-Christian tradition, and many of those who believe it are overtly religious, it has a peculiar property: it can also function as a completely secular political ideology. Even those without any explicit religious faith may accept the secularised form of the myth that promotes America as the land of democracy and freedom and, thus, the embodiment of the hope of humanity. In either case, the myth functions as a compensation for narcissistic inferiority both at the national and the personal level.

AMERICA'S NARCISSISTIC RAGE

The diagnosis of narcissistic grandiosity is confirmed by the reaction of the American government to the 9/11 attacks, which displayed the symptoms of narcissistic rage. The 9/11 attacks appear to have scored a direct hit on America's hidden narcissistic wound and to have evoked an outburst of narcissistic rage. From this perspective, the war on terror is an attempt by the United States to protect its fragile sense of self and to reassure itself of its grandiose claims by reasserting its dominance; for one who does not harbour secret doubt has no need to shout so loudly or act violently to gain acknowledgement from others. In other words, America is acting like a narcissistically damaged man who behaves abusively and violently towards others in order to preserve his endangered and fragile sense of self.

This conclusion is supported by Kohut's descriptions of the characteristics of narcissistic rage (see Chapter 2), which include: 'heightened sadism, the adoption of *a policy of preventive attack*, the need for revenge, and the desire to turn a passive experience into an active one' (Kohut, 1978, p. 639, italics added); and by his observation that:

> Aggressions employed in pursuit of maturely experienced causes are not limitless. However vigorously mobilized, their aim is definite: the defeat of the enemy who blocks the way to the cherished goal. The narcissistically injured, on the other hand, cannot rest until he has blotted out a vaguely experienced offender who dared to oppose him, to disagree with him, or to outshine him.
>
> (Kohut, 1978, pp. 643–4)

In the light of Kohut's remarks, President Bush's 'war on terror' (or terrorism) is clearly an example of narcissistic rage; he adopts a policy of pre-emption and aims to annihilate the abstract noun, terror, rather than a specific concrete enemy. The language in which the war is conceived ensures that it will be limitless, even more so when it is spoken about as a war to destroy evil. Its real aim seems to be to obliterate any opposition to American hegemony or effective criticism of its political, military or economic policies. After all, anyone who dares to resist the United States which, according to the myth of America, is the epitome of righteousness in a wicked world, must themselves be evil. Error has no right and must be crushed so that America may fulfil its grandiose destiny to be the saviour of the world, and its unconscious narcissistic inferiority and sinfulness may be pushed out of sight again.

However, there is no reason why the American quest for world hegemony should be more acceptable to the rest of the peoples of the globe than was the quest for world hegemony of past expansionist empires, such as the Soviet Union and Nazi Germany – which is *not* to say that the United States is either Marxist or Fascist. This observation would be true even if American claims to be the perfect embodiment of freedom and democracy were true, which they are not. No group likes being dominated by another. Of course, if the United States really were the perfect embodiment of freedom and democracy, the problem would not arise because the nations it wished to rule or control would be given a free democratic choice about whether or not to accept its overlordship.

Let us be clear: *hegemony and democracy are incompatible; America can have one or the other but not both.* The fact that so many peoples feel that policies advanced by America or its surrogates, such as the IMF and the World Bank, have been imposed upon them, not merely without their consent but against their active opposition (Stiglitz, 2002; Callinicos, 2003), demonstrates conclusively that the United States' quest for hegemony is imperialist and anti-democratic and, hence, an immoral contradiction of its own highest ideals.

JIHADIST TERRORISM AND NARCISSISTIC RAGE

The idea of a war on terrorism is absurd because terrorism is a method of engaging in conflict, not an entity that can be attacked. To have a campaign to eliminate a specific set of terrorists is another thing altogether. However, any organised assault against terrorists begs the question of the definition of terrorism. As has often been observed, terrorism is in the eye of the beholder and the identification of one group as terrorists and another as, say, 'freedom fighters' depends on the political commitments of those doing the identifying. The chief distinguishing factor of groups that are normally described as terrorist is that they are non-state groups that are involved in violence for a political purpose. As Lee Griffith observes:

> When outside rule is inflicted on a nation or tribe or a community and 'terrorism' is defined as violence by a 'non-state entity,' then *ipso facto*, if any individual from among a colonized people picks up a gun with a political idea in his or her head, he or she is a 'terrorist.' This is sleight of hand, and it is not uncommon in the study of so-called 'terrorism.' The actions of a European power in invading and colonizing another nation is not terrorism because it is an action by a state, but any violent objections from colonized people are now grist for study as 'terrorism.' How people became 'non-state entities' is really outside the purview of this study. Whether even people wish to be a state entity (as some Native Americans did not) has no relevance. And so, we are told, groups ranging from the African National Congress (once 'terrorist,' but no longer so) to Zapatistas engage in terrorism, not due to any particular level of violence they employ, but due to their political status (or lack thereof). (Griffith, 2004, p. 16)

The naming of a group as terrorist is often, therefore, a manipulative political act which is intended to denote their cause as illegitimate before it has even been heard. Certainly, this is the way in which the American government uses the term; and often this usage is tendentious to say the least. Thus, its designation of Palestinian groups as terrorist immediately suggests that their grievances should not be attended to, and its description of certain countries as sponsors of terrorism indicates that they are pariah nations and that their opinions should be ignored. This usage is also nauseatingly hypocritical coming from the government of a country that has a long history of sponsoring terrorism, even according to the normal definition, and of seeking to destabilise governments that have resisted its policies (Blum, 2005).

In some respects a helpful way of discussing the terrorism of al-Qaeda is to use the language of war – the language that it uses itself and that is used in the term 'war on terror' – rather than that of terrorism, and to recognise with John Gray that: 'The attacks on New York and Washington were acts of war – but not war of a conventional kind. They were examples of asymmetric warfare, in which the weak seek out and exploit the vulnerabilities of the strong' (Gray, 2003, pp. 81–2). To adopt such an approach is neither to approve of nor to collude with this method of fighting a war; rather, it is to seek to hold both sides to account by the same moral and religious standards, and to avoid foreclosing the analysis of the conflict by a pre-emptive use of loaded language designed to demonise the enemies of America and to preserve the illusion of American innocence. Having said that, there is also a considerable disadvantage in using the language of war, since to do so is to collude with the claims of both sides: firstly, that the Jihadists are engaged in a war rather than a brutal campaign of terror against innocent people; and, secondly, that America is at war, rather than engaged in a campaign against certain groups of terrorists, and that the government can, therefore, ride roughshod over civil liberties and the rule of law.

But whatever language we adopt, let us apply the same standards of judgement to both sides. *The 9/11 attacks were undeniably evil and should be condemned in the strongest terms.* Lamentably, many American actions in the past have also been on the same moral level, including the promotion of Islamic terrorism in Afghanistan that eventually led to the creation of al-Qaeda. *America's condemnation of terrorism condemns itself.* Such American actions are equally evil. Even so, it must be emphasised, America's sins do not justify, even if they help us to understand, the violence of al-Qaeda.

Many explanations of the genesis of terrorism have been advanced (e.g. Juergensmeyer, 2000/2003; Griffith, 2004), and one factor that is consistently mentioned is the sense of humiliation of those who become terrorists. This need not be a result of personal experience, although it often is; it may also be connected with the marginality or oppression of the religious or ethnic group to which they belong (Juergensmeyer, 2000/2003, p. 197). For this reason the fact that bin Laden comes from an extremely wealthy family does not invalidate this analysis. There is also the possibility (or likelihood?) that familial abuse or individual failure may inspire a terrorist to compensate for personal humiliation by identifying with the cause of his insulted people. Hence, narcissistic rage is as much a feature of the Jihadist opposition to the United States of America as vice versa, especially since Jihadist ideology or theology provides the opportunity for the Islamic terrorist to compensate for humiliation by identifying his or her actions with the will of God. The grandiosity of this identification is amplified by the construal of the present conflict as a form of cosmic war between good and evil. To become a warrior in a cosmic war in defence of one's religion against an enemy who is the embodiment of evil is sufficient compensation for almost anyone's sense of shame. As Mark Juergensmeyer explains:

> These cosmic wars impart a sense of importance and destiny to men who find the modern world to be stifling, chaotic, and dangerously out of control. The imagined wars identify the enemy, the imputed source of their personal and political failures; they exonerate these would-be soldiers from any responsibility for failures by casting them as victims; they give them a sense of their own potential for power; and they arm them with moral justifications, the social support, and the military equipment to engage in battle both figuratively and literally. It is an incendiary combination, one that has led to horrendous acts. (Juergensmeyer, 2000/2003, p. 193)

There is, therefore, a considerable similarity between the psychological motivation of Jihadist terrorists and the American administration, a similarity that is extremely dangerous for the peace of the world. In both there is an identification of their policies and actions with the will of God and ultimate goodness; in both, this identification is a grandiose compensation for narcissistic wounds; in both, the enemy is the epitome of evil; in both, the myth of redemptive violence is implicit in the conviction that the enemy is irredeemable and must be destroyed rather than contained or negotiated with; in both, violence is an expression of narcissistic rage rather than part of a strategic plan to achieve a defined goal; in both, the 'war' is part of a cosmic struggle. As Juergensmeyer explains:

> Everyone has enemies in the sense of opponents, but to become objects of religious terrorism such enemies must become extraordinary: cosmic foes. When Osama bin Laden spoke of America as embodying the 'forces of evil,' he was not just identifying a

problem to which he needed to respond, but a mythic monster with which he had to battle – one that ultimately only divine power could subdue. (Juergensmeyer, 2000/2003, p. 186)

This description could equally well be applied to President Bush's attitude towards bin Laden, except that he seems to believe that American weapons can defeat the mythic monster 'terrorism'.

The absolute nature of the convictions and rhetoric of both of the two main protagonists in the war on terror is extremely disturbing. This is especially so when it is recalled that George Bush holds a very conservative, even fundamentalist, form of Christian belief that anticipates cosmic catastrophe as part of the divine plan for the redemption of the world, a belief shared by many Americans (Northcott, 2004; Griffith, 2004, pp. 178–9; Nelson-Pallmeyer, 2005a, pp. 120–26). From this apocalyptic perspective, the prospect of major world conflict is to be welcomed because it is a sign of the end and a preparation for the second coming of Christ. The return of the Jews to Israel is another sign, and one reason why Christians who hold this conviction are so supportive of the State of Israel and resistant to any suggestion that it should surrender land for peace.

To sum up, when the war on terror is viewed from the standpoint of chosen people theology in conjunction with the psychology of narcissism, it becomes evident that the violent actions of both sides are an expression of narcissistic rage designed to defend or promote a grandiose identification with a divine source of narcissistic value, and that the existence and expansionist intentions of both sides, be it America's quest for world hegemony or the Jihadist quest for a universal Muslim nation, cannot be adequately counteracted unless both this religious dimension and the narcissistic motivation are taken into account. This mixture of narcissism and non-negotiable religious belief – and in this context I take the myth of America to be such a form of religious belief – is extraordinarily difficult to engage with. Any comments that challenge the identification with the divine that protects the underlying narcissistic injury will immediately be rejected, in the same way that an abusive man rejects the attempts of his partner to point out his deficiencies. This is the problem that the rest of the world, and those Americans and Muslims who do not support the prosecution of this 'war', have to deal with.

CONFRONTING INJUSTICE IN ISRAEL–PALESTINE

A similar problem arises with regard to the State of Israel. The situation in Israel–Palestine is highly complex and its interpretation highly contested, but the actions of the Israeli government against the Palestinians often appear harsh, to say the least, and the policy of confiscating Palestinian land is clearly unjust. At the very least, the Israeli government has a case to answer about much that it has done. I have described some of the psychological reasons why Israelis, and Jews more generally, are so often hyper-sensitive to any negative comments made about Israel, including the feelings of shame associated with the Holocaust. However, these reasons do not mean that Israel should be treated differently from other nations when it offends against the basic human rights of Palestinians. The status of Jews as victims of past persecutions does not mean that the present-day behaviour of Jews in Israel is necessarily innocent. To refrain from comment is to muddle the distinction between being Jewish and being Israeli, to collude with the Israelis' mistreatment of Palestinians and, in addition, to treat Israelis as if they do not belong fully to the same moral universe as other nations; in effect, to treat them as an inferior nation who cannot be expected to adhere to the ethical standards that apply to other countries. This is a subtle and disguised but, nevertheless, real form of anti-Semitism. *The idea that Israel should be immune from criticism simply because it is a Jewish state is an inverted form of anti-Semitism.*

It is sad and ironical to observe so many Israeli spokespeople, as well as Jews living elsewhere, attacking those who criticise Israel as being anti-Semitic rather than doing something about the abuses that are being highlighted. In reacting in this way, ironically, they are themselves being anti-Semitic because they are denying their common humanity with the rest of the human race, which is exactly what the Nazis and earlier persecutors of the Jews also denied. In my opinion, one of the best defences against anti-Semitism is for Jews to be acknowledged as the same as everyone else. It is the repeated construing of them as different and 'Other' that makes prejudice, scapegoating and persecution against them possible.

Having said this, it has to be acknowledged that double standards, inconsistencies and hypocrisy abound in the world of politics, and many other nations are not held to account either. There is some justice in Israeli complaints that they are picked on in a way that other nations are not and that other states which commit extremely serious infringements of human rights are ignored. It is also important to hold the Palestinian Authority to account because its actions too often appear corrupt and they have been accused of intimidating their own people and sponsoring terrorism (Manji, 2005, pp. 109–28). As in the case of Jews, the status of Palestinians as victims does not make them either innocent or immune from criticism, and the activities of suicide bombers must certainly be condemned.

In both the short term and the long run, peace between Israelis and Palestinians can only be found through the development of mutual recognition of each other as human beings and the acknowledgement by both sides of the interests of the other. I doubt if it is possible for any solution to be found that would accommodate the various views of what would be a just settlement, let alone one that would at the same time give security to both communities. I do not know whether the best option is a two-state solution or a one-state one in which both parties have equal rights, the latter of which has been suggested by some radical Jews (e.g. Ellis, 2002). Somehow something resembling justice for both communities has to be put together, if peace is to have a chance and Israel–Palestine is not to be condemned, in imitation of Ireland, to another 300 years of inter-communal conflict. What I do know is that the search for peace will only succeed if it is directed at dissolving the cycle of abuse which presently determines the destinies of both Israelis and Palestinians, and gives rise to seemingly endless cycles of violence.

RESPONDING TO THE WAR ON TERROR

So what is to be done about the war on terror? Fortunately, America is not a monolithic entity. Indeed, one of the reasons why it so often resorts to scapegoating is the need to control its inner tensions by projecting the blame for them outwards onto an exterior enemy. True friends of America who, like me, are distressed by her betrayal of her own best ideals, which we share, and wish to recall her to her better self, should remember how many Americans do not sign up to the full-blown myth of America and are ashamed by their government's betrayal of America's tradition of democracy and human rights. Despite what I have said, numerous Americans are personally secure enough not to need the grandiosity of an identification with the chosen people to compensate for unconscious shame or guilt. One can only hope that they will eventually have enough influence to make a difference politically.

In the meantime, the rest of us must take responsibility for our own contributions to the current situation. In what I have written I have been extremely critical of the United States as a country and, in particular, of its current government. The danger in doing so is that one ends up *scapegoating America* for sins and failings of which one's own nation is also guilty. As a Briton, I am in no position to cast stones. It is tempting to deny personal responsibility for the British government's largely uncritical military alliance with America and to blame it all on Prime Minister Tony Blair. However, I have to acknowledge that my membership of this country inevitably compromises me not just in relation to the war in Iraq, but primarily because I benefit from the exceedingly unequal and often unjust relations between this country and the poorer parts of the world. I too am guilty.

Nevertheless, it is necessary to challenge the policies of the current American administration and British government, and one way in which I have attempted to do this is to use my psychological and theological knowledge to debunk the religious rationalisations that are used to support the myth of America and the war on terror. Part of my motivation for writing this book has been to make a small stand against these gross distortions of the Judaeo-Christian tradition, and my hope is that the reader will by now be convinced that the myth of America is a very dangerous self-delusion which the American people must abandon. *There are absolutely no biblical grounds or religious justification whatsoever for the identification of the American people with the chosen people, Israel, Eden, Paradise, the messiah, the saviour of the world, the kingdom of God or the heavenly Jerusalem.* The myth of America is, at best, either a Christian heresy or a secularised form of national ideology and, at worst, a form of idolatry or blasphemy. The rest of the peoples of the world cannot afford to let this myth continue to be propagated, nor tolerate the abuse inflicted on the international community and the resources of the planet in the name of this myth.

In the war on terror there are several parties who may be regarded as engaging in terror, including the United States, Israel, Palestinians and Islamic terrorists. Each of them needs to be held to account for their actions but, as in the case of an abusive man, the one to begin with is the one who has the most power and who, consequently, has the most potential and responsibility to change the situation for the better. Lee Griffith has succinctly summarised what the United States government needs to recognise about terrorism and the effects of its own attempt to fight terrorism:

> The greatest concession to terrorism is mimesis, and it is also the most frequent concession. Insurgents and counterinsurgents, spies and counterspies, terrorists and counterterrorists – even the vocabulary suggests that these ostensible opponents are united by a fraternity of deadly and duplicitous tactics as well as by the shared conviction that horrible actions are sanctified by the noble goals in the minds of the perpetrators. The 'war on terrorism' is violent and punitive. The war will be won by those who are able to exact the higher price in lives and resources, by those who are able to instil the greater fear. In short, the victor in a violent war on terrorism will be the party that is most adept at inflicting terror. The quest to win the war is ultimately nihilistic. If terrorism is to be defeated by exacting the higher price, utilizing the more

efficacious violence and instilling the greater fear, then the war will be won by the party that is able to muster the will and the resources to commit the genocidal and suicidal act of destroying the planet. *The only peace that can come from the effort to oppose terror with terror is the peace of the graveyard.*

(Griffith, 2004, p. 220, italics added)

This quotation also implies the reasons why the myth of redemptive violence does not work: violence does not and never will destroy evil; rather, it creates endless cycles of carnage; and, in the process, deprives the citizens of the militaristic 'Marduk state' intent on destroying evil of their freedoms in the name of security.

This erosion of ancient liberties has already been significantly advanced by the Patriot Act in the United States and the anti-terrorism laws in the United Kingdom. Unfortunately, the idea that the state has the right to defend itself pre-emptively against the possibility of attack is now being applied to internal security, with the consequence that action to restrain citizens is being taken *before they have committed any offence and without the possibility of due legal process*. It is even alleged that the United States is exporting suspects to other countries where they are tortured, a practice known by the appropriately ugly term, 'extraordinary rendition' (LeVine, 2005, p. 214). In the latest attack on the judicial process, President Bush has asked Congress to authorise in the trials of terrorist suspects the use of evidence that has been extracted by 'coercive measures' (i.e. torture) or that the accused person is not allowed to see for national security reasons, even when he faces the death sentence if convicted. Fortunately, several senior Republicans have rejected this proposal (*The Guardian Weekly*, 22–28 September 2006, p. 6). How can a government that is supposed to be committed to freedom and democracy act in these ways? It is imperative that as many people as possible protest both against these infringements of liberty and against the religiously inspired ideology of the government of the United States of America which is used to justify them.

Chapter 13

CONFRONTING THE ABUSIVE GOD

AGAINST CHOSEN PEOPLE THEOLOGY

Protest against the United States or, for that matter, Britain, Israel, the Palestinian Authority, al-Qaeda and other Jihadist groups is necessary, but protest must also be made against the theological roots of violence. As I have shown, a major justification for, and cause of, the violence of America, Israel and Jihadists is chosen people theology. The present situation in Israel–Palestine is a particularly clear indication of the dangers of this theology. A chosen people seeking to establish a homeland in an already inhabited country will inevitably provoke resistance from the indigenous people, which is what has happened as a result of Zionism and the immigration of millions of Jews into the 'Promised Land'. Two peoples claiming the same land cannot both win; either one will eliminate, eject or dominate the other, or some accommodation must be reached whereby they share the land with equal rights. The only alternative is perpetual conflict.

In Israel–Palestine, whatever the rights and wrongs of the present situation, chosen people theology remains a major obstacle to peace, which can only come about as a result of some sort of compromise. On the one hand, the Israeli religious parties, inspired by the Exodus–Conquest narrative, regard the whole of ancient Israel as legitimately Jewish. For example, Rabbi Meir Kahane, leader of the Kach party, who was elected to the Knesset in 1984, supports a policy of ethnic cleansing:

> 'There are not several messages in Judaism,' he explained to an interviewer. 'There is only one. And this message is to do what God wants.' The message was simply this: 'God wants us to live in a country on our own, isolated, so that we have the least possible contact with what is foreign.' That meant that the Arabs must go. The promise to Abraham was as valid today as in the patriarchal period, so the Arabs were usurpers.
>
> (Quoted by Armstrong, 2001, p. 349)

On the other hand, 'Article 6 of the Hamas charter states: "The land of Palestine is an Islamic *Waaf* (Holy possession) consecrated for future Muslim generations until Judgement Day. No one can renounce it or any part of it, or abandon it or any part of it"' (quoted by McTernan, 2003, p. 119). Obviously, these beliefs are irreconcilable; two different peoples occupying the same land holding these beliefs are condemned to unceasing conflict.

The destructive effects of chosen people theology in Israel–Palestine, and the war on terror more generally, raise a crucial theological problem that applies to each of the Jewish, Christian and Muslim religions. The responsibility that all Christians need to accept in resisting the war on terror is to confront not only this theological tradition, but also the presentation of God as violent and abusive with which the existence of a chosen people is so intimately associated. Jews and Muslims must deal with this issue in their own ways in accordance with their own traditions. Here it is only appropriate and possible to address this problem from a Christian perspective. The fundamental theological question which I have arrived at through undertaking this study is this: *Can we any longer either accept or afford the belief that God has chosen one people out of all the others to be his own people, or that God has decided to grant to that people a Promised Land at the cost of the annihilation of its previous inhabitants?* If this theology were limited to the conviction that the chosen people has a special role in making God known to the rest of the nations of the earth, it could be acceptable; but since the idea that there is a chosen people – whichever group has arrogated to itself that privileged status – has so often been joined to genocide and the reversal of victimhood and, thus, also to the cycle of abuse which plagues the globe with violence, how can it be of God?

I need to emphasise that this question is not simply or primarily about the status of the Jewish people before God or the right of ancient Israel to exist, let alone modern Israel. The current political situation has to be resolved with negotiation, compromise and a practical view of what is possible politically. The idea that there is a chosen people is only relevant to this process insofar as it inspires attitudes that make such a solution difficult or impossible to achieve. The fundamental religious and political problem connected with the idea that there is a chosen people concerns the way in which ethnic or religious groups are able to make use of this belief as the basis for the annihilation or oppression of other ethnic or religious groups. As already noted, historically this tendency has been most commonly manifested by peoples other than the Hebrews.

When I began this book, I was very disturbed at recognising the similarities between the behaviour of God as described by the Bible and that of abusive men but, as I have proceeded, I have come to realise that the problem is deeper than merely the violence attributed to God. The Jewish and Christian religions have at their irreducible core the story of the Exodus of the Israelites from Egypt and their invasion and conquest of Canaan, including the genocide of most of its inhabitants. Even if the biblical account is not historically accurate, the biblical depiction of God remains unchanged. For Christians, the issue is confounded by the crucifixion which, in addition, presents God as a child abuser and murderer. Can anyone believe in such a God? Can a religious tradition with such a central narrative continue to be inhabited by one who has woken up to what it means in human terms? This is the agonising question that I now face, and the force of which I hope my readers are also experiencing.

Part of the problem is that the Exodus narrative is central to the capacity of the Judaeo-Christian tradition to resist oppression. This is the primary text referred to by disadvantaged groups when they look to the Bible for the assurance of God's support in their struggles for justice. The self-identification of Christians with the slaves in Egypt – in other words, with the chosen people – has been a major source of sustenance for Black slaves in the southern United States and their successors in the civil rights movement, and for Black theologians (e.g. Cone, 1997). It is also the foundation stone of liberation theology, which has grown out of the struggle for the liberation of the poor in South America from economic exploitation and political oppression by governments that have been supported by successive American administrations. In liberation theology, the poor rather than the rich are the ones to whom God is revealed. They are treated, in effect, as a new chosen people who are guaranteed God's favour because he has adopted an 'option for the poor' (West, 1999). They are functionally equivalent to the Hebrews in Egypt awaiting the liberating intervention of God.

Black, liberation and similar theologies, such as feminist theology, are in danger of repeating the pattern of previous groups who have identified with the chosen people – namely, reversing their victimhood rather than dissolving the cycle of abuse that causes slavery and oppression in the first place. To give them their due, many such theologians are aware of this danger. Even so, once an appeal to the Exodus narrative has been made, it is difficult to prevent an unhealthy identification with the chosen people taking place amongst those who are seeking support from this theological tradition for their resistance to injustice; and there is always an attendant risk that, when the change does take place, the slaves will be transformed into murderous revolutionaries or oppressors themselves or, at least, intolerant and exclusive sectarians. It is essential to remember what happened after the Exodus – the fate of the Canaanites – if it is not to be re-enacted yet again. This is all the more the case when apocalyptic traditions are also appealed to. Jack Nelson-Pallmeyer describes well the dangers of these radical theological traditions:

> Progressive interpreters glorify the Exodus, jubilee, sabbatical, and prophetic traditions, censor the pathological violence of God, and ignore the disturbing ethnocentrism that is central to many of these texts. Others, including many non-violent activists, idealize the apocalyptic tradition because of its clear call to resist empire. Calls to resistance central to the apocalyptic books of Daniel and Revelation are embraced, but apocalypticism's simplistic dividing wall between good and evil and its overwhelming despair concerning history are ignored. The violence of God is minimised or seen as foundational to God's efforts to insure justice. Nonviolent tactics are rooted in expectations of a violent God. Idealized treatments of liberation and apocalyptic themes draw lofty conclusions from skewed readings of selective texts. The pathology of God is ignored or sidestepped. It resurfaces repeatedly, however, in our own hearts and in the life of the world, where the spiral of violence reigns supreme. (Nelson-Pallmeyer, 2001, p. 138)

REVELATION OR PROJECTION REVISITED

In the light of these dangers, how should we engage with the violence described by the biblical text? One approach is to argue that the God of the Bible is not violent. There are two ways of doing this. One is to regard the portrayal of God in the Bible as the product of the projection of human qualities – in other words, to interpret the violence attributed to God in the Bible not as God's violence but as that of human beings. The other is to explain away the apparent biblical attribution of violence to God as a misunderstanding or misinterpretation of the intentions of the text. The first is a strategy adopted by many feminist theologians and others who find the depiction of God as a patriarchal male objectionable. For example, Carole Fontaine describes the Bible as a 'human product': 'the words of elite males projected on to deity to protect and legitimate the powers of patriarchy' (Fontaine, 1997, p. 93), and Stephen Moore describes the God of the Bible as 'a projection of male narcissism' and 'the supreme embodiment of hegemonic hypermasculinity' (Moore, 1996, p. 139; quoted by Pattison, 2000, p. 241).

The implication of this approach is that the biblical account does not truly represent the God it purports to reveal; in other words, that the genuine experience or apprehension of God contained within Judaism and Christianity has been perverted by abusive dynamics within the psychologies of the biblical authors and editors and the religious communities for whom they wrote. Insofar as the Judaeo-Christian tradition contains a genuine experience of encounter with God, it has been interpreted through the lens of frequently abusive social structures and intimate relationships. Consequently, whatever is authentic in the Bible's message of redemption and hope has been heavily obscured, distorted and to a large extent hijacked by interpersonal and societal interactions concerning power and control. This means that the God presented in the Bible and Christian doctrine is to a large extent a product of the abusiveness or victimisation of the faithful within their own communities, rather than being a true portrait of the deity. It seems to me that this conclusion is unavoidable, but the problem with this approach is that it is difficult, if not impossible, then to use the Scriptures as guides to the nature of God, let alone to regard them as revelation.

Thus, for example, many feminists have come to the conclusion that the Christian religion is irredeemably patriarchal and so have decided to abandon it (e.g. Daly, 1973/1985; Hampson, 1990). Others have decided to stay within its confines and sought to reform it from within. One strategy that some have used is to seek a liberative core within the Scriptures to which they can appeal. For example, Rosemary Radford Ruether has argued that: 'whatever diminishes or denies the full humanity of women must be presumed not to reflect the divine or an authentic relation to the divine' and, conversely, 'what does promote the full humanity of women is of the Holy' (Ruether, 1983, p. 19). This seems to me to be a reasonable criterion. However, ironically, she identifies the prophetic liberating traditions as 'a norm within Biblical faith by which the Biblical texts themselves can be criticised. To the extent to which Biblical texts reflect this normative principle, they are regarded as authoritative. On this basis,' she concludes, 'many aspects of the Bible are to be frankly set aside and rejected' (Ruether, 1983, p. 23). In the light of our earlier analysis of the abusiveness of God within the prophetic traditions, Ruether's reliance on them appears misplaced to say the least; very little of the Bible will be left by the time she has applied her criterion of acceptability to it. Even less will remain if we excise chosen people theology and the Exodus–Conquest tradition from the Bible.

There is a further problem with this method: if one decides what the text is allowed to say before one reads it, it is impossible for the text to challenge one's presuppositions. If the Bible does contain some kind of revelation from God, we must be prepared to be disturbed and confused, even angered and insulted by it. This is not possible if we have already edited the 'word of God' to suit our preconceptions. Furthermore, if we proceed in this manner, the text ends up having no authority and no revelatory ability. It is we who judge the text, not the text that judges us. God is Other; stranger than we can possibly imagine; she will not fit into our categories or definitions; it escapes our images; he tortures our intelligence. No nicely tamed God whom we can understand and live comfortably with is either the true God or of any use to us in the complexity, joy and pain of human existence. One might as well abandon both Judaism and Christianity altogether than attempt to live with such an inauthentic domesticated facsimile of this wild primeval mystery.

Even so, the adoption of some *a priori* assumption about what the Bible would have to say if we are to deem it an authentic witness to a God of love is probably unavoidable. I admit that I have taken as my own pre-supposition the idea that such a God would not reinforce but seek to counteract the cycle of abuse, and have used the empirical consequences of belief in God as a means of judging the authenticity of the various ways in which God is described within the Bible. This is my equivalent to Ruether's criterion for discerning what is of God in the Bible. The difficult task we face is to read the Bible in a discriminating manner, allowing ourselves to be challenged by what is uncomfortable within it, but also confronting the text itself with our knowledge of its origins and of the human condition; while at the same time recognising that we do not and cannot understand God, and all our conclusions about the nature of the deity must be open to revision.

The second strategy for engaging with the violence described by the biblical text is one adopted, for example, by J. Denny Weaver, who argues that God is not violent, and presents interpretations of such 'obviously' violent passages as the book of Revelation that plausibly support this opinion (Weaver, 2001, pp. 20–33; cf. Griffith, 2004, pp. 203–18). Although I am intrigued by this approach, I am not completely convinced. It strikes me that this and other such attempts by contemporary theologians and others to establish the non-violence of God (e.g. Girard, 1987; Wink, 1992; Schwager, 2000) may well be subtle versions of the moral defence, intent on preserving God's innocence at the cost of humanity's guilt. In any case, even if in some texts the apparent violence of God can be argued away, the general presentation of God as violent is so ubiquitous in the Bible that it is not credible to dispense with it altogether. A further difficulty is that, even if all the violence attributed to God by the Bible could be reasoned away, the Bible would become utterly incoherent. The image of God presented by both the Hebrew

Bible and the New Testament is irreducibly connected to the covenant relationship, the theology of the chosen people, the gift of the Promised Land and the expectation of reward and punishment by God, whether in this life or the next. If the biblical picture of the nature of the deity's relationship with human beings loses these essential theological foundation stones, it is difficult to see what would be left. And it is not possible to declare the God of the Bible innocent of violence without detaching him from this central theological tradition which, as we have seen, is soaked in violence.

A similar obstacle to regarding the God of the Bible as not violent is its overwhelmingly predominant presentation of him as a patriarchal male. We have seen how much patriarchal masculinity is associated with the ability to be violent and how easily men's narcissistic deprivation or wounding moves them to compensate for their sense of shame through violence. The depiction of God as a patriarchal male, therefore, unavoidably associates him with the violence that is intertwined with patriarchal masculinity. Indeed, it is very likely that God is viewed in this way precisely because the biblical authors were, as far as we know, men who constructed their conception of God as a mirror-image of their own psychology and social identity.

Moreover, because the world in which we live is itself violent and it is God's creation, the problem of theodicy cannot be solved simply by declaring the God of the Bible innocent of violence, even if that declaration were plausible. We still have to deal with the fact that we live in a world full of disease, suffering and death, and that most of this is inherent to the structure of the cosmos. The doctrine of original sin has historically acted as a form of the moral defence to blame humanity for the 'disorder' in creation rather than the Creator. However, one of the consequences of Darwinism is that this defence no longer works because 'evil' existed before the human race evolved. Creationists object to the theory of evolution because it challenges the literal truth of the Bible, but it is comparatively easy to accommodate the idea that the creation of life happened gradually through evolution compared with the difficulty that this hypothesis presents to the traditional Christian understanding of redemption. Remarkably, this difficulty is largely ignored by theologians and church authorities who, for the most part, continue to refer to 'the Fall' as if it were an historical event.

The problem is that, if Adam and Eve never existed, there never was an original sin. Hence, the whole theological superstructure built upon the idea of original sin collapses. Paul's central interpretation of the saving work of Christ on the cross, as the new Adam who reverses the disobedience of the old Adam through his obedience on the cross, is meaningless. So is Augustine's idea that we are all born guilty because of inherited sin. There was no sin to inherit and, therefore, we cannot be justly condemned to hell for it, even if the idea of inherited guilt is thought to be just. Furthermore, humans cannot be blamed for the 'fallen' state of the world. Whatever is wrong in the structuring of life, including the existence of carnivores, disease, suffering and death, all existed long before the human race came into being. God must take responsibility for them all. Once the doctrine of original sin is rejected as the explanation of the 'fallen' state of the earth, the Creator has to be held responsible for the innate 'evil' and violent properties of the creation – and the animal world is intrinsically violent.

Nevertheless, theologians may seek to preserve the idea of original sin by regarding it as a symbol of the human predicament: Adam and Eve represent Everyman and Everywoman rather than being historical figures, and the Fall is a pictorial or symbolic way of talking about the distortions of human nature and the limitations on human freedom. There is much value in this approach, and there is a continuing and very important debate in the human sciences as well as in theology and philosophy about the capacity of humans to act freely. However, this is a separate question from whether or not they are responsible for the existence of evil in the world, and should not be confused with it.

What is more, even if we do explain away the violence of God as either a projection or a misinterpretation of the biblical text, there still remains the formidable problem for theodicy of accounting for why a non-violent and non-abusive God has allowed him- or her- or itself to be portrayed by such deeply destructive images, and ones, furthermore, that have been used to justify the violence done by the multitude of 'chosen peoples' who have soiled the divine name with blood. Ultimately, we are left with the choice of abandoning the God of the Bible or of seeking to address him, knowing that the tradition through which we engage with him often presents him as abusive and violent. We may be sceptical about the accuracy of this presentation, but we cannot simply excise the objectionable parts of the tradition. Rather, we need to wrestle with the biblical and theological depiction of this God in an attempt to discern the elusive reality to which it witnesses. In doing so we can learn a great deal from contemporary Judaism.

A THEOLOGY OF PROTEST

The Jewish theologian David Blumenthal has written a most moving and helpful book, *Facing the Abusing God: A Theology of Protest* (1993), comparing the Jewish experience of the Holocaust with a child's experience of paternal abuse. Although these experiences are radically different in degree, the individual effects of being exposed to them have much in common; and viewing God through these two lenses at the same time shows how very appropriate is the analogy of God as an abusive father. In the light of the Holocaust, the Jewish tradition of protest that stretches back to the complaining psalms and Job has been renewed. For many Jews, it is the only standpoint from which to address God whilst retaining their own integrity. I suggest that it may be very helpful for Christians to stand alongside our Jewish cousins in faith and imitate their stance. Blumenthal describes how one can engage with the abusive God:

> One cannot forgive an abusing f/Father. This is the classical position of religious thinkers in our tradition from Job to Elie Wiesel. It is also one of the lessons we learn from psychotherapy with adult survivors of child abuse and the holocaust. Rather, we will try to accept God as God is; we will protest our innocence, as our ancestors and greatest thinkers have done. And we will accuse God of acting unjustly, as fully and directly as we can, as our greatest poets and sages have done. We cannot forgive God and concentrate on God's goodness. Rather, we will try to accept God – the bad along with the good – *and* we will speak our lament. We will mourn the bad, and we will regret that things were, and are not different than they are. This face-to-Face alone will enable us to maintain our integrity, even though it leaves an unreconciled gap between us and God. These steps alone will enable us to have faith in God in a post-holocaust, abuse-sensitive world. Unity and reconciliation are no longer the goal; rather, we seek a dialogue that affirms our difference and our justness, together with our relatedness to God. (Blumenthal, 1993, p. 266, italics in original)

Even though we Christians were not the victims of the Holocaust, and some of us were perpetrators, the theological problem facing the Jewish people is one we share with them. Compare the following words of the Christian feminist theologian Elizabeth Johnson with the quotation from David Blumenthal:

> Radical suffering afflicts millions of people the world over in intense and oppressive ways. In face of one innocent child, described so graphically by Dostoevsky; in face of the unfathomable degradation of the Jewish holocaust narrated so searingly by Elie Wiesel; in face of the boundless affliction of a freed slave woman explored so hauntingly by Toni Morison; in face of these and all singular and communal ills which plague living creatures in history, the idea of the impassible, omnipotent God appears

riddled with inadequacies. The idea of God simply cannot remain unaffected by the basic datum of so much suffering and death. Nor can it tolerate the kind of divine complicity in evil that happens when divine power is conceived as the force that could stop all of this but simply chooses not to, for whatever reason. A God who is not in some way affected by such pain is not really worthy of human love and praise. A God who is simply a spectator at all of this suffering, who even 'permits' it, falls short of the modicum of decency expected even at the human level. Such a God is morally intolerable.

(Johnson, 1992, p. 249; quoted by Nelson-Pallmeyer, 2001, pp. 297–8)

It may seem crazy to continue to hang onto a religious tradition that is as seriously flawed and compromised as the Christian one is, and whose God is such an ambiguous and unreliable figure. However, the option to abandon it is not a real one for those of us who have also found grace and forgiveness and meaning within it. The conundrum we face is that this religion has had the capacity in our own lives to be redemptive, liberating and transformative, even though it may also have been condemning, restrictive and regressive. If we can accept this ambivalence, and be aware of the dangers contained within it, this tradition is, I believe, still capable of being a source of good rather than evil. But this is only possible if we are able to protest like Blumenthal and other Jewish theologians of the Holocaust. We need to hold God to account like Job and the Psalmists, and not submit until, like Job, we have forced God to encounter us in the whirlwind. And even if the whirlwind is not an answer, at least we will have an honest relationship with the One who overwhelms us. In the meantime, along with protest, Qoheleth's scepticism and ability to live with ambivalence is a good stance to adopt towards the Mystery, as long as we also pick up his underlying, if muted, profession of faith. If we proceed in this manner, we will avoid engaging with God through the psychology of the cycle of abuse; in which case, a genuine relationship with the deity in which we can maintain our integrity becomes possible.

THEOLOGY AND PEACE

When I began this book I naively planned to finish it with a section on the theology of peace. The process of writing it has brought me to a point where I am incapable of producing one or, at least, not one that immediately looks like a theology of peace. Therefore, rather than producing a theology of peace, I want to concentrate on how Christian theology can promote peace rather than violence. The first contribution of theology is to be honest about the prominence of violence in the Christian religion. If nothing else, I hope that this book will have made it clear that Christianity is not 'an innocent religion of peace' in contrast to Islam which is 'a primitive, intolerant religion of violence that justifies terrorism'. Let's have no more of this nonsense. *Christianity is at least as capable as Islam of promoting violence* and, historically, has often been less tolerant and more likely to engage in persecution than Islam.

In *The Cost of Certainty* I argued that Christianity needs to face its shadow side if it is to be reformed (Young, 2004, pp. 94–122). Much of this book has been a description of the Christian shadow. It is shocking, shaming and disheartening to recognise just how much evil has been produced in the name of the Christian God, and how the origins of this evil lie in the core doctrines of the faith. I have repeatedly stressed this point because it is so easy to evade it. However, now is the time to take a different approach and to ask to what extent the violence inspired or justified by appeal to the biblical text is actually supported by it.

Chosen people theology is the major theological source of violence that I have identified. *According to the Bible, there is only one chosen people, the Jews.* No other ethnic group has any biblical grounds for asserting that it is the chosen people. Furthermore, the theory of supersession in the New Testament does not say that the Christian Church has replaced the Jews as the chosen people, let alone as a political entity. Although, according to the New Testament, the promises made to the ancient Hebrews have been transferred from them to Christians, Christians look to the establishment of the kingdom of God and the revelation of the Heavenly Jerusalem at the end of time, not to the foundation of a kingdom like other kingdoms in this world now. The relationship of the kingdom of God to the current political and social order is a matter of dispute in the Christian tradition, but nowhere does the New Testament envisage the setting-up of Christians as a chosen people in a particular nation state. Hence, the use of the Old Testament promises to the Hebrews as a justification for Christian chosen people theology, and the occupation of one or another 'promised land' by one or another latter-day group of Christian 'Israelites', is completely illegitimate, and a gross and frequently evil abuse of Christian theology.

Chosen people theology is only possible because of the use of typology. Typology is an aspect of the spirituality of identification, the attribution of biblical prototypes to a contemporary situation. By definition, typology is an innovation; it appeals to the biblical text but it *cannot* be justified by it, since it is the interpreter who is making an identification between the biblical narrative and the current context, not the Bible itself. There is, therefore, *absolutely no biblical authority* for any particular typological interpretation apart from those made by the New Testament itself. Thus, there is no biblical justification for any of the typological identifications made in the myth of America, nor for the identifications of the British, the Germans, the French, the Russians, the Afrikaners, or the Ulster Protestants with God's chosen people, nor for the identification of the Emperor Constantine or any of his successors or any other ruler with the Lord's anointed. Seen in this light, all of these typological identifications are the result of the self-assertion of the races or rulers concerned. Their appeal to divine writ to justify their claims to worldly authority is not only erroneous, but also presumptuous and arrogant, and sometimes idolatrous or blasphemous as well.

A giant step forward towards reforming Christianity as a religion of peace would be to ban the use of typological interpretation altogether. This would have very far-reaching implications, since much Christian theology is based on typology, but it would at a stroke take away the major tactic that enables groups to arrogate to themselves a divine fiat to their power and the violence that they use to gain and maintain it. Unfortunately, there is no space here to examine what Christian theology would look like without typology, but the development of such a theology is a task that urgently needs to be performed.

Alongside the banning of typological interpretation, there needs to be a concerted attempt to eradicate the spirituality of identification. This is a much more difficult task, since identification is a very significant means through which believers use their faith to compensate for their emotional and social inadequacies. Again, there is no space here to examine this further. In *The Cost of Certainty* I suggested Christians should develop a theology and spirituality of uncertainty to counteract the spirituality of identification (Young, 2004, pp. 123–79). I refer the reader to what I said there. In essence, we need to live with the assumption that we cannot be sure what the Bible is saying and that our ideas about God are provisional and liable to revision. In addition, we need to accept that our behaviour is more likely to resemble that attributed to the Pharisees in the Gospels than that of the apostles; in other words, we are more likely to be using our religion for self-assertion and to justify the lives we live than to be genuinely following Christ. To adopt such an attitude is quite a severe form of asceticism and can, I believe, provide a secure foundation for a contemporary spirituality that promotes peace.

THE CROSS AND PEACE

It is important to recognise that, as well as its potential to encourage violence, Christianity is also capable of promoting peace; and there are places in the contemporary world, such as South Africa, where the

Christian Church has played a really important role in producing peace out of a context of conflict. Central to this ability to promote peace is the cross. The cross is as irreducibly fundamental to the Christian religion as the Exodus is to Judaism. We cannot dispense with it without dispensing with the religion itself, and yet it is such an objectionable image and so liable to generate abuse of all kinds amongst Christians. I have concentrated on the negative or shadow side of the story of the crucifixion because it is essential for Christians to recognise the violence at the heart of their religion and its capacity to produce violence, oppression and abuse. Even so, there is something about the cross and the pattern of self-sacrificial submission to God that it represents which can be radically redemptive and transformative of human relations. I am aware that, in my concern to draw attention to the dangers inherent in many Christian interpretations of the cross, I may have understated the radically transformative potential of the cross, as well as of much of Jesus' teaching if it is read apart from the influence of the psychology of abuse. Now is the time to remedy that deficiency.

In my comments on the kenosis–exaltation paradigm I drew attention to the danger that it may lead to a reversal of victimhood as a result of believers identifying themselves not only with Christ's submission and crucifixion but also with his return to rule in power. This identification is, of course, completely illegitimate and without foundation. If Christians are destined to share with Christ in his kingdom, that is an eschatological reality which cannot be identified with any present-day political structure. When this is remembered, the Philippians passage remains a potent witness to the potential of the cross to counteract both the reversal of victimhood and mimetic rivalry. As Walter Wink comments:

> Philippians 3:21 further specifies: Christ will transform the world 'by the power that also enables him to make all things subject to himself.' The paradox of the cross, however, prevents this from being just another dream by the powerless of a reversal of power. The one who subjects all things to himself is precisely the same one who abandoned all mimetic rivalry with God – 'who, though he was in the form of God, did not regard equality with God as something to be exploited' – and emptied himself of all desire to dominate, taking the form of the oppressed, identifying himself with the enslaved, and suffering a criminal's death (Phil. 2:6–8). Subjection to such a ruler means the end of all subjugation. The rulership thus constituted is not a domination hierarchy but an enabling or actualizing hierarchy. It is not pyramidal but organic, not imposed but restorative. It is presided over by naked,

defenceless truth – the Crucified – not by a divine dictator. Christ makes all things subject to himself, not by coercion, but by healing diseased reality and restoring its balance and integrity.

(Wink, 1992, pp. 82–3)

The refusal of Jesus to be caught up in the cycle of violence between the Romans and those Jews who sought to resist them violently, and his witness to non-violence as a means of responding to oppression remain extremely relevant to the contemporary world. If we read the New Testament from this perspective and avoid identifying ourselves with Jesus in his exaltation, the imitation of Christ may be a very constructive means of advancing peace.

In my view, the most positive way of interpreting Jesus' ministry and death is to see them as witnessing to a God whose power, as Nelson-Pallmeyer expresses it, 'is invitational and not violent or coercive' (Nelson-Pallmeyer, 2001, p. 347). However, such a perspective can only be maintained if it is accompanied by a profound rethinking of the New Testament's witness to Jesus. It requires a recognition that the Christian Scriptures (and many traditional interpretations of them) were as thoroughly influenced, indeed perverted, by the psychology of abuse and its potential to give birth to violence as the Hebrew Scriptures were before them. Even so, in both sets of sacred writings there is a genuine, if often obscured, witness to a God who is non-violent and genuinely loving, and who is working to redeem the human race from the cycles of violence and abuse to which it is so often subject. Potentially at least, we have in the cross a clear indication that God refuses to compel us to love her or him. As Burton Cooper describes it:

> Jesus on the cross presents his failure to God. It is the failure of suffering love to coerce a loving response. But this defeat on the cross redefines failure for the Christian – and for the church. In his defeat, Christ denies the identification of God's power with co-ercion. Now it is a sign of failure to resort to coercive powers. In his defeat at the hands of the strong, Christ makes it a victory to identify with and care for the weak. Now it is a sign of failure to live with indifference to the suffering of the weak.

> (Cooper, 1998, p. 123; quoted by Nelson-Pallmeyer, 2001, p. 347)

This understanding of the cross does not answer all the problems for theodicy of the failure of God to intervene to prevent the Holocaust and other disasters, but it does suggest that there is a feasible approach other than protest to the crisis for theology provoked by such events. Perhaps, what we need to do is to hold these two perspectives in tension: continue to protest against the violent, coercive and arbitrary God, whilst holding on to the hope that God is actually not like that at all, but non-violent and invitational: suffering at the hands of the violence of his creatures, and yet turning that apparent defeat into a victory over the destructive tendencies in the human heart that are lived out in the cycle of abuse in human relationships. For myself, only a God who is free from the dynamics of abuse and refuses to impose his will by force is able to redeem humanity from patterns of domination and to inaugurate a realm of peace.

The cross can only be a model of such a transformation if the denial of self-assertion entailed in following Christ is the result of genuine self-giving by believers who are sufficiently psychologically mature, with a sufficiently developed sense of self-value, to be able to sacrifice themselves without doing so as a consequence of experiences of neglect or abuse. In other words, when self-sacrifice is freely chosen, without compulsion and outside the cycle of abuse, it is capable of being genuinely redemptive for both the individuals concerned and human communities. The key point for a spirituality of peace is to ensure that this is the case. This concern should be central to all pastoral care and spiritual guidance.

The problem is that the language of self-sacrifice is very easily colonised and used in the service of those who seek power over others, and is often adopted as a tool of individual or corporate control. As we have seen, this process is recorded over and over again in the Bible and has been lived out repeatedly in Church history. When we recognise the frequently abusive nature of both text and tradition, it becomes possible to begin to extricate their witness to authentic and healthy self-sacrifice from their advocacy of submission to violence and threat.

Despite my criticisms of the selectivity of Rosemary Radford Ruether and some other feminist theologians, we do need to exercise some form of discrimination in approaching the biblical text. If we begin by recognising that not only our own interpretations of the Bible but also the sacred Scripture itself are likely to be the products of human psychology, social position and ideological interests, then it becomes possible to open ourselves to the possibility that they may also contain a divine challenge interwoven with the human context of its delivery, one that may be discovered through our engagement with these documents. This potential cannot be isolated from the texts as they are but must be discerned within them, often as a hint or a fleeting insight or a surprising action. Regrettably, there is no space here to explore further how this may be done. We are faced with a very difficult and paradoxical task. As Mary Anne Tolbert says with regard to feminist biblical interpretation, we are challenged: 'To understand the same God as enemy and friend, as tormentor and savior, to read the same Bible as enslaver and liberator' (Tolbert, 1983, p. 126). Liberating authentic spiritual growth, through such an engagement with the biblical text, from the controlling, abusive and violent dynamics associated with the Christian religion and its institutions is, I believe, an essential and urgent task for all Christians to engage in. We owe it to ourselves, but much more importantly we have a responsibility to undertake this task for the peace of the world.

A final point to note is that, even if the New Testament in various places does depict God as violent, the right to use violence is *reserved to God alone*. He may use it to redeem his faithful from oppression or to exercise judgement but, with hardly any exceptions, the New Testament calls Christians to follow in the non-violent path of Jesus of Nazareth – the cleansing of the temple notwithstanding. Thus, there is no justification for any merely human leaders to arrogate to themselves the right to exercise violence in the world as God's representatives (Desjardins, 1997, p. 72). Whether God is regarded as non-violent or is expected to exercise violence on behalf of his devotees, Christians are not justified in using the Bible to justify their own violence. In view of this fact, I want to end with some words from Miroslav Volf which are particularly apt for the war on terror, and which indicate what Christians are called to do in the practical world of politics – even if, unlike Volf, they do doubt the justice and presence of God:

> This is what Jesus Christ asks Christians to do. Assured of God's justice and undergirded by God's presence, they are to break the cycle of violence by refusing to be caught in the automatism of revenge. It cannot be denied that the prospects are good that by trying to love their enemies they may end up hanging on a cross. Yet often enough, the costly acts of nonviolence become a seed from which the fragile fruit of Pentecostal peace grows – a peace between people from different cultural spaces gathered in one place who understand each other's languages and share in each other's goals. (Volf, 1996, p. 306)

References

Altmann, W. (1994), 'A Latin American Perspective on the Cross and Suffering', in Y. Tesfai (ed.), *The Scandal of the Crucified World: Perspectives on the Cross and Suffering* (pp. 75–86), Maryknoll, New York, Orbis Books.

Anselm, St (1909), *Cur Deus Homo?*, Edinburgh, John Grant.

Armstrong, K. (2001), *The Battle for God: Fundamentalism in Judaism, Christianity and Islam*, London, HarperCollins.

Ateek, N. S. (1989), *Justice and Only Justice: A Palestinian Theology of Liberation*, Maryknoll, New York, Orbis Books.

Aulen, G. (1970), *Christus Victor: An Historical Study of the Three Main Types of the Idea of the Atonement*, London, SPCK.

al-Banna, H. (1978), trans. Charles Wendell, 'Between Yesterday and Today', in *Five Tracts of Hasan al-Banna: A Selection from the Majmu 'at Rasa'il al-Imam al-Shahid Hasan al-Banna'*, Berkeley, University of California Press.

Barber, B. R. (2004), *Fear's Empire: War, Terrorism, and Democracy*, New York & London, W. W. Norton & Co.

Bauckham R. (2001), 'Revelation', in J. Barton & J. Muddiman (eds.), *The Oxford Bible Commentary* (pp. 1287–306), Oxford, Oxford University Press.

Blum, W. (2005), 'A Concise History of US Global Interventions, 1945 to the Present', in B. Hamm (ed.), *Devastating Society: The Neo-Conservative Assault on Democracy and Justice* (pp. 204–46), London & Ann Arbor, MI, Pluto Press.

Blumenthal, D. R. (1993), *Facing the Abusing God: A Theology of Protest*, Louisville, Kentucky, Westminster/John Knox Press.

Boesak, A. A. (1976), *Black Theology and Black Power*, London, Mowbray.

Brogan, H. (1999), *The Penguin History of the United States of America* (2nd edn), London, Penguin Books.

Brown, J. C. & Bohn, C. R. (eds.) (1989), *Christianity, Patriarchy, and Abuse: A Feminist Critique*, New York, The Pilgrim Press.

Brown, J. C. & Parker, P. (1989), 'For God So Loved the World?', in J. C. Brown & C. R. Bohn (eds.) (1989), *Christianity, Patriarchy, and Abuse: A Feminist Critique* (pp. 1–30), New York, The Pilgrim Press.

Brueggemann, W. (1984), *The Message of the Psalms: A Theological Commentary*, Minneapolis, Augsburg Publishing House.

Brueggemann, W. (1997), *Theology of the Old Testament: Testimony, Dispute, Advocacy*, Minneapolis, Fortress Press.

Olivia Carr (2005), 'Domestic Violence – Survivors' Voices', in *Feedback* 10:3, 2–7.

Callinicos, A. (2003), *An Anti-Capitalist Manifesto*, Cambridge, Polity.

Chomsky, N. (2003), *Power and Terror: Post 9/11 Talks and Interviews*, New York, Seven Stories Press/Tokyo, Little More.

Chomsky, N. (2005), 'Wars of Terror', in B. Hamm (ed.), *Devastating Society: The Neo-Conservative Assault on Democracy and Justice* (pp. 185–203), London & Ann Arbor, MI, Pluto Press.

Cooper, B. (1988), *Why God?*, Atlanta, John Knox Press.

200 REFERENCES

Cone, J. H. (1969), *Black Theology and Black Power*, New York, The Seabury Press.

Cone, J. H. (1997), *God of the Oppressed* (revised edn), Maryknoll, New York, Orbis Books.

Crenshaw, J. L. (2001), 'Job', in J. Barton & J. Muddiman (eds.), *The Oxford Bible Commentary* (pp. 331–55), Oxford, Oxford University Press.

Cross, F. M. (1973), *Canaanite Myth and Hebrew Epic: Essays in the History of the Religion of Israel*, Cambridge, Massachusetts, Harvard University Press.

Daly, M. (1973 & 1985), *Beyond God the Father*, London, The Women's Press.

Dark, D. (2005), *The Gospel According to America: A Meditation on a God-blessed, Christ-Haunted Idea*, Louisville, Kentucky, Westminster/John Knox Press.

Dell, K. J. (2003), 'Job', in J. D. G. Dunn & J. W. Rogerson (eds.), *Eerdmans Commentary on the Bible* (pp. 337–63), Grand Rapids, Michigan & Cambridge, UK, Eerdmans.

Desjardins, M. (1997), *Peace, Violence and the New Testament*, Sheffield, Sheffield Academic Press.

de Zulueta, F. (1993), *From Pain to Violence: The Traumatic Roots of Destructiveness*, London, Whurr Publishers.

Easlea, B. (1983), *Fathering the Unthinkable: Masculinity, Scientists and the Nuclear Arms Race*, London, Pluto Press.

Ela, J.-M. (1988), *My Faith as an African*, Maryknoll, New York, Orbis Books.

Ellis, M. C. (2002), *Israel and Palestine Out of the Ashes: The Search for Jewish Identity in the Twenty-First Century*, London & Sterling, Virginia, Pluto Press.

Emmerson, G. I. (2001), 'Ruth', in J. Barton & J. Muddiman (eds.), *The Oxford Bible Commentary* (pp. 192–5), Oxford, Oxford University Press.

Esposito, J. L. (2002), *Unholy War: Terror in the Name of God*, Oxford, Oxford University Press.

Fairbairn, W. R. D. (1952), *Psychoanalytical Studies of the Personality*, London & New York, Tavistock/Routledge.

Faludi, S. (1999), *Stiffed: The Betrayal of the Modern Man*, London, Chatto & Windus.

Farrell, W. (1994), *The Myth of Male Power: Why Men Are the Disposable Sex*, London, Fourth Estate.

Fiorenza, E. S. (1983), *In Memory of Her: A Feminist Reconstruction of Christian Origins*, London, SCM Press.

Fontaine, C. R. (1997), 'The Abusive Bible: On the Use of Feminist Method in Pastoral Contexts', in A. Brenner & C. R. Fontaine, *A Feminist Companion to Reading the Bible: Approaches, Methods and Strategies* (pp. 61–83), Sheffield, Sheffield Academic Press.

Freeman, C. (2003), *The Closing of the Western Mind: The Rise of Faith and the Fall of Reason*, London, Pimlico.

Freeman, D. (1991), *Victim Power, Guild of Pastoral Psychology Pamphlet 238*, London, Guild of Pastoral Psychology.

Fukuyama. F. (1992), *The End of History and the Last Man*, London, Hamish Hamilton.

George, T. (1988), *Theology of the Reformers*, Nashville, Tennessee, Broadman Press / Leicester, UK, Apollos.

Gerstenberger, E. S. (2002), *Theologies in the Old Testament*, London & New York, T. & T. Clark.

Giladi, G. N. (1990), *Discord in Zion: Conflict between Ashkenazi and Sephardi Jews in Israel*, London, Scorpion Publishing.

Gilligan, J. (2000), *Violence: Reflections on Our Deadliest Epidemic*, London, Jessica

Kingsley Publishers.

Girard, R. (1987), *Things Hidden since the Foundation of the World*, trans. S. Bann & M. Metteer, London, The Athlone Press.

Girard, R. (1988), *Violence and the Sacred*, trans. P. Gregory, London, The Athlone Press.

Godsi, E. (2004), *Violence and Society: Making Sense of Madness and Badness*, Ross-on-Wye, PCCS Books.

Goldner, V., Penn, P., Sheinberg, M. & Walker, G. (1990), 'Love and Violence: Gender Parodoxes in Volatile Attachments', in *Family Process*, Vol. 29, No. 4, 343–64.

Goldner, V. (1998), 'The Treatment of Violence and Victimization in Intimate Relationships', in *Family Process*, Vol. 37, No. 3, 263–86.

Gray, J. (2003), *Al-Qaeda and What It Means to Be Modern*, London, Faber & Faber.

Gray, J. (2004), *Heresies: Against Progress and Other Illusions*, London, Granta Books.

Griffith, L. (2004), *The War on Terrorism and the Terror of God*, Grand Rapids, Michigan & Cambridge, UK, Eerdmans.

Gunn, D. (2003), 'Jonah', in J. D. G. Dunn & J. W. Rogerson (eds.), *Eerdmans Commentary on the Bible* (pp. 699–702), Grand Rapids, Michigan & Cambridge, UK, Eerdmans.

Gutiérrez, G. (1974), *A Theology of Liberation: History, Politics and Salvation*, trans. & ed. C. Inda & J. Eagleson, London, SCM Press.

Habeck, M. (2006), *Knowing the Enemy: Jihadist Ideology and the War on Terror*, New Haven & London, Yale University Press.

Hamm, B. (ed.) (2005), *Devastating Society: The Neo-Conservative Assault on Democracy and Justice*, London & Ann Arbor, MI, Pluto Press.

Hampson, D. (1990), *Theology and Feminism*, Oxford, Basil Blackwell.

Hardin, M. (2000), 'Sacrificial Language in Hebrews', in W. M. Swartey (ed.), *Violence Renounced: René Girard, Biblical Studies, and Peacemaking*, Telford, PA, Pandora Press US.

Hauerwas, S. (1985), *Against the Nations: War and Survival in a Liberal Society*, Minneapolis, Chicago & New York, Winston Press.

Hauerwas, S. (2004), *Performing the Faith: Bonhoeffer and the Practice of Nonviolence*, London, SPCK.

Hopkins, J. M. (1995), *Towards a Feminist Christology: Jesus of Nazareth, European Women, and the Christological Crisis*, Grand Rapids, Eerdmans.

Huntingdon, S. P. (2002), *The Clash of Civilizations and the Remaking of the World Order*, London, The Free Press.

Jacobson, N. & Gottman, J. (1998), *Breaking the Cycle: New Insights into Violent Relationships*, London, Bloomsbury.

Jarick, J. (2003), 'Ecclesiastes', in J. D. G. Dunn & J. W. Rogerson (eds.), *Eerdmans Commentary on the Bible* (pp. 467–73), Grand Rapids, Michigan & Cambridge, UK, Eerdmans.

Jenkins, A. (1990), *Invitations to Responsibility: The Therapeutic Engagement of Men who Are Violent and Abusive*, Adelaide, South Australia, Dulwich Centre Publications.

Johnson, E. A. (1992), *She Who Is: The Mystery of God in Feminist Theological Discourse*, New York, Crossroad.

Juergensmeyer, M. (2003), *Terror in the Mind of God: The Global Rise of Religious Violence* (3rd edn), Berkeley, Los Angeles & London, University of California Press.

Kagan, R. (2003), *Paradise and Power: America and Europe in the New World Order*, London, Atlantic Books.

Kahn, A. (1984), 'The Power War: Male Response to Power Loss under Equality', in

Psychology of Women Quarterly, 8(3), 234–47.

Kapuści nski, R. (2002), *The Shadow of the Sun: My African Life*, London, Penguin Books.

Kaufman, M. (1994), 'Men, Feminism, and Men's Contradictory Experiences of Power', in H. Brod & M. Kaufman (eds.), *Theorizing Masculinities* (pp. 142–63), Thousand Oaks, California, Sage.

Keen, S. (1992), *Fire in the Belly*, London, Piatkus.

Kelly, J. N. D. (1977), *Early Christian Doctrines* (5th edn), London, Adam & Charles Black.

Kiernan, V. G. (2005), *America: The New Imperialism: From White Settlement to World Hegemony*, London & New York, Verso.

Kimmel, M. S. (1994), 'Masculinity as Homophobia: Fear, Shame, and Silence in the Construction of Gender Identity', in H. Brod & M. Kaufman (eds.), *Theorizing Masculinities* (pp. 119–41), Thousand Oaks, California, Sage.

Kirwan, M. (2004), *Discovering Girard*. London, Darton, Longman & Todd.

Kohut, H. (1978), 'Thoughts on Narcissism and Narcissistic Rage', in P. H. Ornstein (ed.), *The Search for the Self* (Vol. 2) (pp. 615–58), Madison, Connecticut, International Universities Press.

La Guardia, A. (2001/2003), *War without End: Israelis, Palestinians and the Struggle for a Promised Land*, St Martin's Griffin, New York, Thomas Dunne Books.

Lazare, D. (1996), *The Frozen Republic: How the Constitution is Paralyzing Democracy*, New York, Harcourt & Brace.

Lee, J. (1992), *At My Father's Wedding: Reclaiming our True Masculinity*, London, Piatkus.

LeVine, M. (2005), *Why They Don't Hate Us: Lifting the Veil on the Axis of Evil*, Oxford, One World.

Lewis, B. (2002), *What Went Wrong? Western Impact and Middle Eastern Response*, London, Phoenix.

Lewis, B. (2004), *The Crisis of Islam: Holy War and Unholy Terror*, London, Phoenix.

Liechty, J. (1995), 'Christianity and Identity in Ireland: A Historical Perspective', lecture given at Christianity, Culture and Identity Conference, ECONI, 4 November.

Lieven, A. (2004), *America Right or Wrong: An Anatomy of American Nationalism*, London, HarperCollins.

Lind, M. C. (1980), *Yahweh is a Warrior: The Theology of Warfare in Ancient Israel*, Scottdale, Pennsylvania & Kitchener, Ontario, Herald Press.

Lochery, N. (2004), *Why Blame Israel? The Facts Behind the Headlines*, Cambridge, Icon Books.

Longley, C. (2002), *Chosen People: The Big Idea that Shapes England and America*, London, Hodder & Stoughton.

McDonald, P. M. (2004), *God and Violence: Biblical Resources for Living in a Small World*, Scottdale, Pennsylvania & Waterloo, Ontario, Herald Press.

McGlinchey, P. (1996), 'The Threefold Cord: The Fusion of Patriotism, Violence and the Gospel in Ireland', in *Frontiers: Evangelical Perspectives on Faith and Society*, Autumn 1996, 36–42.

McTernan, O. (2003), *Violence in God's Name: Religion in an Age of Conflict*, London, Darton, Longman & Todd.

Maimela, S. S. (1994), 'The Suffering of Human Divisions and the Cross', in Y. Tesfai (ed.), *The Scandal of the Crucified World: Perspectives on the Cross and Suffering* (pp. 36–47), Maryknoll, New York, Orbis Books.

Manji, I. (2005), *The Trouble with Islam Today: A Wake-Up Call for Honesty and Change*, Edinburgh & London, Mainstream Publishing.

Meth, R. L. (1990), 'The Road to Masculinity', in R. L. Meth & R. S. Pasick (eds.), *Men in Therapy: The Challenge of Change* (pp. 3–34), New York & London, The Guildford Press.

Meth, R. L. & Pasick, R. S. (eds.), *Men in Therapy: The Challenge of Change*, New York & London, The Guildford Press.

Micklethwait, J. & Wooldridge, A. (2004), *The Right Nation: Why America is Different*, London, Allen Lane.

Miller, A. (1987), *For Your Own Good: The Roots of Violence in Childrearing*, London, Virago.

Miller, A. (1990), *The Untouched Key: Tracing Childhood Trauma in Creativity and Destructiveness*, London, Virago.

Miranda, J. P. (1982), *Communism in the Bible*, London, SCM Press.

Moane, G. (1994), 'A Psychological Analysis of Colonialism in an Irish Context', in *Irish Journal of Psychology* 15, 2/3, 250–65.

Moltmann, J. (1974), *The Crucified God: The Cross of Christ as the Foundation and Criticism of Christian Theology*, London, SCM Press.

Moore, S. (1996), *God's Gym*, London, Routledge.

Nasr, S. H. (1990), *Traditional Islam in the Modern World*, London & New York, Kegan Paul International.

Nelson-Pallmeyer, J. (2001), *Jesus against Christianity: Reclaiming the Missing Jesus*, Harrisburg, Pennsylvania, Trinity Press International.

Nelson-Pallmeyer, J. (2005a), *Saving Christianity from Empire*, New York & London, Continuum.

Nelson-Pallmeyer, J. (2005b), *Is Religion Killing Us? Violence in the Bible and the Quran*, New York & London, Continuum.

Neumann, E. (1973), *Depth Psychology and a New Ethic*, San Francisco, Harper Torchbooks.

Niditch, S. (1995), *War in the Hebrew Bible: A Study in the Ethics of Violence*, New York & Oxford, Oxford University Press.

Northcott, M. (2004), *An Angel Directs the Storm: Apocalyptic Religion and American Empire*, London & New York, I. B. Tauris.

Owen, W. (1985), *The Poems of Wilfred Owen*, J. Stallworthy (ed.), London, The Hogarth Press.

Pattison, P. (2000), *Shame: Theory, Therapy, Theology*, Cambridge, Cambridge University Press.

Perdue, L. G. (1991), *Wisdom in Revolt: Metaphorical Theology in the Book of Job* (*Journal for the Study of the Old Testament* Supplement Series 112, Bible and Literature Series 29), Sheffield, The Almond Press.

Prinsloo, W. S. (2003), 'Psalms', in J. D. G. Dunn & J. W. Rogerson (eds.), *Eerdmans Commentary on the Bible* (pp. 364–436), Grand Rapids, Michigan & Cambridge, UK, Eerdmans.

Real, T. (1997), *I Don't Want to Talk about It: Overcoming the Secret Legacy of Male Depression*, Dublin, Newleaf.

Real, T. (2002), *How Can I Get through to You? Reconnecting Men and Women*, Dublin, Newleaf.

Rose, J. (2005), *The Question of Zion*, Princeton & Oxford, Princeton University Press.

Rosenthal, D. (2005), *The Israelis: Ordinary People in an Extraordinary Land*, New York, Free Press.

Ruether, R. R. (1983), 'Feminist Theology: Methodology, Sources and Norms', in R. R. Ruether, *Sexism and God-Talk: Towards a Feminist Theology* (pp. 12–46), London, SCM Press.

Ruth, S. (1988), 'Understanding Oppression and Liberation', in *Studies* 99, 434–43.

Sardar, Z. & Wyn Davies, M. (2002), *Why Do People Hate America?*, Cambridge, Icon Books.

Sardar, Z. & Wyn Davies, M. (2004), *American Dream, Global Nightmare*, Cambridge, Icon Books.

Scheuer, M., 'Anonymous' (2005), *Imperial Hubris: Why the West is Losing the War on Terror*, Washington, D.C., Potomac Books.

Schwager, R. (2000), *Must There Be Scapegoats? Violence and Redemption in the Bible*, Leominster, Gracewing / New York, Crossroad.

Sobrino, J. (1978), *Christology at the Crossroads*, Maryknoll, New York, Orbis Books.

Sobrino, J. (2003), *Witnesses to the Kingdom: The Martyrs of El Salvador and the Crucified Peoples*, Maryknoll, New York, Orbis Books.

Southwell, P. J. M. (2001), 'Jonah', in J. Barton & J. Muddiman (eds.), *The Oxford Bible Commentary* (pp. 593–5), Oxford, Oxford University Press.

Stiglitz, J. (2002), *Globalization and its Discontents*, London, Penguin Books.

Tolbert, M. A. (1983), 'Defining the Problem: The Bible and Feminist Hermeneutics', in M. A. Tolbert (ed.), *The Bible and Feminist Hermeneutics, Semeia* 28, 113–26.

Tesfai, Y. (1994), Introduction in Y. Tesfai (ed.), *The Scandal of the Crucified World: Perspectives on the Cross and Suffering* (pp. 1–16), Maryknoll, New York, Orbis Books.

Volf, M. (1996), *Exclusion and Embrace: A Theological Exploration of Identity, Otherness, and Reconciliation*, Nashville, Abingdon Press.

Walker, L. E. (1984), *The Battered Woman Syndrome*, New York, Springer Publishing Co.

Washington, J. (1986), *A Testament of Hope*, New York, Harper & Row.

Wallis, J. (2005), *God's Politics: Why the Right Gets It Wrong and the Left Doesn't Get It*, San Francisco, Harper San Francisco.

Weaver, J. D. (2001), *The Nonviolent Atonement*, Grand Rapids, Michigan & Cambridge, UK, Eerdmans.

Weems, R. J. (1995), *Battered Love: Marriage, Sex, and Violence in the Hebrew Prophets*, Minneapolis, Fortress Press.

West, G. (1999), 'The Bible and the Poor', in C. Rowlands (ed.), *The Cambridge Companion to Liberation Theology* (pp. 129–52), Cambridge, Cambridge University Press.

West, G. (2003), 'Ruth', in J. D. G. Dunn & J. W. Rogerson (eds.), *Eerdmans Commentary on the Bible* (pp. 208–12), Grand Rapids, Michigan & Cambridge, UK, Eerdmans.

Westerholm, S. (2004), *Perspectives Old and New on Paul: The 'Lutheran' Paul and His Critics*, Grand Rapids, Michigan & Cambridge, UK, Eerdmans.

Wiesel, E. (1960), *Night*, trans. S. Rodway, New York, Bantam Books.

Wiesel, E. (1979), *The Trial of God*, New York, Schocken Books.

Wink, W. (1992), *Engaging the Powers: Discernment and Resistance in a World of Domination* (*The Powers*, Vol. 3), Minneapolis, Fortress Press.

Yoder, J. H. (1994), *The Politics of Jesus: Behold the Man! Our Victorious Lamb* (2nd edn), Grand Rapids, Michigan, Eerdmans/Carlisle, UK, Paternoster Press.

Young, J. (2004), *The Cost of Certainty: How Religious Conviction Betrays the Human Psyche*, London, Darton, Longman & Todd.

Index